Outlaw Capital

Outlaw Capital

EVERYDAY ILLEGALITIES AND THE
MAKING OF UNEVEN DEVELOPMENT

JENNIFER L. TUCKER

THE UNIVERSITY OF GEORGIA PRESS
Athens

© 2023 by the University of Georgia Press
Athens, Georgia 30602
www.ugapress.org

Set in 10.25/13.5 Minion 3 Regular by Kaelin Chappell Broaddus

Most University of Georgia Press titles are
available from popular e-book vendors.

Printed digitally

Library of Congress Cataloging-in-Publication Data

Names: Tucker, Jennifer L., author.
Title: Outlaw capital : everyday illegalities and the making of uneven development / Jennifer L. Tucker.
Description: Athens : The University of Georgia Press, [2023] | Series: Geographies of justice and social transformation ; 59 | Includes bibliographical references and index.
Identifiers: LCCN 2023002348 | ISBN 9780820364476 (hardback) | ISBN 9780820364483 (paperback) | ISBN 9780820364490 (epub) | ISBN 9780820364506 (pdf)
Subjects: LCSH: Capitalism—Moral and ethical aspects—Paraguay—Ciudad del Este. | Informal sector (Economics)—Paraguay—Ciudad del Este. | Community development, Urban—Paraguay—Ciudad del Este. | Ciudad del Este (Paraguay)—Economic conditions. | Ciudad del Este (Paraguay)—Social conditions.
Classification: LCC HC223.C58 T83 2023 | DDC 330.9892—dc23/eng/20230215
LC record available at https://lccn.loc.gov/2023002348

For my parents, who taught me to care deeply about the world and believe in justice

CONTENTS

ACKNOWLEDGMENTS

"Knowledge itself is a social accomplishment," says the feminist scholar Dorothy Smith (1987, 72), signaling vast relational webs behind all projects of knowing. This book is no exception.

I owe so much to so many in Ciudad del Este. My debts are especially deep to a great many street vendors in Ciudad del Este who shared their stories—and their *tereré*—with me over countless visits. I have sought to be a worthy vessel for their stories. I learned from more of them than I can name here, but an especially heartfelt thanks goes out to Alva, Ariel, Atanasio, Carlos, Cristina, Elida, Eusebio, Jorge, Julio, Lina, Luisa, Mabel, Matilde, Merci, Miguel, Miriam, Norma, Pavi, Petrona, Plácida, Reina, Rober, Rosa, Ruben, Sara, Trifom, Yonny, and Zuni. Many community leaders in Ciudad del Este also generously helped me make sense of the city, including Emilio Achinelli, Nani Arrua, Hugo Cárdenas, Ruben Cardoso, Paraguayo Cubas, Dolly Galeano, Alberto Gómez, Wilfrido González, Alfredo Mesa, Javier Miranda, Fernando Paredes, Tony Santamaría, Miranda Silva, and Juan Vásquez. I am eternally grateful to Elida and Norma for their generous hospitality. They shared both their homes and their knowledge of the city with me.

I'm grateful to the Geographies of Justice and Social Transformation series editors for believing in this project, especially for Sapana Doshi's mentorship and Mick Gusinde-Duffy's editorial stewardship. It's an honor to be published in the key venue for engaged geography and urban studies scholarship alongside exemplar scholars who demonstrate how theory matters in our struggles for social justice.

It's hard to write books and near impossible, I reckon, to write one without the support of a solid writing group. Manisha Anantharaman's and John Stehlin's brilliance and steadfast spirit of care have seen this project from messy dissertation to published book. I value our commitment to each other's work over the long term. It has also been a privilege to share the writing process with Naomi Adiv, Freya Knapp, Kristen Nelson, Stephanie Sevall, Nomi Stone, and Lani Tsinnajinnie. At different moments and in different ways, they helped me stick with writing. Good writing requires many drafts, which in turn require many readers. I am grateful for generous and insightful feedback from Christian Anderson, Ricardo Cardoso, Daniel Cockayne, Tara Cookson, Ryan Devlin, Julie Gamble, Vinay Gidwani, Brian Goldstein, Sophie Gonick, Carlo Inverardi-Ferri, Julie Klinger, Sarah Knuth, Mukul Kumar, Victoria Lawson, Aman Luthra, Lizzy Mattiuzzi, Sergio Montero, Linda Peake, Fernando Rabossi, Malini Ranganathan, Lana Salman, Cheryl Mei-ting Schmitz, Oscar Sosa López, and Matt Wade, among others.

The good fairy of graduate students was working overtime when I pulled together my dissertation committee of intellectual powerhouses who are also just wonderful people. Teresa Caldeira offered invaluable guidance while modeling impeccable standards of scholarship. Early on, Ananya Roy helped me see knowledge production and academic practice as political projects. I remain challenged by Gillian Hart's probing questions about critical concepts adequate to the specificity of place and history. At Berkeley, I also benefited from the kind, insightful mentorship of Charisma Acey, Peter Evans, Jake Kosek, Jane Mauldon, Raka Ray, Victoria Robinson, Stephen Small, and Clare Talwalker. Thank you all.

This project was supported by the generosity of researchers at the Centro de Análisis y Difusión de la Economía Paraguaya (CADEP) who offered research assistance, insights, connections, and valued desk space in Asunción. I am particularly thankful for the support of Fernando Masi, who—despite a busy research itinerary—willingly gave astute, long-form responses to my questions, predictably leading me in unpredictably interesting directions. I also want to thank Carolina Balmori for research assistance and Rosa Verza and Gloria Correa for making me feel welcome. While my take is somewhat different from that of most researchers at CADEP, I hope this book will spark useful discussions in a spirit of engaged pluralism.

I owe much to a small cadre of critically minded scholars of Paraguay who remind me of the importance of producing knowledge from Paraguay: Gustavo Codas, Joel Correia, Juan Carlos Cristaldo, Christine Folch, Carlos Gómez Florentín, Ignacio González Bozzolasco, Kregg Hetherington, José Tomás Sánchez, and Gustavo Setrini. I feel particularly lucky to have shared Ciudad del Este as a field site with Caroline Schuster, a kindred spirit and generous colleague.

Three close friends in Paraguay brought joy, comfort, and intellectual stimulation over fifteen months of fieldwork: Sofía Espíndola, Mariana Lagada, and Ariel Álvarez. With you I feel at home. Sofía, your insightful anthropological deconstruction of *everything* is a solace. Mariana and Ariel, where else could I find concert-quality birthday serenades and encyclopedic knowledge of Ciudad del Este? My guest room is ready for you all. I am also grateful for the gracious hospitality of the Cocuesta family.

My debts to friends in Paraguay extend back almost two decades. Many of those friends are in Mbocayaty del Yhaguy, a small community with a high concentration of big-hearted folks: Nã Antola and family; Rumi, Adan, and Sabrina; Don Castro and family; the teachers, staff, and students of Colegio Río Negro; Sulma and family; Elva and Jasmine; Ana Gillen and family; Lucila Rodríguez and family; Muñeca; and so many more. A special thanks also to the Brizuela family: with your extended clan, I can count on delicious *sopa*, a warm bed, and warmer friendship in at least three different Paraguayan cities.

Even within the neoliberalizing university, spaces for critical thought and action bloom. I am grateful for the connections, conversations, and frictions that emerged with sharp thinkers in these spaces of hope, including the Berkeley PhD room; the SSRC International Dissertation Research Fellowship workshop; the Politics of Scale workshop organized through Berkeley Global Metropolitical Studies; the 2014 Relational Poverty Network conference; the UN-Habitat Hub on Informal Urbanism; GenUrb (Urbanization, Gender, and the Global South: A Transformative Knowledge Network); the 2019 Comparative Urbanism: Global Perspectives conference; Colectivo Guara; Women in Economic Geography; and the panels, email threads, and Zoom calls behind the Work Outside the Wage Antipode symposium.

In the University of New Mexico's Department of Community & Regional Planning, I have been blessed with an amazing set of colleagues who model engaged scholarship and action. I am especially thankful for the invaluable mentorship of Renia Ehrenfeucht and Claudia Isaac. Thank you, Moises Gonzales, Laura Harjo, Ted Jojola, Caroline Scruggs, and Lani Tsinnajinnie for making service to the university both productive and enjoyable. I am also grateful to CRP students who constantly challenge me to more fully live my ethics of action inside and outside the classroom.

Research assistance from Thainara Granero de Melo helped shape my argument about the racialization of Paraguay and Paraguayans from Brazil; I'm excited about our ongoing collaborations. I am also grateful for the research assistance of Melisa Casarrubias and Laura Rilqulime, the transcription assistance of Sanie Molina and Mariela Cuevas, the bibliographic support of Hally Bert, and the assiduous competence of Rosa Palau at the Museo de la Justicia.

This project was made possible by several grants and fellowships. The Social Science Research Council's International Dissertation Research Fellowship and the Fulbright Fellowship provided generous funds for extended fieldwork. I also benefited from two Foreign Language and Area Studies Research Fellowships for language study. The Berkeley Dissertation Completion Fellowship and Berkeley Center for Race and Gender provided support for writing.

With books, interconnection takes material form, challenging the stodgy academic notion of sole authorship. Without the smarts, support, time, and care of so many, this book would simply not exist. All oversights and errors are my own.

Outlaw Capital

INTRODUCTION

Dionel Pérez, the president of a local chamber of commerce in Ciudad del Este, Paraguay, is a man who gets things done.[1] Pérez called me in October 2013, three days after the municipality evicted a group of hawkers occupying a contested land parcel called the Nine Hectares (Nueve Hectáreas), which was slated for shopping mall development. "I need to talk to you as soon as possible, in person," he emphasized.[2] His chamber promotes a brand of formalization that protects the profits of Ciudad del Este's border trade by slashing taxes on the import and fast reexport of electronics and other high-value merchandise. Bordering both Brazil and Argentina, Ciudad del Este is a strategic location for this sort of trading economy, and the city has earned a reputation as the "largest illicit economy in the hemisphere."[3] It draws elite businessmen from Lebanon to Seoul, small-scale Brazilian traders called *sacoleiros*, and Paraguayan street vendors. Cutting taxes eliminates the temptation to smuggle, advocates like Pérez argue. It also, in effect, legalizes contraband, as businesses trade without contributing much to state coffers.

Just outside the chamber's office, I walked past the armed, unsmiling security guard to take a rickety elevator to the chamber's office. The secretary, a poised young woman in a tight skirt, ushered me into Pérez's office. Even without her towering high heels, she was taller than Pérez, a self-assured Central American of small stature and immaculate dress. He spoke in short, bold declarations, a style of speech unburdened by questions: "I'm going to cut to the chase. We need to talk in confidence," he said to me. "The municipality asked me to speak with you. They know you were at the occupation of the Nine Hectares." Punching numbers into his cell phone, he said to me abruptly, "Don't say a word. I'm calling Arturo from the municipality. I'm going to put it on speaker phone.

FIGURE 1. A map of Ciudad del Este and the Tri-Border region; cartography by Alicia Cowart

FIGURE 2. *Sacoleiros* carry merchandise across the International Friendship Bridge; copyright Reuters

"Arturo. How are you. So the American woman was at the invasion yesterday. Is that so."

Arturo responded, "Yes. She was seen there with Muñoz."

I watched this staged glimpse of powerful men discussing my presence in the city with surprise. I had sought access to both the municipality and the opposition: street vendors and anticorruption activists rebelling against governing logics that shuttled between caretaking and coercion, between contingent protection and life-threatening evictions. "Well," I thought to myself, "it looks like I have lost access to the municipality."

I had been at the occupation, the bold but brief protest of the most marginalized vendors, hawkers who sold sweatshirts, socks, or thumb drives from shoulder bags. Officially an illegal or semilegal presence, hawkers were still ubiquitous; they were tolerated but also harassed by municipal officials and some established street vendors who resented the competition. By occupying the Nine Hectares, these vendors demanded that urban development benefit poor Paraguayans. They envisioned a state-owned vending space for the working poor, fulfilling the mandate that expropriated the land for this purpose in 1990.

A coalition of vendors and anticorruption activists disagreed over the best strategies for claiming the land. Tired of negotiations, the political operative Raul Muñoz had organized the occupation. I joined Raul as he rallied different contingents of protesters, choreographing their entry onto fenced-off land to set up camp. We stopped as Raul encouraged a group of women and their children from poor, underserviced neighborhoods not far from the city center. Their pragmatic loyalty to Raul held despite rumors that he had sold out his past constituents—informal lottery ticket sellers. Other leaders only organized with established vendors who could claim a specific spot in the street market, excluding these itinerant hawkers. I left the occupation a few hours later with high hopes that it represented a reckoning over the Nine Hectares, as well as bigger questions over who benefits from urban development.

Later that evening a journalist called me: "Let's go! They are evicting them right now!" Soon I was watching as a municipal lawyer oversaw legally questionable evictions.[4] Raul's sidekick and a few others lay on the ground, resisting arrest in front of a banner that read, "Expropriated by law for street vendors!" I watched, dismayed, as armed police officers manhandled protesters. Young women cried out, "Have a heart! We are poor!" and "I have five children to feed!" A crowd of more-established vendors watched from their tin-roofed stalls, despite the late hour. Someone shouted, "¡Fuera, mondaha!" (Get out, thieves), as another shouted, "¡Campesinos!" (Peasants), casting the poor families as outcast interlopers.

I recalled this scene in Pérez's office as he hung up the phone. He said, "You see. So it is best that you stop attending these protests. They invade private property. They are not real street vendors; they are just riffraff. The municipality doesn't like that you are there. So you will stop going to these things." My stomach sank as I assessed the turn of events. How far would the forms of security provided by whiteness and a U.S. passport extend? Studying street vendors and urban development meant also studying contraband, and everybody knew that contraband profits flowed through the municipality. A local reporter, a French anticorruption consultant, and Raul Muñoz had all received death threats for asking too many questions. A journalist once told me, "It's more dangerous to report on contraband than drug trafficking."

"Am I in danger?" I asked Pérez.

"Oh no, of course not. I would not stand for that. That's not the issue."

"Well, if I'm not in danger, then I want to understand the city from all sides," I said. "These vendors and their protests are part of the democratic process."

Pérez frowned, dissatisfied. "OK, but you won't talk to the press. Say you are doing a study, but you won't speak to the press."

Two years later, a mall called Shopping Paris towered in the very spot of Raul's occupation. Two half Eiffel Towers were awkwardly attached to the front facade in a brash reference to a Eurocentric modernity. Profits from the so-called black market, what I call *outlaw capital*, both built the mall and circulate through it. Many shoppers and traders avoid tariffs by using an underground transport network to move purchases across the border. Yet the mall looks legal. We recognize malls as the urban form of the modern city and read them as a sign of progress.

Ciudad del Este was, however, a globally integrated hub city long before the construction of frontier malls. The city may not look like the high-tech ports associated with globalization like Oakland and Vancouver, yet through the tumult of vending stalls, dirt roads, poor riverfront barrios, clandestine ports, and rundown shopping galleries the border economy nonetheless moves consumer goods worth billions of dollars. Yet places like Ciudad del Este are written out of most globalization stories and dismissed as spaces of lawlessness.

The study of Ciudad del Este makes plain the centrality of gray spaces and transgressive practices to the social reproduction of capitalism, a complex, historically produced, densely interconnected set of social relations manifesting differently across geography. In what follows, I argue that places like Ciudad del Este are zoned as sites of transgression, places cast out of thought even as they are crucial to the social reproduction of capitalist life. This means that

FIGURE 3. Shopping Paris; courtesy of Mariana Lagada

transgression is a key logic of accumulation. In working against powerful spatial stories that ignore or marginalize places like Ciudad del Este, I aim to show that this city is an expression of globalized capitalism rather than its corrupt antithesis. Contending with the rise of outlaw economies and the forms of political power they authorize is urgent for those desiring to plot pathways to more just urban worlds. I begin here with a brief overview of Ciudad del Este's border trade, situating it in global and regional trends, and then outline the main themes of the book: the making of outlaw economies, their expression in particular spatial forms, and their contestation by ordinary workers.

The Rise and Fall of a Hub City

"Here, everybody sells," proclaimed Emilio, a longtime street vendor and my friend's brother, when he picked me up from the airport upon my arrival in 2011 to begin this project. As we drove past vast monocultures of soybeans on the eighteen-mile ride to the city, he conveyed something of the city's heartbeat with his stories of the hard work and sacrifice behind his family's successful climb to a precarious perch in the Paraguayan middle class.[5] Indeed, Ciudad del Este buzzed with the commercial activity of thousands of street vendors and small-scale Brazilian buyers. About a million people live in the three cities of the Tri-Border Area—as it is called by the U.S. security apparatus—where

Paraguay, Argentina, and Brazil meet. The brisk border trade dominates the economic life of both Ciudad del Este and the Brazilian city of Foz do Iguaçu across the bridge.

Despite the decline in trade since the heyday of the 1980s and 1990s, the city certainly felt to me like a hub, with about five thousand street vendors selling within the eight square blocks of the *microcentro*, Ciudad del Este's center city. They occupied every possible inch of street and sidewalk space, many with vending infrastructure they built themselves incrementally over time. Tarps and tin roofs protected vendors against rain and the fierce Paraguayan sun, shading narrow corridors and strips between vendors' stalls and storefronts. Vendors share this urban space with hawkers, taxi drivers, and money changers. Business owners complain about losing street-front visibility as vendors block store entrances. Parts of the market felt to me like an overcrowded labyrinth, its darkened pathways stacked high with fake Gucci handbags, fishing rods, pirated CDs, cheap lingerie, and contact lenses to lighten brown eyes. A few shiny malls that symbolize reform contrast with a ramshackle warren of vendors' stalls and shopping galleries the size of city blocks, some spiderwebbed with pirated electrical connections. The hustling street commerce structuring the city center quickly gives way to rutted dirt roads and barrios of self-built shacks, many without running water or electricity. By 4:00 in the morning the market is in full swing as *sacoleiros* start shopping early in order to make the return trip to Foz do Iguaçu on the same day. By 4:00 in the afternoon the city quiets as low-wage municipal workers in orange jumpsuits methodically clean the streets from the detritus of the day's commerce.

Small-scale vendors and traders in the popular economy often bent or broke rules to avoid taxes and secure the urban spaces that enabled access to these trade flows. I use the term *street illegalities* to describe the popular, bottom-up economies through which ordinary Paraguayans and Brazilians captured some value from this global trade route. My use of the term also emphasizes the publicity of this work, as street vendors and *sacoleiros* rely on public spaces for their livelihoods, spaces that are in plain view, whereas elites have more resources to hide their illegalities out of sight.

Sacoleiros travel up to two thousand miles from the northeastern Brazilian cities of Recife and Fortaleza to buy cheap goods for resale; these arduous, risky trips have gotten riskier as the Brazilian state cracks down on "ant contraband" (*contrabando hormiga*), especially in the post-9/11 security era. This metaphor invokes the toil and scale of the trade: long individual journeys that together trace well-worn trails, the ant tracks of globalization. An intricate division of labor concentrates the risks of rule-breaking—the moment of illegal

FIGURE 4. Streets and sidewalks bustling with commerce in Ciudad del Este's city center; photo by author, 2013

FIGURE 5. Street vendors' stalls; photo by author, 2015

FIGURE 6. An itinerant hawker sells fruit to vendors; photo by author, 2013

border-crossing—onto traffickers, usually poor Paraguayans and Brazilians. Indeed, the city has been described as a prime example of globalization from below because regular people, not just transnational conglomerates, capture some of the value moving through world-spanning, post-Fordist economic forms.[6] This bottom-up framing draws our attention to the ways that the work of small-scale vendors, *sacoleiros*, taxi drivers, and others help produce the city and its profit potential.

Petty traders are joined by authorized large-scale importer-exporters and unauthorized *contrabandistas* who profit through arbitrage, that is, by taking advantage of price differences across space and between different markets.[7] Chapter 1 describes these dynamics in detail, using the term *extralegal* to underscore the mix of legalized and rule-breaking practices along gradients of transgression that confound the legal/illegal binary. For instance, customs agents clear cargo planes full of high-value merchandise by weight, a practice called *undervaluation*. By skirting customs categories, importer-exporters and specialized middlemen divert money from state coffers into their own pockets.

The volume of trade is astounding. Since the mid-1990s, the value of legal reexportation has fluctuated between U.S.$1 billion and $5 billion.[8] Educated guesses as to the annual value of contraband suggest it equaled or exceeded registered trade through the early 2000s, at times exceeding the country's GDP.[9] The precise trade volume is not knowable, but these estimates underscore its vast scale. One persistent rumor imagines Ciudad del Este as the third largest commercial economy in the world, after Hong Kong and Miami. Trade flows have dropped considerably in recent years, especially following the coronavirus crisis, but the city continues as a reexportation engine.

Ciudad del Este has long been global. This history confounds the stereotype of Paraguay as isolated or as an aberrant exception to regional trends, imaginaries I analyze in the next chapter. *Sacoleiros* move cell phones manufactured in Shenzhen, China, and handbags carried through Chile's free-trade zone in Iquique to street markets in São Paulo. Unsmiling money changers manage the fluctuations of four different currencies, while street vendors closely track the dips and rises of the Brazilian real, which impact their daily earnings. Brazilian and Chinese capitalists invest in frontier factories, malls, and high-rises. Cargo planes packed with electronics arrive direct from Hong Kong.

Scholars from the region, especially Eric Gustavo Cardin, Rosana Pinheiro-Machado, and Fernando Rabossi, astutely analyze the popular elements of the trade route.[10] They also document the dislocations wreaked by its criminalization over the last twenty years.[11] Their research is an essential view into Brazilian and Chinese sites along the trade route, places outside the scope of my research. My urban approach adds an analysis of the co-constitution of the trade route and the city, as late capitalism relies on and produces gray spaces of profitable transgression. It also offers an account of the various powers of transgressive practices—both spatial and economic—and demonstrates the key contradictions of outlaw capital: tens of thousands of poor street vendors and traders depend on the border economy, yet outlaw capital also reproduces stark inequalities and undermines democracy. Even further, I show how class conflict conditions contests over the boundaries of legality in both spatial and economic practice.

By the time I arrived to conduct fieldwork in 2011, intense pressures threatened the entire economic base of the city. The legal flexibilities that created openings for ordinary Paraguayans and Brazilians to benefit from globalized flows had become a liability. In the Islamophobic post-9/11 milieu, the U.S. security apparatus interpreted the presence of Lebanese traders as inherently threatening, intensifying pressures for border controls. Within Paraguay, proposals to draw foreign direct investment in *maquilas* (factories) presented the hope—and fantasy—of formalized production and waged job opportunities. Neoliberal trade liberalization put downward pressures on Brazilian tariffs, threatening the city's arbitrage potential. At the same time, proposed duty-free zones in Brazilian frontier cities threatened the city's economic viability as Brazilian policymakers sought to absorb these trade routes into Brazil. In addition, a corporate-led intellectual property rights movement, backed by the World Trade Organization, equated copies and trademark violations as criminal, launching a disciplinary antipiracy discourse targeting some of the goods and the workers moving through this trade circuit.[12] As this powerful antipiracy discourse criminalized *sacoleiros*, regional pressures for trade liberalization slowly eroded the arbitrage opportunities the Paraguayan state had studiously constructed over the decades.

Unsurprisingly, these contradictory reform efforts imagine and act on elite and street illegalities quite differently. I found that elite networks, even those connected to contraband, were better positioned to rewrite the rules of the game and less likely to become objects of reform than marginalized street vendors. I saw this most clearly in studying how an urban growth coalition that I call the *merchant bloc* successfully legalized part of the electronics trade, even though these were forms of commerce once considered contraband. Indeed, this was a big win for Pérez and his chamber of commerce, as they led a campaign to slash taxes and tariffs on the movement of electronics through national territory without contributing much to state coffers, actions that were also once labeled as contraband. Ex-president Horacio Cartes, for his part, secured political pacts to protect the contraband networks that moved the cigarettes produced in his frontier factories. As some illegalities were formalized and some criminalized, reform pushed much of the popular economy (sometimes designated as the informal economy) underground, intensifying a range of risks faced by small-scale workers.

The rise of Ciudad del Este as a contraband hub was made possible by authoritarian state projects, a story I detail in chapter 2. Paraguay's authoritarian president, Alfredo Stroessner, held office from 1954 until 1989 and sought regional economic integration with Brazil, founding the port town that would later become Ciudad del Este. In the 1950s, with intellectual support from the International Monetary Fund, he liberalized trade, cut taxes, and reduced tariffs to among the lowest on the continent, creating the conditions for the arbitrage economy. In the 1960s state modernization projects built urban infrastructure essential to the border trade, including Highway 2 and the International Friendship Bridge. Divvying access to lucrative contraband routes among his allies helped Stroessner stabilize his political alliances, and so he famously called contraband "the price of peace."[13] These *contrabandistas* smuggled luxury goods like perfume, whiskey, and cigarettes. Lebanese traders set up shops that became cornerstone businesses, importing name-brand goods, often from Miami, through Panama's free-trade zone in Colón or Paraguay's customs warehouse in the port of Paranaguá, Brazil. Taiwanese and Chinese migrants soon settled in the city, sourcing goods from China's emerging export processing zones.

Ciudad del Este was therefore shaped by and in turn influenced regional political-economic trends. The 1970s and 1980s were marked by the consolidation of neoliberalism, a suite of economic policies like austerity and deregulation, as well as practices of economizing political reason.[14] Emblematically, in authoritarian Chile, Augusto Pinochet launched neoliberal experiments with guidance from Chicago school economists, making plain neoliberalism's birth through state violence. U.S. foreign policy and global institutions like the World Bank promoted neoliberal reforms—the Washington Consensus—as a universal path toward national economic development. While these reforms may have increased aggregate economic growth, they also intensified inequality and social dislocation. Social movements across Latin America rebelled against these dislocations, so, as Fernando Coronil (2011, 237) has suggested, the "ideological supremacy of neoliberalism did not last long in Latin America."

Economic shocks and the rollback of social welfare measures pushed many into make-do worlds of informalized work, including street vending and the fast-growing *sacoleiro* circuit, which, by the 1990s, was booming. At the same time, the consumerist ethos spread, and consumption increasingly became a means for the poor and working classes to claim membership in an urban modernity. The China–Paraguay–Brazil trade network thus provided both much-needed income-generating opportunities and consumption subsidies for a growing class of urban consumers, especially in Brazil.

By the 1990s governments across the continent had moved away from U.S.-backed dictators to wide-ranging experiments with democracy. These experiments flourished in the 2000s as left-wing pink tide governments from Argentina to Venezuela invested in social programs, redistribution, democratic experimentation, cultural rights, and state-led economic management.[15] Bold and imperfect, these projects reduced poverty as social movements led by historically marginalized social groups challenged subordination and exclusion. Pink tide governments varied considerably but shared a growth-with-redistribution political-economic model. Described as neodevelopmentalism, this export-oriented model generated economic growth through extraction.[16] It was dependent on global commodity prices and vulnerable to inevitable economic crises. Rather than hooking political membership to waged work (the model in North Atlantic countries), state income supports like cash transfers amplified the purchasing power of the poor and working classes, generating some of the consumer demand necessary to keep up the endless growth cycle.

With President Fernando Lugo (2008–12), Paraguay briefly joined the pink tide. His 2012 ouster foreshadowed new strategies of regional right-wing statecraft, namely, the parliamentary coup in which the removal of an elected president was hidden behind a veil of legality.[17] His removal from office also highlights revanchist reactions to even modest attempts to challenge the power of entrenched elites and more equitably distribute social wealth, key dynamics in the expansion of the authoritarian Right across Latin America and, indeed, in the rise of Trumpism in the United States. Writers with the Argentine Colectivo Situaciones frame the dilemmas of the regional conjuncture as an impasse rather than as the more common "transition to democracy" because the twinning of colonial-authoritarian power and global capitalist exploitation has so stunted the forms of collective political-economic power and emancipatory imagination necessary for transformation.[18] Throughout this book I argue that part of this impasse is the constitutive nature of elite illegalities and the structured forms of misapprehension that normalize or obscure them.

Outlaw Economies under Neoliberalism

Outlaw economies are central to global capitalism. This assertion is almost banal, as the power and reach of outlaw economies generate relentless media attention, populate film storylines, and garner the attention of anthropologists, criminologists, and sociologists. Indeed, more than a decade ago anthropologist Carolyn Nordstrom (2007) coined the term *il/legal* to describe the interpenetration of illegality and rule-breaking throughout a social field of legitimated economic practices. However, research on the urban dimensions of global capitalism has yet to fully contend with cities like Ciudad del Este: a motor of commodity circulation constructed extralegally and from the bottom up, not just the top down. These shadow worlds constitute a significant share of global economic activity even as measurement of their size is an impossible task.[19]

Across the Americas and beyond, overlapping crises today condition life. Crises open up spaces for extralegal economies. Neoliberalism's deregulatory impulse opens up new spaces for illegal, illicit, and criminal economic activities as it promotes the free movement of capital, even as states invest in militarized policing and border controls to limit the free movement of people. Decades of neoliberal austerity have also undermined the social capacities of states, expanding the need for bottom-up worlds of rule-breaking work. As these informalized and criminalized worlds of work meet urgent livelihood needs, they are especially important during economic downturns. The centrality of these economies means that ordinary people's everyday lives are intertwined with contraband, drug trafficking, and the like.[20] On a global scale, extralegal trade moves consumer goods worth billions, even trillions when estimates include drugs and other illegalized commodities.[21] This vast scale underscores that illicit and illegal economic organizations like contraband networks, drug traffickers, and cartels shape globalized capitalism as much as so-called legal firms through economic relations that are transnational, diverse, and responsive.[22] Today's glut in production and overcapacity in manufacturing may even invite the intensification of outlaw economies as investors struggle to find legal and profitable investments over an already staggering global GDP of U.S.$87 trillion in 2019.[23] As investigative journalist Dawn Paley demonstrates, the war on drugs is actually a war on people aimed at opening up new spaces for profitable, "formal" investment by clearing land-based communities from Colombia to Mexico.[24] Drug economies, furthermore, work in a "symbiotic relationship" with neoliberal economic forms like NAFTA, while the widespread involvement of state officials in drug trafficking has led some to describe places like Mexico as a narco-state.[25]

Illicit flows of money further intertwine with other financial transactions. Institutionalized corporate tax evasion through offshore accounts—"advanced business services" in corporate parlance—shelters about U.S.$2.6 trillion for Fortune 500 companies and shapes regulatory landscapes.[26] It also remains largely unpunished. Drug money also helped shore up the global economic system in the wake of the 2008 financial crisis.[27] Antonio Maria Costa, former executive director of the United Nations Office on Drugs and Crime (2002–10), reflected that money from the drug trade funded the interbank loans necessary to keep some banks afloat as the global economy faltered.[28] One journalist commented that money from drug gangs "appear[s] to be one of capitalism's global savings accounts."[29] A few years later, the U.S. attorney general found that British megabank HSBC had laundered money for drug cartels. Traffickers designed specialized cash boxes sized to fit HSBC teller windows for regular deposits of hundreds of thousands of dollars.[30] The deposit boxes passing between the hands of the trafficker and teller suture the underworlds of drug money to the vaunted worlds of finance, mundane actions that turn dirty money clean. In a decision epitomizing the deep race-class biases of the legal system, the U.S. Justice Department opted to fine HSBC U.S.$1.9 billion (about five weeks of the bank's income), with no serious penalties for executives.

State power is intertwined with these processes rather than outside of them. A critical, processual take on state power contests the dominant view across the social sciences that outlaw economies thrive where the state is weak or absent.[31] This weak state perspective argues that outlaw economies thrive in spaces where the sovereignty of the state wanes or where governance fails.[32] Instead, what is at stake is the coexistence of multiple forms of political authority, pluralisms that dominant Western theories of state and governance struggle to see.[33] As I argue throughout this book, outlaw economies co-constitute with state power. At the most abstract level, states *produce* illegality and crime with the power of defining boundaries between legal and illegal.[34] This frame is an essential starting point, but we need to zoom in to see how the social construction of legality articulates historically specific practices of power that support some economic projects over others. Drawing on Charles Tilly's (1985) argument that early European states were formed through protection rackets and war, Alan Karras (2010) argues that smuggling helped construct modern states. Indeed, smuggling was so central to the political-economic formation of the United States that Peter Andreas (2013, 3) suggests that the "oft-celebrated rise of American capitalism" should be understood as contraband capitalism. Others demonstrate that profits from drug trafficking helped consolidate global capitalism, emblematically with British war ships forcing open China to the sale of opium, the proceeds of which propped up the British Empire.[35] Assumptions that outlaw economies thrive in spaces of so-called state absence belie these histories and overlook how state formation works alongside and through illicit organizations. Instead, state formation is contested, ongoing, and processual.[36] This book unpacks the relationships between outlaw capital and state power, which are also questions of their relationship to class power.

I define outlaw capital as a mode of accumulation that negotiates profits and distributes rents from legal transgression. The terms *negotiate* and *distribute* emphasize that outlaw capital does not organize the production of surplus value; instead, outlaw capitalists capture value.[37] Such transgressive forms of profitability require camouflage, or what I have come to think of as *obscuration*. This term means "the action of hiding or concealing something" and emphasizes that profitability via transgression requires varied forms of masking.[38] Outlaw capital works through situated deals, bribes, and schemes. Deals are the transgressive practices producing profitability, and bribes are part of the transaction costs. The term *scheme* is inspired by the Paraguayan term *esquema* and describes the enabling alliances that connect state agents to economic actors. Dealmaking and alliances are situated and shifty, made possible through personal relationships rather than the logics of abstraction and commensurability that characterize finance capital.[39] Conceptually, then, outlaw capital is a form of capital. Like Marx's general category of capital, outlaw capital is both a social relation and the product of that relation in the form of profits from extralegal economic practices. In a similar vein, Teo Ballvé (2019, 218) shows that narco-capital has its own logics, a quantitative difference that is realized through massive profit margins in the drug trade alongside a qualitative difference that involves the necessity to "remove the blockage of illegality" through laundering and land deals.

Appropriation and dispossession have always been core logics of capital.[40] Capitalism continually renews its conditions of possibility by capturing or colonizing hitherto uncommodified spheres of life, from stealing Indigenous land for resource extraction to commodifying clean air through carbon markets. These enclosures are an ongoing process rather than a founding moment.[41] Unlike what Marx called the "silent compulsion" of normalized wage exploitation (to which many of us consent), these enclosures often require violence and coercion not uncommonly abetted by state action.[42] These processes of *accumulation by dispossession*, rather than value creation, are the "dominant form" of accumulation under late capitalism (Harvey 2003, 153), a seismic reframing of Marxism's historic focus on production and labor, narrowly defined. This framing centers resistance movements to dispossession as key to anticapitalist politics. Yet accumulation by dispossession holds together many divergent processes, from land grabs to pension privatization to gentrification.

These specific dynamics of outlaw capital merit attention so we can better appreciate capitalism as a complex and mutating social formation working through worlds beyond waged and productive labor. With the concept "accumulation by extra-economic means," Jim Glassman (2006, 617) gathers enclosures and forms of accumulation enabled by the uncompensated but essential (gendered and racialized) work of social reproduction.[43] The tag "extra-economic" emphasizes processes internal to capitalism but outside the wage relation, a key distinction, given the decline of waged work and production as capitalism's central pivots. Outlaw capital is a mode of accumulation by extra-economic means.[44] Rather than enclosing an easily identified commons, accumulation by transgression *captures* or *redistributes* revenue streams through illegalities.[45] Of course, capitalists break the law often, but with outlaw capital, transgression creates the conditions for profitability. Thus, I argue that *accumulation by transgression* is the core logic of outlaw capital, a means of valuation that captures rents through rule-breaking and dealmaking.[46] This framing helps specify the elite illegalities, political alliances, and everyday practices of value capture at work in extralegal economies in Ciudad del Este and beyond.

These modes of accumulation are central to capitalism rather than an aberration or deviation. The relations that construct and obscure outlaw capital are both material and epistemological. "Everybody knows," street vendors would say to me when I asked how they knew that contraband profits flowed through the municipality or that the president cut deals with cops and naval officers to protect the clandestine transit networks that moved his cigarettes. In this book, I argue that there is a fatal intertwining of outlaw capital, how we know it, and how it escapes being known.

Social hierarchies of class, race, and gender all play vital roles in these dynamics. Indeed, race and racism are constitutive of outlaw capital's social relations. Theories of racial capitalism from the Black radical tradition explain how capitalism incorporates and depends on the "devaluation of nonwhite bodies," as Laura Pulido (2017, 525) argues. From its origins, capitalism tended to "differentiate—to exaggerate regional, subcultural, and dialectical differences into 'racial' ones," as Cedric Robinson (1983, 26) argues.[47] Capitalism requires and produces stark, life-taking inequalities, for it is by moving through these hierarchies of difference that capital accumulates. As Jodi Melamed (2015, 77) explains, "Racism enshrines the inequalities that capitalism requires."[48]

Race mediates powerful discourses of legitimacy and corruption. These discourses sort celebrated places, peoples, and forms of economic practice from those that are condemned. Racial regimes operate differently in different places. In old apartheid states like the United States and South Africa, where many theories of racial capitalism originate, rigid, legalized hierarchies of racial difference excluded those assessed as nonwhite through pseudometrics like the one-drop rule, even as membership in the category of white slowly expanded.[49] Across Latin America, social hierarchies operate through a more flexible "pigmentocracy" that correlates light skin and perceived proximity to Europeanness with higher social status.[50] Latin Americans of all colors also negotiate their position in a global field of Eurocentrism and Euro-American cultural hegemony. In all cases, racism produces the social categories of race. This analysis challenges the prevailing view that perceived racial differences produce racism.[51]

Bringing theories of racial capitalism to the study of outlaw capital helps clarify why and how street illegalities are punished while elite illegalities are protected or even celebrated. As I show, elite networks rely on racialized modes of obfuscation to hide and legitimate their transgressions. Learning from the Paraguayan vernacular critique of *blanqueamiento* (whitening), as well as scholars of racial capitalism, I analyze how epistemologies of whiteness justify elite illegalities and enable the deadly scapegoating of those marked disposable, via racialized logics, who are also those disproportionately dependent on criminalized worlds of work. I argue that this death-dealing articulation cannot be understood apart from racialization as a dynamic that undergirds law and policy. This articulation also animates epistemologies in imagining a bounded, legal economy that can be separated from a criminal one.

As a key node of outlaw capital, Ciudad del Este is a privileged place from which to ask big questions about its forms, functions, logics, and consequences. Indeed, accumulation by transgression now appears to be entrenched in the conditions of late capitalism, a process I explore in the book's conclusion. The story of Ciudad del Este's rise from a tiny river port town to a global contraband hub is important on its own terms. Furthermore, thinking from this place and alongside the everyday struggles of the city's ordinary workers can teach us about global capitalist transformation writ large.

Contraband Urbanism

In Ciudad del Este, the border economy grew up with the city as an entangled mix of legal trade and smuggling built from the bottom up, not just the top down, by street vendors and Brazilian traders. Enabling these commodity circulations requires infrastructure and investment in physical space.[52] Indeed, the force of the border trade shaped the built environment, producing urban infrastructures oriented toward enabling commerce both registered and off the books. Yet the spatial productions and politics of outlaw economies are not well understood. Disciplines like geography and urban studies—equipped to analyze the social production of space—remain "almost entirely undisturbed" by research in anthropology, sociology, and criminology that details the power and reach of extralegal economies.[53] Security scholars, for example, have observed how these "nimble, dispersed, adaptive networks" concentrate in particular places but tend to imagine locally produced "lawless zones" and "partial state degradation" exploited by bad actors.[54] These approaches underappreciate the relationships between outlaw capital, political power, and urban space while at the same time they create an unhelpful disciplinary division of intellectual labor that separates the study of cities of poverty from investigations of "world-class" cities of industry or technology. Ciudad del Este links these worlds, connecting iconic zones of manufacturing in China's Pearl River Delta to major urban hubs like São Paulo.

This book tackles the urban dimensions of extralegal trade economies, studying both the built form of Ciudad del Este and the practical forms of knowledge that enable it.[55] I follow the spatial turn in the social sciences and scholarship influenced by the French theorist Henri Lefebvre, which demonstrates that the environments we occupy are historically and socially produced. Each society produces a particular kind of space, urban environments that both reflect and influence social values.[56] The social dimensions of power embedded in this informal trade city are particularly important because most critical research on global capitalism focuses on production, what Marx called the "hidden abode," to emphasize production as the real political-economic motor behind the more visible worlds of exchange, that is, buying and selling. While his adversaries, the classical political economists, focused on exchange, Marx insisted on the centrality of the social relationships of production as the site of alienated labor and value creation. Merchants, as scholars like David Harvey (2017, 36) insist, "by and large create no value." Instead, they merely support the realization of value by moving goods swiftly to market, as capital—value in motion—changes forms from money to commodity back to money plus profit.

But realization is not a seamless process. Cities have long been key to global geographies of commerce. From Italian merchant cities to the entrepôt port towns of China, traders congregate, negotiate, sell, and organize transport, shaping spaces and subjectivities along the way. Merchants also shape law, policy, and statecraft.[57] Today, globalized trade requires the fast movement of consumer goods and production inputs across vast economic space. This "lively system" prioritizes moving commodities as a national security imperative, applying the logics of war to the practices of trade.[58] In this global system, the distributive city is a new niche: sophisticated logistics hubs oriented around the circulation of goods.[59] In places like Oakland, California, unionized dock workers use cybernetic ID cards to access securitized space where they unload container ships with high-tech machines. But there is also a world of commodities moved by people. It runs along unexpected paths, like the China–Paraguay–Brazil trade route, allowing some in these spaces to profit. The distinct spatial forms, modes of social control, and labor processes along these routes circulate an astounding volume of goods. As a contraband powerhouse, Ciudad del Este is a privileged site from which to study the logics, practices, and consequences of extralegal trade economies.

In the city, contentious political struggles shape who has access to border profits. If economic practices are always spatial, whose practices will be banished, outlawed, or targeted for reform? At the city scale, the built environment funnels *sacoleiros* and shopping tourists to sites of sale and consumption, carving out a shifting geography of profit possibilities. I learned the stakes of these microgeographies while chatting with a respected cell phone vendor in a choice location outside a busy shopping gallery. "I could sell my vending spot [*mi puesto*] tomorrow for $10,000," he commented, describing elaborate workarounds that would enable him to transfer his vending claim to another, even though sidewalk space is officially public and nonexchangeable.[60] Other vendors confirmed this price, putting the under-the-table square footage value of prime vending space in Ciudad del Este on par with cities like Tokyo and Tel Aviv.[61] The steep price of a small slice of sidewalk helps explain why struggles over the form and future of the city are so intense.

Attention to the social production of space challenges dominant assessments that interpret Ciudad del Este's commercial frenzy and irregular occupations of city space as a lack of urban planning. By their nature, urban reforms upend one spatial arrangement of the city's economy to promote another, benefiting some and hurting others. The projects I observed proceeded in fits and starts. Plans changed constantly. Vendors' associations, municipal officials, and private developers negotiated constantly, sometimes in back rooms and sometimes through protests designed to garner press attention. Provisional deals rather than master plans or official public processes guide development across the city. Yet this too is the "public production of space," that is to say, urban planning, as I have argued elsewhere.[62]

This framing of the social production of space also helps us see the impossibility of reading transgression or compliance off of urban forms. Indeed, the malls promoted by the merchant bloc broke zoning codes, environmental laws, and development restrictions. While traders move fake Gucci handbags and Johnny Walker whiskey through clandestine ports, buyers can make these purchases in high-end shopping malls like Shopping Paris. Yet most mainstream globalization stories split apart malls from clandestine ports by celebrating the former, condemning the latter, and misunderstanding both. I came to think of these stories as discourses of disconnection because they misread global and interconnected economic relationships as local forms of corruption or backwardness. Instead, infrastructures of authorized commerce are intertwined with spaces of contraband across scales. Just as frontier malls depend on clandestine ports, signature spaces of globalization like special economic zones (SEZs) use zones of transgression like Ciudad del Este.

While I center Ciudad del Este, I do not propose adding something that we might call an informal trade city to urban typologies. Urban typologies are the impulse of global urbanism, the hegemonic form of depoliticized, market-oriented urban development. Global urbanism, as "loose bundles of ideas and practices," assumes that the trajectories of a small number of North Atlantic cities are both desirable and universally applicable even as these reforms often entrench inequality and uneven development, as Eric Sheppard, Helga Leitner, and Anant Maringanti (2013, 894) argue. Urbanism as a field of action-enabling knowledge is what Lefebvre (2003, 23) calls a "blind field," that is, a structured form of misapprehension that obscures how space is produced as a "class strategy" (157). Oriented toward securing the conditions of economic growth without regard for the social consequences, global urbanism's blind field obscures outlaw capital.

Urbanization is a complex, differentiated set of processes with impacts extending beyond the juridical boundaries of any given city. Lefebvre (2003, 1) captured these dynamics in saying that "society has been completely urbanized." The category of the urban instead of the city emphasizes these processes as geographically extensive, historically produced, and intertwined with capital accumulation. Any space is always an unfinished product of countless interrelations, the site of multiplicity and therefore of political possibility, as we learn from Doreen Massey's (2005; see also 2004) work on the relational production of space.[63] Places are nodes in networks of expansive sociospatial processes, like trade routes connecting far-flung East Asian factories and Brazilian consumers. This relational approach emphasizes how multiscalar relations come together to construct a particular place, from the global to the hyperlocal.

Feminist and postcolonial thinkers emphasize that alongside and through global capitalist urbanization other systems of domination and resistance are at work. These differences take many forms, including cultural forms and social hierarchies like race and gender, as well as historical differences resulting from imperial geographies of uneven development. Theorists in the planetary urbanization school or Marxist geographers like David Harvey posit universal or general processes of capitalist change, which produce "an infinite variety of physical city landscapes and social forms."[64] Gillian Hart (2016) and other feminists critique these approaches for ascribing determinative power a priori to the forces of capitalist urbanization and for not seeing the force of forms of difference like race and gender.[65] The local in these models can only resist, not generate. In contesting this from various vantage points, feminist and postcolonial scholars insist that difference is constitutive—it is an active, generative force.

The study of the forces that collide in this unexpected border town can help illuminate how the trajectories colluding here are shaped by places elsewhere: the street markets of Brazil, the production rhythms in East Asian factories, a family in Lebanon missing their father but enjoying the privileged life supported by his electronics import-export business. Furthermore, this study can help us analyze how illegalities shape urban spaces, global trade networks, and the far horizons of the politically possible. While this story is grounded in Ciudad del Este, the insight that uneven development zones certain places as sites of profitable transgression can be applied to other places, including border towns, smuggling centers, and tax havens, as well as to supposed paragons of legality like "Londongrad," where city planners protect the dodgy money of Russian billionaires with an accommodating legal regime, even offering "golden visas" to those who invest U.S.$1.3 million.[66]

Popular Economies

The everyday practices of ordinary Paraguayans helped to build Ciudad del Este into a vibrant trade city as working-class Brazilians traveled the tracks of ant contraband, stitching together the cities along the trade route. The dynamics of this frontier trading hub differ from many Latin American cities where street vending is common, yet we can still learn from the histories and struggles of street vendors in Ciudad del Este. I highlight street vendors' claims to urban livelihood rights as a useful intervention in theories and practices of urban life. Critical researchers from Latin America use the frame of *popular economies* to emphasize these worlds as more-than-economic and as a "field of dispute," to use Verónica Gago's (2018, 34) term, because these economies contest the distribution of the social surplus.[67] This framing is crucial because the global urban majority—poor city dwellers in the Global South and North—depends on unwaged work outside state labor protections. Today, the paradigmatic worker is not a unionized factory man but rather a woman hustling as a street vendor or waste picker, juggling multiple debts to fund the tools of her trade, and bearing the inevitable risks of her work alone or with the support of similarly strapped family and community. In most places, unwaged work is now the norm rather than a temporary stage along a pregiven developmental path heading inexorably toward formal employment.[68] Indeed, secure, unionized, well-paid employment as the median form of work was limited to so-called developed countries for a few postwar decades, and then with significant racialized and gendered exclusions.[69]

Street vending is often included in the category of informal work, which encompasses a wide range of income-generating activities outside of the wage relation and state labor protections.[70] In South American countries, participation in nonagricultural work designated as informal ranges from around 40 percent in countries like Chile and Brazil to more than 70 percent in Paraguay.[71] The study of popular economies also reveals that informal workers produce value. The work of waste pickers, for example, reduces the cost of public waste management services by diverting recyclables away from landfills. Informal firms produce goods cheaply, reducing costs for formal, capitalist firms that depend on these inputs.[72] Vendors and traders along the China–Paraguay–Brazil trade route move merchandise cheaply through global space, subsidizing consumption.

Some observers describe informal worlds of work as spaces of survival, arguing that late capitalism expands *surplus population*, a term Marx used to describe those unnecessary to the exigencies of capital.[73] Mike Davis (2006, 178) exemplifies this view, arguing that "informal survivalism" strips labor of historical agency as tough competition fractures the working class. Under the brutal logics of late capitalism with chronic job scarcity and intensifying inequality, he argues, those engaged in informal survivalism can focus only on the daily struggle, as they lack energy and resources to invest in transforming the conditions of their lives and labor. The problem with this view is that it reads political potential off of structural location, ignores the power of organized informal workers, and reifies the industrial proletariat as the subject of history, a bleak proposition given the decline of waged work.[74] The informal survivalism perspective also underappreciates the multiplicity of work worlds, which are also modes of making life.[75] Popular economies are necessary spaces of livelihood, complex systems of redistribution, and community networks that can be tapped in times of need.[76] Under the condition of calamitous state disinvestment from collective life, what geographer Ruth Wilson Gilmore (2007, 178) calls "organized abandonment," popular economies provide a buffer against outright destitution.

Informal work is also important as a permanent feature of capitalist economies.[77] Yet informal work is consistently devalued, dismissed as survivalism, or described as impermanent. Contesting this deficit framing highlights a key contradiction not often explicitly named in the extensive literature on informal work. Capitalism—especially today's predatory neoliberal forms—creates the conditions that impel people to work informally, even as the value produced by these workers is often appropriated, as I detail in other work.[78] Nancy Fraser (2014, 59) captured this relationship of appropriation when she described how capital "siphons off value" from informalized work worlds. Thus, like a

Möbius strip, wageless workers are at once inside and outside: they are simultaneously marginalized as they also produce value, construct urban spaces, and defend their right to livelihood in cities with urban policies that often seek to banish the poor rather than support their flourishing.

While contesting the deficit framing of these economic worlds, it is also essential not to romanticize them. Popular economies are complex and contradictory, combining individualism and community, competition and collaboration, autonomy and drudgery.[79] They are spaces of care and commoning, just as they can involve exclusions, harms, and hierarchies. Desiring a counterforce outside capitalist social relations, some theorize popular economies as a "counterpoint to capitalist economic rationality" or sites of unproblematic resistance.[80] But romanticized framings of "solidarity economies" can impose an ideal standard that actually existing social worlds rarely meet. Such framings can also overlook how these economic worlds are intertwined with capitalist social relations.[81] Thus, our theories of popular economies must be able to track their imbrications with capitalism writ large. For instance, the extension of private credit, sometimes backed with proof of state income supports, opens up popular economies to relations of accumulation and wealth extraction.[82] Popular economies also enable the social reproduction of workers and thus are a condition of possibility for work designated as productive.

Of course, vendors within Ciudad del Este are not homogeneous. Their earnings, tenure security, and politics vary widely. Some vendor politics are exclusionary or reinforce common notions of the deserving poor or the productive citizen. Others foster new ways of thinking about urban life, livelihood, and the right to the city. I think of these latter practices as insurgent in the sense outlined by Faranak Miraftab (2009): they are counterhegemonic, transgressive, and imaginative, promoting worlds otherwise. The role of the intellectual is to analyze new forms of exploitation and dispossession, expose the tensions within movements challenging inequalities, and, as Gago (2017, 26) argues, lift up that which "antagonizes and . . . ruins, spoils, and/or confronts that supposed hegemony [of neoliberalism]." Thus, I prioritize—without romanticizing—the claims of poor Paraguayans to explore their useful urban epistemologies.

Methodology

With a fake Gucci handbag from the street market slung over my shoulder, I walked to an interview across town from the quiet neighborhood where I lived with friends. Inside the bag I stuffed a pair of high heels alongside my voice recorder and several notebooks, the stock-in-trade of ethnographers. Heels, painted nails, and lipstick symbolized my performance of professional femininity, a self-conscious tactic of gender conformity I hoped would help me stick out a bit less as I sought to establish connections across the city. I slipped on the heels before walking through the wrought-iron municipal gates erected to protect government officials from protesting publics. I waited fifteen minutes before being called to the office of the mayor's assistant. He looked my tall frame up and down as I walked in, commenting, "You must play basketball."[83] I tried not to cringe as I shook his hand. "Your handshake is much too strong for a woman," he declared, settling in behind his desk before adding, "What can I do for you today?"

Across fifteen months of ethnographic fieldwork between 2011 and 2015, my gringo accent, gender expression, U.S. citizenship, and blue eyes always marked my presence as embodiments of my outsider status. My negotiations of these lines of difference shape the partial, embodied knowledge claims outlined in this book. After all, there is no unmarked body from which to produce detached, objective, unbiased theories of the world. All knowledge is partial, embodied; it is made from somewhere and some*body*.[84] And so white skin, along with the UC Berkeley logo on my business card, often coded me as a legitimate researcher, opening some doors while closing others. My U.S. passport provided a measure of safety as I navigated the fraught waters where political authority and extralegality mix. I felt these forms of protection in Pérez's office as he staged his call to the city official, telegraphing his message to me: "You are being watched." In short, my positionality shaped what I could and could not see. While I was not invited into some of the key spaces of contraband, I still learned something of its logics, logistics, politics, and consequences.

Ethnography transforms life experience into data in a political economy of knowledge production that is often extractive. Researchers backed by universities in the Global North can turn ethnographic encounters into beneficial products like books. In contrast, the benefits to our interlocutors are less clear. Scholarly agendas usually operate through time frames and logics that do not coincide with those on the front lines of late capitalism, like campaigning street vendors' organizations. Obdulio, a street vendor you will meet in chapter 4, often chided me, once commenting, "Doctora, while you work up your study, your patient is dying." I hope this book makes visible—for it cannot resolve—the ethical dilemmas of studying across the power-laden differences so well documented by feminist ethnographers.[85]

I returned to Paraguay for dissertation research four years after I finished a two-year stint there as a Peace Corps volunteer. It made sense to return to a country I knew well. Yet my return was also predicated on my relationship with a dubious development organization forged out of Cold War paranoia and seen by the likes of George W. Bush as a vehicle for spreading the "compassion of our country to every part of the world."[86] Given the tenacious, bipartisan proclivity of U.S. foreign policy to confuse compassion with empire and plunder, I feel the weight of my association with this imperial institution. While serving as a volunteer, I published an essay for an in-house magazine titled "A Case against the Peace Corps" in which I reflected on the links between altruistic agency, U.S. imperial interests, the Peace Corps, and American "cultural arrogance," as I called it then. Perhaps I returned to Paraguay seeking exoneration. Yet anthropology, geography, urban planning, and area studies are also caught up in imperial histories and legacies of epistemic violence.[87] Leaving the world of international development to study it cannot eradicate complicity, for the critic and practitioner are likewise bound up in social relations of capitalism and empire.

As an antiracist feminist who dreams of worlds beyond capitalism, I stand with ordinary workers and their everyday struggles to earn their daily bread in a hard city. My political commitments inevitably shaped each stage of the research and writing process, including the methodologies and myriad decisions that make up any research project. In particular, the gaze of this project is turned to both elite practices of power and everyday spaces of sociality and survival. This approach acknowledges the oft-forgotten truth that poverty is produced in relation to spaces of wealth, privilege, and protection (and, further, that these relationships are often forged through violence). I see these commitments and research ethics as a strength. While I cannot offer a comprehensive story (no one can), I hope to offer a useful one that demonstrates the power and politics of outlaw capital.

While outlaw economies work by being hard to see, their dynamics are also open secrets to those who negotiate shifting legalities in their work on the street. Ethnographic attention to the street economy, then, provides an important window into the border economy more broadly, as street vendors have useful, albeit partial, knowledge of its workings. Even more, it is an ethical commitment to learn from those on the front lines of this instantiation of racial capitalism. Thus, ultimately, I will also argue that street vendors' embodied knowledge is a useful vantage point from which to construct ethical urban epistemologies. I choose to lift up street vendors' challenges not because these are the only or even the most forceful dynamics at work but because transformative change requires training ourselves to see and foment small rebellions and epistemological disputes that contest the naturalized terrain of that which is taken for granted. This is the intellectual work of good critical social theory. I also prioritized participant observation with street vendors for pragmatic reasons: it was harder to access spaces of elite illegalities, as the powerful have the means to hide and protect their transgressions, while the poor—spatially segregated into public spaces for livelihood and work—break the rules in plain sight.

I also take seriously the productive power of this place. Critical and post-colonial urban theorists emphasize how our theories of the world are always shaped by the places from which we make them. All knowledge is situated. Acknowledging the imprint of place on theory challenges the Eurocentrism of dominant urban canons and their easy claims that placeless theories produced out of a few North Atlantic cities produce universal frameworks. Feminist and postcolonial scholars have demonstrated that by "seeing from the South" we do not merely add empirical variation from southern cities to established—even entrenched—urban theories. Instead, we need a more inclusive register of the sites of theory making along with methods attentive to history, place, and power.[88] Indeed, for many readers outside South America, Ciudad del Este may be symbolically "off the map," as Jennifer Robinson (2002, 535) might say. Yet materially, it is a crucial node in globalized capitalism. Building theory from Ciudad del Este thus holds the potential to generate better systems of explanation. Grounded in this intellectual lineage, this book argues that Ciudad del Este expresses and shapes globalized capitalism.

All economies, including outlaw ones, are the result of countless everyday interactions across scales organized by everyday practices and regimes of knowledge. This ethnographic account of outlaw capital centers everyday life, a domain that is at once concrete and abstract. This is a Lefebvrian—rather than an anthropological—perspective, emphasizing that everyday life expresses contradictory dynamics: it is "colonized by capitalism," as Stuart Elden (2004, 117) says. It can also be the ground of transformation, of more emancipatory ways of being, building, and becoming. I use the ethnographic orientation of defamiliarization to take apart various forms of urban knowledge regarding the border city, including its raison d'être (its reason for being).[89] I brought this sensibility of defamiliarization to interviews with a range of municipal and national state actors, as well as to a key chamber of commerce for electronics importer-exporters.

Contraband economies and outlaw capital are ghostly: they operate in the shadows and draw power from being hard to see. They do not exist on official maps, and they escape national customs accounts of imports and exports. They also challenge many mental maps of what economies should look like. The abstract models employed by economists and development experts wildly misread the everyday messiness of economic life in places like Ciudad del Este. These models cannot see how outlaw capital works through norms of protection, prosecution, invisibility, and immunity that tend to protect the well-off and expose the already vulnerable. Ethnographic attention to the everyday making of outlaw economies, then, is a key counterpoint to these official stories.

I studied different spaces of commerce, from the more expected (malls, vending stalls, shops, and street corners) to the perhaps less expected (clandestine ports, the International Friendship Bridge, and the Paraná River). I spent countless hours talking to street vendors and others whose work centered on the street: association leaders, taxi drivers, and political brokers known as *operadores*. I also interviewed frontier businessmen about the histories and logistics of the border trade and observed the daily workings of Pérez's controversial chamber of commerce. While contraband works by being hard to see, it nonetheless leaves archival traces in USAID reports, leaked U.S. Embassy cables, and the Stroessner-era state security documents colloquially known as the Archives of Terror, which are usually used to find information about U.S.-backed state violence and extrajudicial killings. My official affiliation with the economic think tank Centro de Análisis y Difusión de la Economía Paraguaya (CADEP) helped me understand the maze of regulations delineating how commodities are supposed to move through national space. A CADEP research assistant and I compiled a fifty-year history of the complex, contradictory statutes and laws governing reexportation. I also interviewed national government officials, policymakers, ministry heads, and elected representatives.

Furthermore, in addition to these efforts, I also observed key spaces of contestation: the waiting rooms of the municipal Office of Urban Development (Dirección de Área Urbana), everyday enforcement encounters enacted on the street, and sporadic public protests. Following a wave of evictions in the street market in 2013, I accompanied three groups of vendors as they negotiated for permission to sell again from the street market. I also shadowed municipal officials during a campaign to "order and clean up" city streets called the Thirty-Day Plan (Plan de Treinta Días). I historicized the decades-long conflict over urban development on the Nine Hectares and a multiday bridge blockage in 2001 that shuttered the city and paralyzed national exports. I focused on several differently scaled formalization efforts that expressed wildly different views of the good city: (1) a project to register and recognize some street vendors' claims to space called the Pilot Plan (Plan Piloto); (2) Pérez's project to formalize the electronic trade through the near elimination of taxes and tariffs; and (3) a binational effort to register and tax *sacoleiros* called the Unified Tax Regime (Régimen de Tributo Unificado, RTU).

I conducted interviews and fieldwork in Spanish and the Indigenous language of Guaraní, widely spoken by mestizo Paraguayans. Guaraní persisted despite its prohibition under Stroessner, and it remains the language of the heart for the popular classes, while Spanish is the language of bureaucracy and power. The widespread embrace of an Indigenous language by mestizos—90 percent of Paraguayans speak Guaraní—is unique in the Americas. Colonialism more commonly assimilates those with mixed Indigenous and Iberian heritage into Spanish or Portuguese. Yet while Paraguayan culture valorizes Guaraní language and mythology as a cornerstone of national culture, members of the country's eighteen Indigenous groups face intense exclusion and discrimination. I learned Guaraní as a commitment to a place not my own and to many generous friends and interlocutors. It was a small step toward what postcolonial scholar Gayatri Chakravorty Spivak (2007, 103) calls "deep language learning," the laborious process of accessing different epistemologies, worldviews, and "cultural infrastructures," which often cannot be understood without linguistic competence. Access across difference is always incomplete; the goal is not total knowledge but cultural, historical, and spatial literacy. Speaking Guaraní sometimes helped me fast-track the process of establishing connections. In other moments, skeptical vendors or municipal employees rebuffed my attempts to connect across difference through Guaraní. By responding to me in Spanish they marked a boundary and located me on the other side.

A Map of the Argument

Outlaw Capital ultimately argues that the transgressive is constitutive of global capitalism. It charts new articulations of this old phenomenon, including how accumulation by transgression is a process that builds cities and conditions conflicts over urban futures. I tell this story from an understudied city: a motor of global commodity circulation constructed extralegally and from the bottom up, not just the top down. Multiple sectors target the city for reform, attempting to banish spaces and practices labeled as corrupt or informal yet also seeking to preserve the commodity flows that sustain the city. The class-based results of these struggles criminalized the popular economy while legalizing or protecting elite illegalities, a process of "whitening" or laundering licit outlaw capital. Understanding the capacities unleashed by outlaw capital's logics and political coalitions is necessary if we want to chart pathways toward more just cities.

Chapter 1, "Notorious Markets," describes how Ciudad del Este works as a motor for the circulation of commodities. It also analyzes the spatial imaginaries that misconstrue the sources of this city's power. Like more well-studied and high-tech distributive cities, Ciudad del Este moves an astounding quantity of goods but through extralegal practices and spaces. Tax evasion, arbitrage, dealmaking, and other flexibilities—along with state projects to support the trade—produced place-based profits for the powerful and precarious incomes for *sacoleiros* and street vendors. Most English-language writing sensationalizes the city as a space of lawlessness. At work are spatial imaginaries that, while operating from different vantages, all explain the sources of lawlessness locally as a trait of Paraguayan culture. In historicizing the racialization of Paraguayan space, the chapter argues that these spatial imaginaries misinterpret the logics of capital at work but still shape policy and practice.

Chapter 2, "Contraband Urbanism," argues that Ciudad del Este is an urban expression of outlaw capital. *Contraband urbanism* describes the spatial forms of a hub city in extralegal trading circuits. It also describes a suite of political strategies and ways of knowing innovated by the merchant bloc. The built environment of the informal trade city aims to circulate commodities cheaply, relying on streets, sidewalks, and the river as spaces of commerce. Extending theories of the social production of space, I examine four key spatial forms: clandestine ports, busy streets, vendors' stalls, and frontier malls. Although clandestine ports are open secrets, effectively zoned as off-limits to reporters and researchers, they are connected by commodity flows to East Asian factories, frontier shopping malls, Brazilian street markets, and Paraguayan customs offices. For their part, the spatialities of the popular economy conflict with the aesthetics promoted by global urbanism. Yet spaces that look legal, like the mall, require and produce spaces of contraband like clandestine ports. Indeed, global urbanism produces superficial forms of urban knowledge that tend to infer legality and legitimacy from visual cues and aesthetic registers laden with race-class biases, what I call the *antipoor epistemology*. Showing how contraband urbanism works as a form of governance, the chapter pushes Lefebvre's framing of urbanism as a blind field so that it can be relevant to urban spaces he did not consider, like the informal and so-called unplanned cities of the Global South.

Chapter 3, "Schemes and State Power," develops a historical framework of territorial and frontier development to explain the surprising rise of Ciudad del Este. The chapter explains the seeming paradox that the high modernism of Paraguay's postwar authoritarian regime produced a city that became known as "liberated territory," a zone of profitable wildness.⁹⁰ I draw out the state-making dynamics of outlaw capital, detailing the long, messy transition from plantation-based extraction to state-sponsored contraband (mixed with legal reexportation). Contesting narratives of eastern Paraguay as a space of state absence, I show that outlaw capital thrives precisely because of state projects. While state modernization projects—city building and urban infrastructure—sought to establish a state presence on the frontier, they had the surprising effect of decentralizing access to contraband. Economic forms have shifted since brutal yerba mate plantations dominated the region, but one through line is *esquemas* (schemes), which connote alliances connecting politicians and other elites with law-breaking profiteering, including contraband. I tell this story through the rise of the merchant bloc and their spatial power grab as they claimed control over the border trade and successfully unhooked Ciudad del Este from national oversight.

Chapter 4, "Urban Livelihood Rights," emphasizes the range of creative strategies street vendors use to defend the popular economy, arguing that we can learn from their urban epistemologies and ethics. In a place where urban planning proceeds by dealmaking and uncertainty, vendors engaged the mutable boundaries of formality and legality through social fields adjacent to the law, including public discourse, spatial practice, and emotional politics. I intentionally lift up the most insurgent practices to foment our collective political imagination. Vendors often ground their claims in demands for dignified work, not legal compliance. By claiming urban space as a means to livelihood, vendors highlight its use value. At the same time, the most marginalized women vendors display their vulnerabilities and maternal responsibilities to reactivate dependencies with local municipal actors, not to stake claims as rights-bearing individuals. These women invoke a shared condition of vulnerability and need as the condition for urban belonging, not legal compliance or individual rights. Taken together, these politics push us to take more seriously an urban epistemology of use, livelihood, and care.

Chapter 5, "Enclosure Devices," examines how illegalities worked as a terrain of class conflict as multiple pressures rerouted trade and criminalized the *sacoleiro* circuit. The chapter demonstrates how the merchant bloc discursively constructed the boundaries of the informal economy and the so-called competitive, global city to protect some of its own illegalities. In their framing, malls and the new Qin Yi textile factory stand in for formalization and progress. Yet the Qin Yi factory relies on *sacoleiros* and clandestine networks to distribute its products. Arguing for tax breaks, the electronics reexportation sector successfully changed legal codes to protect its economic forms, even as formalization projects criminalized the *sacoleiro* circuit. Even further, efforts to reform the city ultimately undercut the forms of flexibility at the root of the border trade, especially the flexibilities within the popular economy, thereby demonstrating the antipoor biases of urban policies promoted in the name of global legitimacy.

Outlaw economies are notoriously hard to study, yet their import must not be underestimated. Indeed, outlaw capital may be playing an underappreciated role in the terrifying rise of authoritarian populisms across the Americas, dynamics I explore in the conclusion. I hope this book offers insights into the stakes of these transformations, as well as into the pitfalls of legalistic, rule-of-law policy frameworks that come out of anticorruption discourse and Eurocentric theories of the state, frameworks that elide the centrality of elite illegalities to the multiple historical agencies of capitalism. Instead, centering illegalities as a terrain of race-class conflict—a key theme of the book—offers a better starting point for social movements demanding economic redistribution and racial justice. I hope this book inspires the critical analytic perspectives and radical political imaginations necessary for efforts toward worlds otherwise.

CHAPTER 1

Notorious Markets

On a flight to Asunción in 2015, I sat next to a white woman from Ohio, Elisa, a naturalized Paraguayan married to a successful Paraguayan businessman. We chatted about Elisa's strong connection to Paraguay, rooted in her childhood as a diplomat's daughter under the long-ruling dictator Alfredo Stroessner and a comfortable life in the Asunceño upper class. When I shared my research in Ciudad del Este, a frown flashed across her face, and her chattiness faded fast. Her husband leaned into the conversation, commenting that the city ran on contraband and pirated CDs. Elisa concluded, "I always tell people that Ciudad del Este *isn't* Paraguay," abruptly shifting the conversation. Elisa saw the city as a problem. She sought to exile Ciudad del Este from her imagined national community by constructing it as somehow outside of the real Paraguay. Their passing comments suggest that anxieties about extralegality motivate this desire to set Ciudad del Este apart.

Over empanadas, I shared Elisa's comments with Sofía Espíndola, a researcher and friend. Espíndola recounted growing up in another frontier boomtown that, like Ciudad del Este, drew rural migrants expelled from the countryside by industrial agriculture. But with few waged jobs and industrial agriculture's extended assault on the smallholder farm economy, the survival of so many depended on the border economy. Espíndola argued that Elisa's imaginative exclusion of the frontier from the space of the nation represented a common, situated discourse: a view from the capital city. She described a kind of yellow journalism among reporters based in Asunción who delighted in scandalous stories of drug running and contraband through frontier cities but sought distance from their object of ridicule.[1] These "stigmatizing narratives," or *narrativas estigmatizantes*, as she called them, imaginatively confine illicit trade to border cities and then sever those spaces from a socially constructed understanding of the so-called real Paraguay.

Academic perspectives often reinforce these stigmatizing narratives. At an academic conference in southern Paraguay, an Argentine sociologist frowned as he commented on my research: "But Ciudad del Este is a monster." He dismissed the trade city as a hypercapitalist distillate of the self-interested, competitive hustle. Even the go-to *Paraguay Reader*, published by Duke University Press, addresses the rise of Ciudad del Este with a reprint of a five-page hyperbolic *Financial Times* article and a mere paragraph of editorial context.[2] In this narrative, a "city of hustlers" was "hacked out of the jungle," while a local "culture of graft" continues to thwart various formalization efforts.[3] Stories like the *Financial Times* article depict the autonomous rise of a deviant city. The book's editors—respected academics at U.K. universities—acknowledge Ciudad del Este as one of Paraguay's main economic engines but suggest that the stigmatizing hyperbole of the *Financial Times* article is a sufficient explanation for understanding the city and its various powers.

Stigmatizing narratives work through a collective denial of the links between the capital city and the frontier: circulations of wealth, relationships of political power, discourses of nationhood, circuits of development expertise. They also deny the struggles of border town residents for whom smuggling is the only buffer against destitution. I came to think of these narratives as spatial imaginaries with important political lives. In the same way that "territorial stigmatization" denigrates ghettos and slums, these hyperbolic narratives of Ciudad del Este spatialize a so-called cultural dysfunction, in this case, corruption and lawlessness, discursively confining them to particular spaces imagined as underdeveloped or unimportant to the core workings of capitalism.[4]

In working against these stigmatizing narratives, this chapter offers a counterstory of Ciudad del Este as a site of global interconnection, an eminently modern node in global geographies of trade and commerce. I argue that the story of its making offers an important window into the power of actively produced gray or transgressive spaces within contemporary capitalism. After previewing the power of the narratives that stigmatize Ciudad del Este, I outline a two-part framework for analyzing Ciudad del Este's role in geographies of global trade. First, I discuss theories of dependency and uneven development, approaches focusing on material, political-economic forces. To trace how these material processes are understood, imagined, and misconstrued, I rely on theories of spatial imaginaries within racial capitalism. In the next section, I describe the actually existing economic practices that make this place work. Then I turn to the stigmatizing narratives that dismiss Ciudad del Este as a corrupt site of lawlessness and argue that racialized discourses of corruption and legitimacy are constitutive in shaping both the border economy and efforts at reform. I show how the views of elites in the capital city, the Brazilian media, and U.S. free-trade advocates are distinct yet converge in the identification of local sources of lawlessness. Both regional and neocolonial spatial imaginaries construct corruption as a trait of Paraguayan culture and space, ignoring the ways the city and the border trade are produced relationally across extensive geographies of commerce and globalized capitalism. Disavowing these material realities requires a blindness to the many points of interconnection along this key global trade route. These discursive dismissals are both spatial and racial. Part of outlaw capital's power is this discursive field of misapprehension. By drawing from rich intellectual lineages critiquing racial capitalism, I argue that the local critique of *blanqueamiento* (whitening) can help us assess how forms of obscuration hide the spoils of outlaw capital. In later chapters, I show how reforms motivated by stigmatizing narratives hurt ordinary Paraguayan vendors and small-scale Brazilian traders while legalizing or protecting elite illegalities.

Situating a "Notorious Market"

U.S. policymakers and journalists writing in English condemn Ciudad del Este. The Office of the U.S. Trade Representative (USTR) exemplifies this trend, listing Ciudad del Este as one of the world's nineteen "notorious markets" or sites selling counterfeit goods.[5] This designation certainly captures the centrality of the city in global trade networks, even as the USTR identifies popular markets like Ciudad del Este, La Salada outside Buenos Aires, and Tepito Market in Mexico City as problematic places. In the USTR's analysis, these markets host activities that "harm the American economy," challenge corporate control of brands and patents, and subvert the global economic order.[6] As an agency with "direct ties to industry," the USTR expressly aims to protect the profitability of transnational corporations, so places listed as notorious markets become the focus of U.S. foreign policy pressure.[7] The listing itself reveals the powerful forces behind the narratives stigmatizing Ciudad del Este. Indeed, journalistic research published by the U.S. National Defense University Press identified Ciudad del Este as a hub in "geographies of badness," a place of global interconnection where illicit activities concentrate.[8] There is a kernel of truth to these representations, as transgressions concentrate in particular places, as well as at particular moments, like the crony capitalist looting across Russia after the fall of the Berlin Wall and human trafficking at the U.S. southern border. Yet the notorious markets perspective traffics in stereotypes of defective cultural propensities, failed states, and the therapeutic effects of free markets. Instead, this chapter offers framings that show how spaces supposedly outside of or irrelevant to capitalism's core processes are, in fact, central. Critical urbanists have been arguing for new kinds of mappings, ones that go beyond the dominant hierarchies of world cities and manufacturing hubs (organized by urban planning) and megacities (targeted for development intervention).[9] These perspectives are crucial for my purposes because Ciudad del Este also defies simple categorization within urban studies and geography literatures, challenging academic expectations of urban development and capitalist change. This informal trading hub is not a celebrated world city in the way that London, Tokyo, and New York are command-and-control centers of finance capital. Nor is it a megacity of the so-called developing world, cities that are often mischaracterized as slumdog dystopias.[10] Ciudad del Este has not garnered the attention of geographers or urban studies scholars, yet the city materially links sites of production, including SEZs in East Asia and consumers in cities like Rio and São Paulo. This book relies on critical historical and spatial approaches to argue that Ciudad del Este has been *made* as a zone of transgression not through defective cultures of corruption but through its historical production by multiscalar forces that are at once material and imaginative, forces that are at work locally, nationally, and extranationally.

DEPENDENCY AND UNEVEN DEVELOPMENT

Development under capitalism is constitutively uneven, producing interconnected landscapes of wealth and poverty, opportunity and vulnerability, protection and premature death.[11] Uneven geographical development links economic growth in rich countries to the underdevelopment of poorer countries due to both the living legacies of colonial extraction and the everyday operations of a deeply biased global trade system.[12] The resulting landscapes are at once patterned and contingent.[13] Thus, *interconnection* produces unevenness and inequality, an observation that bears repeating, given the dominant view that better integration into globalized capitalism will yield uplift and economic development.

Critical accounts of global capitalism contest Eurocentric stage models of development, perspectives shared by capitalism's champions and some Marxists.[14] With metaphors of ladders or stages of development, stage theories locate the sources of historical capitalist change exclusively in the Global North, places also assumed to give the universal form to which other places—most places—only provide modifications or empirical variations. This "colonizer's model of the world" assumes that modernity and capitalist change diffuse outward from Euro-America, or so-called developed countries, which then claim the knowledge, capacity, and authority to exact political-economic changes the world over.[15] Fernando Coronil (1996, 57) calls this "occidentalism," a conception of the world that "separate[s] the world's components into bounded units; disaggregate[s] their relational histories; turn[s] difference into hierarchy; [and] naturalize[s] these representations."

Dependency theory offers a powerful critique of stage theories. Created in the crucible of the rebellious 1960s, dependency theorists sought to understand the specific economic formations characteristic of Latin American countries, as insertion into the global economy on subordinated terms seemed to *underdevelop* Latin American countries rather than produce economic growth. They studied chronic underemployment, the superexploitation of labor, and the intense class stratifications of economies largely based in the exportation of natural resources or primary goods. *Dependistas*, as the Latin American members of the dependency school were called, contested modernist economic theories that posited that the development trajectories of Western countries map a universal pathway along predetermined stages of growth in which competition, technological innovation, and specialization ineluctably lead to economic growth, thanks to the magic of comparative advantage. Foreshadowing contemporary efforts to decolonize knowledge, Marxist *dependistas*, especially radical thinkers like Theotônio dos Santos, Ruy Mauro Marini, and Vania Bambirra, refused to assume a European-given norm and instead foregrounded complex national-global interrelations.[16] They argued that internal dynamics—class structure, specific national histories, and production dynamics, as well as the social movements of the oppressed—interacted with external forces, including global political-economic relations. Crucially, *dependistas* highlighted the transfer of surpluses—that is, social wealth—from peripheral countries in Latin America to core countries in the Global North. Core countries extracted surplus in a range of ways, including profit remittances, royalties and debt payments, and declining terms of trade.[17] Egyptian economist Samir Amin (1976) tracked unequal exchange in which workers earning low wages in the Global South bought expensive goods produced by higher-paid workers in the Global North, such that northern countries extracted value from their southern counterparts.[18] In 2012 the estimated value of this south-to-north transfer was U.S.$1.46 trillion, more than eleven times the value of foreign aid moving in the other direction.[19] Dependency theorists thus insisted that extractive and coercive relations are at the core of capitalism.

Without fully acknowledging the complexity of these lineages of dependency theory, Marxist geographers also argue that the ordinary processes of capitalism produce geographic unevenness.[20] Marxist geographers focus on capitalism's crisis tendencies and internal contradictions to argue that competition conflicts with capital's tendency toward monopoly power, that the drive to fix capital in space conflicts with its unfettered mobility to follow profit margins, and that the need for consumers with spending power to feed a demand-driven economy conflicts with wage stagnation and the exploitation of labor. In an influential treatise, Neil Smith (1986, xii) argues that uneven geographical development inevitably results from the dialectical tension between "differentiation and equalization of levels and conditions of development." Capital requires fixed infrastructural investments, locking it in place, but capital also requires mobility to follow profit margins as competition and the spatial division of labor make production cheaper elsewhere. Capitalism thus restructures geographical space. Economic geographers also importantly nuanced the politics of scale by challenging the assumption that the nation-state is the primary unit of development.

Geographers of uneven development also sought to grapple with the spatial reorganization of production, which intensified in the 1970s. Deindustrialization and outsourcing moved manufacturing from cities in the Global North to places across the Global South with lower costs due to very low wages, weak labor protections, and lax environmental laws. As Doreen Massey (1995) has shown, this reworked spatial division of labor reorganized the distribution of economic functions across geographies.[21] Decentralized production processes generated geographically stretched commodity chains connecting inputs, production, distribution, and consumption.[22] These production geographies shift constantly as capitalists seek places with higher profit possibilities and, in moments of crisis, rework existing spatial relations. Firms compete for places along these production networks with higher profit margins, margins produced through state policies, low wage rates, monopoly powers, techno-organizational strategies, and the like. It is not preordained that a given place is slotted into a particular spot in this hierarchy of functions and profits. Indeed, the hierarchy is constantly shifting. But the hierarchy itself is a necessity of capitalism.[23] Workers are active agents in sculpting this mosaic even as struggles are fought on terrains not of our choosing.[24]

Uneven development therefore produces places like Ciudad del Este, a key hub facilitating global trade networks. Ciudad del Este drew merchants through material and geographic factors, including proximity to Brazilian markets, profitable legal flexibilities, extensive trade knowledge, and useful relationships built through contraband and legalized reexportation. Yet powerful narratives frame Ciudad del Este as underdeveloped, corrupt, or lawless while construing the border trade as deviant or structurally irrelevant to globalized capital.

SPATIAL AND RACIAL IMAGINARIES

Spatial and racial imaginaries are implicated in the stigmatizing narratives that locate Ciudad del Este as a place of deficiency or corruption. Spatial imaginaries are powerful stories with force in the world. The news stories and policy reports that opened this chapter all communicate implicit spatial imaginaries. These representations matter: they influence the production of city space and pave pathways for particular kinds of economies. Drawing from a Lefebvrian understanding of the social production of space, Wendy Wolford (2004, 410) defines spatial imaginaries as "cognitive frameworks, both collective and individual, constituted through the lived experiences, perceptions, and conceptions of space itself." They are a key constituent of common sense, following Antonio Gramsci. Stuart Hall (1986, 20) describes common sense as "practical and popular forms of consciousness" commonly used to make sense of the world in ways that are always historically produced and contested and that are made up of both useful forms of social critique and misapprehensions.

Commonsense notions of economic legitimacy—the fuzzy line between criminal and entrepreneur—are racialized. These racialized processes criminalize the livelihood strategies of the poor while protecting the illegalities of the rich. Indeed, processes of racialization are inseparable from struggles over which kinds of work are valued and which are poorly paid, unpaid, or criminalized. These imaginative hierarchies are also spatial. Indeed, racial capitalism generates value by moving through socially produced inequalities between human communities. At the same time, its authorizing epistemologies disavow the inequality-generating dynamics of capital by constructing hierarchies of valued workers. These epistemologies imagine the productive versus the indolent, the entrepreneurial versus the criminal, the deserving versus the undeserving. These characteristics are then falsely mapped onto race, gender, and other forms of difference. Indeed, the history of capitalism is one of introducing divisions within the working class. Silvia Federici (2004, 63) writes that the long history of this "accumulation of differences and divisions" required two centuries of witch hunts and other strategies to devalue women's work, autonomy, and knowledge. Today, these hierarchies of valued bodies and valuable labor loosely affiliate with imaginations of productive and legal economic activities and their associated spaces.[25]

The Paraguayan vernacular *blanqueamiento* (whitening) critiques the ways that wealth and whiteness work to substantiate elite claims to social legitimacy by obscuring their transgressive profiteering. For members of the largely light-skinned Paraguayan elite, legitimacy attaches more to who people are than to what they do. Of course, whiteness is much more than a privileged subject position. Whiteness is a system of historically produced power relations, an ontology, and an epistemology. Legal scholar Cheryl Harris (1993) teaches us how whiteness is a form of property, an argument she meticulously traces through U.S. colonial property and slave law, which excluded Africans from membership as self-sovereign persons in the polis and refused to recognize Indigenous land claims. This bloody history binds whiteness to land theft and exclusion-based forms of property.[26] Indeed, in his analysis of institutional racism in the United States, George Lipsitz (2011, 3) describes whiteness as a "racial cartel" that hoards resources while masquerading behind mythologies of personal responsibility, meritocratic advancement, methodological individualism, and (until recently) color blindness. Indigenous and Black studies have produced libraries of evidence of the countless ways law, policy, everyday practice, and notions of white personhood normalize Black and Indigenous dispossession, enslavement, exploitation, and, indeed, genocide.

Although racial regimes vary across the Americas with important regional differences, racial categories emerged to control labor, steal land, and justify violence.[27] The eliminatory work of settler colonialism in the United States disappears Indigenous life and land claims, as systems of chattel slavery used racist hierarchies to mark Africans as enslavable, dynamics that are also important in Brazil. *Mestizaje* (race mixing) across Latin America involved different kinds of violence, namely, forced assimilation and the systematic rape of Black and Indigenous women by European men.[28] The wealth coercively extracted through slavery and colonialism across the Americas played an essential role in the consolidation of early capitalism.[29]

Across South America, racial identification is contextual and fluid, operating through gradations of skin tone rather than a white/nonwhite binary.[30] Racial regimes affiliate with antipoor epistemologies to justify the hoarding of wealth and life opportunity among a tiny, largely light-skinned elite. Alongside significant national differences, there is a tendency across Latin America to imagine hierarchies of worth based on proximity to Europeanness, distance from indigeneity, and attainment of the class signifiers of urban life. Through the mid-twentieth century, modernization projects sought national progress through forms of racial whitening realized through state efforts like race categorization in national censuses and policies promoting European immigration.[31] These epistemologies of whiteness construed national progress as distance from Indigenous and Black culture, assigning light-skinned elites the task of moral and cultural uplift.[32] Sometimes Latin American race theories celebrate mestizos, as Mexican nationalist José Vasconcelos ([1925] 1997) did in his glorification of the "cosmic race." Other times, they denigrate mestizos as "ex-Indians who had abandoned their proper natural/cultural environment" by relying on spatial imaginaries linking whites to cities and Indigenous people to the countryside.[33]

As I demonstrate, marking Paraguayans as racial others authorizes stigmatizing narratives that ultimately contribute to the misapprehension of the role of outlaw capital in the global economy. The imagination of Paraguayans as a racial other was constructed historically through the specificity of regional racial regimes, including anti-Indigenous racism. It also expresses differently in different places, as American attitudes about Paraguay and perspectives of race are different from Brazilian ones, for instance. Paraguay is strongly marked by Indigenous culture and is the only country in Latin America where the mestizo majority speaks an Indigenous language. Indeed, Guaraní persisted even in the face of Stroessner-era prohibitions, which banned Guaraní from schools, public spaces, and government offices. Spanish and Portuguese dominate among mestizos in most other Latin American countries. Southern Cone countries like Argentina and Chile celebrate European immigrant histories or, in the case of Brazil, colonial legacies linking elite families back to Portugal. Today, the Brazilian media often emphasize this distinction, calling Paraguayans "Guaraní people" and Paraguay "Guaraní territory" (without any suggestion of land return to First Peoples).[34] These specific racial regimes shape the narratives that imagine Ciudad del Este as a spatial expression of lawlessness. Before I trace this history, I turn to actually existing economic practice in this border town.

Profit-Making and Rule-Breaking in a Trade City

Since the city's midcentury founding, large- and small-scale trade circuits have run through the city. Paraguayan street vendors and shop owners sell to Brazilian traders called *sacoleiros*, who resell merchandise for a profit on the street in cities across Brazil.[35] Large-scale wholesalers, importer-exporters, and *contrabandistas* also participate in the trade. Indeed, the city is like a switchboard, redirecting some commodities from corporate container ships, cargo trucks, and airplanes to individual petty traders who have little start-up capital and low-tech means of moving goods.

A cottage industry of logistics caters to border traders: hotels, restaurants, storage centers, and transportation networks. In 2015, within Ciudad del Este, fleets of twenty-five hundred taxis, eight hundred motorcycle taxis, and eighteen hundred vans vied for parking spaces and riders.[36] Rumors described full-service transportation logistics: businesses arranged for taxi drivers to transport merchandise to clandestine ports, traffickers to ferry it across the river, and Brazilian workers to deliver packages the next morning to hotel rooms in Foz do Iguaçu. Indeed, a whole economic world supports the *sacoleiro* circuit. These everyday mobilities sutured together street markets in Paraguay and Brazil as ant contraband traced trails available for others to follow, even as it soon became the target of state condemnation and criminalization. The appendix captures some of the economic vocabulary that describes these specialized labor niches.

Traders, small and large, profited through arbitrage, that is, they took advantage of price differences across space and between different markets. Different sources generated these price differences. *Contrabandistas* evaded tariffs and taxes, creating profit opportunities by breaking the law. The Paraguayan state studiously created a low-tax environment to promote reexportation (also called triangulation). Street vendors and shop owners rarely charged sales tax, a competitivity strategy that helped earn the city a reputation as the world's largest duty-free zone. This slogan captured the experience of buyers who paid very low or no taxes. And the phrase traveled, repeated often by journalists and academic researchers and even headlining the second paragraph of the city's Wikipedia entry.[37] But the city has never been a duty-free zone. The widespread uptake of the phrase captures the divergence between everyday economic activities and what is supposed to happen according to the law.

Border traders used metaphors of gray to describe the legal flexibilities behind their work and the way that transgression opens spaces of profitability.[38] This language captures extralegality as a spectrum of intensities rather than a binary of legal/illegal that is indexed with metaphors of black/white. In the strategy of undervaluation (*subfacturación*)—colloquially known as *la tablita* (the little tablet)—customs officials cleared entire containers of high-value electronics by weight, underreporting the value of merchandise in order to slash tax bills.[39] Customs officials, traders, customs brokers, and political fixers split the savings diverted from state coffers. One reporter estimated the take at U.S.$500,000 per plane, about U.S.$5 million monthly.[40] If smuggling directly violates legal codes, undervaluation is more ambiguous in the way that it works in concert with state agents and laws. Reflecting on undervaluation, one merchant commented to me, "If you don't buy in the gray, you can't compete," concluding that everyone avoided paying the full suite of taxes.[41] Paying all the taxes would raise the prices on products and therefore put rule followers at a competitive disadvantage, he insisted.

Proximity to Brazilian markets worked as a sort of spatially fixed asset. During the 1960s, Brazil, like other Latin American countries, protected its nascent national industry with high tariffs on imported goods, which peaked at more than half of import value. This development strategy—import substitution industrialization (ISI)—paired high tariffs with strong state policies and subsidies to nurture homegrown manufacturing and attract foreign direct investment.[42] Paraguay's population of fewer than two million in the 1960s meant that its small domestic market could not generate the demand necessary to make ISI work. Indeed, under the terms of a 1956 International Monetary Fund stabilization plan, rather than implement ISI, Paraguay instead set the conditions for reexportation by eliminating export tariffs and reducing import taxes.[43] Brazil's high tariffs also created arbitrage possibilities. Traders imported goods to Paraguay under relatively low tariffs and smuggled or transported them into Brazil, where they resold the goods at higher prices. With the circulation of billions of dollars of consumer goods, the possibilities for place-based profits in Ciudad del Este became considerable. In the language of economic geographers, the city generates land rents, that is, profits flowing from the ownership of or access to a particular space or place-bound resource.[44] City planners have long sought to capitalize on the city's particular competitive edge, its "magnificent geographical location," and its "accumulated experience as a commercial center that yields comparative advantages and competitivity," as described in a 1997 planning document.[45]

The reexport economy garnered significant political support as allies of the urban growth coalition I call the *merchant bloc* built a regulatory architecture to support it, a story I tell more fully in chapter 3. Other sectors opposed the border trade. The small industrial sector argued that it hurt local manufacturing. Economists in the treasury department worried about the hit to tax revenues. In battles over the appropriate role for reexportation in national economic development, the merchant bloc labeled these concerns as *fiscalista* (fiscalist), overprioritizing tax revenue generation and undervaluing the importance and contribution of reexportation.

Despite these tensions, state policies actively promoted reexportation, setting up special tax advantages for companies that import goods into Paraguay for reexportation to end consumers across borders. Since the 1990s, registered reexportation moved goods worth between U.S.$1 billion and $5 billion annually.[46] Indeed, in the last three decades, 80 percent of Paraguay's exports to Brazil, Argentina, and Uruguay were reexports, not national products.[47] A USAID-funded report concluded that reexportation "always had a legal regime in Paraguay that changed and responded to particular economic moments."[48] Thus, while stereotypes depicted the city as a space of lawlessness, as outside of state control, Paraguay policymakers helped set the conditions that generated a profitable border economy.

Paraguayan policymakers used two different legal strategies to create arbitrage opportunities: a list-based strategy and a spatial strategy. Both strategies required state officials to negotiate trade policies with Brazil and then, later, with Mercosur, a regional customs union between Brazil, Argentina, Paraguay, and Uruguay. In the 1960s traders imported luxury goods like whiskey and cigarettes from Miami through Asunción or Puerto Presidente Stroessner. Traders paid a low transit tax on items on a special list (*despachos en tránsitos*) rather than the full suite of taxes and tariffs. Over time, traders pressured lawmakers to add new items to this list. In the 1970s state regulators included more goods in the reexportation trade, spawning a series of exceptional import-export regimes. The most important was the Tourism Regime (Régimen del Turismo), which lowered taxes and tariffs on a list of select consumer goods. As the name implies, officially the policy was aimed at shopping tourists who purchased goods for personal consumption. The codes and practices nevertheless diverged, as many Brazilians bought goods for resale back home.

The spatial strategy also designated exceptional spaces of commerce for reexportation. In making these zones subject to different trade rules, politicians created differentiated state space. For a brief period, the Tourism Regime was both a spatial and a list-based strategy, initially limited to Puerto Presidente Stroessner and the northern border town of Pedro Juan Caballero, as well as, later, to the southern border town of Encarnación.[49] Then, for a short period in the early 1980s, the Tourism Regime required that all reexportation commerce circulate through a duty-free zone, the Zona Franca Internacional, a monopoly concession operated by a firm called Busines [sic] Company. With its clumsy use of generic English-language terms for commerce, the firm bid for legitimacy. In practice, Busines Company regularly skirted the law, as traders used their warehouses as contraband way stations, a "breach of fiscal obligations," as the Finance Ministry dryly observed in a resolution revoking the concession.[50]

Even as regional economic conditions changed, threatening the arbitrage base of the trade, Paraguayan state policies continued to back reexportation. By the 1980s Brazil had abandoned ISI and lowered import taxes. Paraguayan lawmakers responded by introducing new strategies to keep reexportation viable. Beginning in the 1970s, the overall burden of reexport taxes and tariffs trended sharply downward.[51] In the 2000s the four Mercosur countries (Brazil, Argentina, Paraguay, and Uruguay) consolidated a regional customs union premised on open borders and free trade. Mercosur's regional trade framework threatened to extinguish the price differentials behind reexportation. At the same time, U.S. foreign policies pressured states to combat counterfeiting and contraband, and Brazil tightened border controls, threatening the trade route. But state authorities successfully extracted concessions in international negotiations to retain list-based arbitrage opportunities.[52]

Seeking to maintain their competitive edge, the merchant bloc fought for tax breaks as a pathway to formalization and a means to maintain the city's competitivity. Sometimes Paraguayan state officials agreed, describing tax relief for the import-export sector as a solution to contraband. In 1972 a presidential decree argued that "tax concessions for certain products have been the most effective measure to counteract operations at the margin of legal tax provisions."[53] The dry language covers the colorful reality: the extent of contraband alongside the policy decision to set taxes based on businesses' "willingness to pay," as it is called in microeconomics. Forty years later, I took notes on a PowerPoint presentation by a Ministry of Industry and Commerce representative proposing the same state strategy. Describing her proposal to reenergize the border trade, she asked, "At what point do we need to have taxes so that there isn't undervaluation?"[54] In chapter 5 I explore how electronics importer-exporters successfully equated formalization with low taxes to slash total taxes to under 5 percent.[55] Thus, one state strategy brings contraband inside the law, legalizing the circulation of consumer goods through national territory and across the border without paying much in taxes. When turned toward elite illegalities, policymakers legalize what was once illegal.

It is not easy to make sense of these economic worlds in part because contraband practices work by being hard to see. They are often supported by explicit or tacit state support, and the relationships between contraband and public officials are kept out of public view, even as they are open secrets. Rule-breaking takes many forms, from trafficking to selling goods without charging sales tax to squatting a space on the sidewalk in order to sell jump drives to shopping tourists. Crucially, the powerful have the means to hide and protect their transgressions, while the poor—spatially segregated into public spaces for livelihood and work—must break the rules in plain view.

While Paraguayan state policies created the conditions for the profitability of the border trade, the trade remained dependent on regional economic and political conditions. It depended on the purchasing power of Brazilian consumers, itself subject to various factors like border controls, currency exchange rates, and the dependency of the Brazilian economy on commodity prices. A strong Brazilian real and a weaker dollar increased the purchasing power of *sacoleiros* who bought from venders selling in U.S. currency; a strong dollar, however, could result in precipitous drops in trade. Consumer demand also drove the trade network. The cheap distribution network, enabled by legal flexibilities, helped Brazilians access cheaper consumer goods, which in effect provided a consumption subsidy. In the Brazilian economic crisis of debt and hyperinflation between 1981 and 1994, self-identified middle-class Brazilians in São Paulo, aspiring to a "First World modernity," used contraband merchandise to perform a threatened class identity.[56] In the 2000s the redistributive policies of the Workers' Party (Partido dos Trabalhadores, PT) governments under presidents Lula da Silva (2003–10) and Dilma Rousseff (2011–16) enhanced the purchasing power of the working class. With increased spending power, marginalized social groups could demonstrate their self-worth by buying things, a fragile form of "inclusion via consumption."[57] However, PT governments also tightened border controls and reduced taxes and tariffs, undermining the arbitrage basis of the trade. The weakened trade position of the city faltered further during Brazil's recession in 2015 and 2016. The city's 1990s boom soon skittered toward bust.

Stigmatizing Narratives

In this section, I discuss in turn spatial imaginaries at the national, regional, and global neocolonial scales. Although these representations differ, Ciudad del Este is imagined as a spatial manifestation of lawlessness through narratives of local deviance without attention to the ways the city and the border trade are produced relationally across extensive geographies of commerce and globalized capitalism. I start with stories like Elisa's that sever Ciudad del Este from the imagined national space of Paraguay. Then I analyze racialized imaginations of Paraguay and Paraguayans from Brazil and the disavowals they enable. I conclude by reflecting on the forms of blindness inherent in the developmentalist spatial imaginaries of U.S.-backed interventions. Taken together, these spatial imaginaries contribute to the criminalization of the popular border economy while authorizing some forms of elite illegalities (stories I tell more fully in subsequent chapters).

NATIONAL SPATIAL IMAGINARIES

"What the fuck has happened to my country?" laments the private detective Martín Olmedo in the opening line of *El último vuelo del pájaro campana* (The last flight of the bellbird), by journalist Andrés Colmán Gutiérrez (2007, 13), a novel critical of development in Paraguay. "Here the world ends," Martín comments as he leaves the capital city, Asunción, invoking a spatial division between urban modernity and a rural, backward past. Throughout the novel, Martín battles against the return of Stroessner, whom Martín calls "the Tyrannosaurus," flagging him as a relic and marking authoritarian practices as unmodern. The battle for democracy boils down to a conflict between a past that refuses to die and the forces of liberal modernity. The author, Colmán Gutiérrez, is a respected journalist living in Asunción. The anthropologist Kregg Hetherington (2011) argues that Colmán Gutiérrez exemplifies the urban intelligentsia, a group Hetherington calls "new democrats" because these liberal modernizers claim they are democracy's rightful stewards.[58] Claiming that the worlds outside the capital are not worlds at all, Colmán Gutiérrez implies that the spatial boundaries of democratic potential align with the city limits of Asunción.

El último vuelo del pájaro campana also maps a peculiar territoriality of illicit networks. Martín finds transnational criminality on the ranch of Don Pablo Ferreira in the countryside. Ferreira is a Brasiguayo, a Brazilian-born, naturalized Paraguayan with strong cultural ties to his homeland. Martín's guide, Willie, explains the spatiality of the *fazenda*, the Portuguese term for "plantation": "'[This is] the *"fazenda"* or ranch Ipanema of Don Pablo Ferreira,' Willie explained. 'It has more than 300,000 hectares. Half is in Brazil and half in Paraguay. *It's like a separate country*. His people can cross the border, bringing across anything they feel like. The ranch has several airports hidden in the woods. Huge warehouses where merchandise arrives directly from Miami, Hong Kong, Malaysia, Singapore, and Taiwan'" (Colmán Gutiérrez 2007, 151, emphasis added, my translation).

The novel relies on powerful, submerged spatial imaginaries to construct the unruly frontier as outside the nation and beyond state control. Resonating with Elisa's desire, Willy's comment that "it's like a separate country" distinguishes a real Paraguay from spaces of illicit economies where transnational contraband cartels link up with military generals. Don Pablo Ferreira's "separate country" spans two nation-states, an economic space conjured as in but not of the Paraguayan nation. This fantastical parastatal territory does not correspond to actual frontier spatial formations, eliding the key role of border towns. By locating elite illegalities in the countryside, Colmán Gutiérrez reinforces the strong associations between rural spaces and the past. This spatial imaginary marks contraband economies and their supportive spaces as remnants of prior eras rather than as constitutive of urban modernities. At work then is a spatiotemporal imagination that splits off the frontier economy from the space of the nation and then casts it as backward, as if it belongs to a bygone era. Politically, this spatial imaginary overlooks capitalism's cozy cohabitation with illiberal practices.

REGIONAL SPATIAL IMAGINARIES

Popular Brazilian conceptions associate Paraguay with counterfeiting, contraband, corruption, and backwardness.[59] Brazilian researcher Carolina Samara Rodrigues (2015, 1) summarizes these regional stereotypes of Paraguay as "the country of *muamba*, defeat, contraband and piracy."[60] *Muamba* is likely a Kimbundu word from what is now Angola for food or a basket for transporting goods, a word brought to Brazil by stolen Africans on slave ships. In the intervening centuries, the word's meaning has transmuted to signify something shoddy, counterfeit, or contraband, and Paraguay, as a place, is particularly associated with *muamba*.

This assessment of Paraguayans as culturally predisposed to lawlessness and corruption is racialized. A small 1996 note in a Brazilian newspaper under the heading "Programa de índio" (Indian program), for example, discussed an actress on a shopping trip to Ciudad del Este accompanied by cartoons of a shirtless figure with a feathered headdress and long braid holding a bag, following a sign pointing toward Paraguay.[61] The caricature of a stereotyped "Indian" uses anti-Indigenous racism to mock the trip across the border into "Indian Country." The derogatory expression "programa de índio" indicates uninteresting or unproductive activities, and this unvarnished anti-Indigenous racism implies that Europeanness, with its Protestant work ethic and wage labor, is the standard of civilization. This narrative claims the authority to pass judgment on other lifeworlds, very often assessing Indigenous lifeways as idle and indolent.

The racialization of Paraguay has a long history. In his iconic book, *Open Veins of Latin America: Five Centuries of the Pillage of a Continent*, Eduardo Galeano (1975, 191) interpreted eighteenth-century Paraguay as "Latin America's most progressive country" because its model of autarkic, debt-free development represented a threat to British imperialism and free trade through the power of example.[62] The insular, nationalist ruler José Gaspar Rodríguez de Francia (1814–40) refused foreign investment and promoted homeland ranches for national food production while building impressive ironworks and the continent's first railroads. Leaders within imperial and expansionist Brazil, however, did not interpret Paraguay's "admirable level of development" as a success, as a Brazilian journalist and historian explains. Instead, they saw Paraguayan self-sufficiency as a "barbaric peculiarity," a cultural disposition to "abuse, theft and corruption."[63]

Brazilian state propaganda mobilized these racialized discourses in the lead-up to the War of the Triple Alliance, which set Paraguay against Brazil, Argentina, and Uruguay (1864–70). Brazil's imperial elites of Portuguese descent asserted their role as the bearers of civilization against Hispanic barbarism, as historian José Murilo de Carvalho (1998) notes, envisioning their project on the grand scale of the South American continent and placing Paraguay on the negative side of the civilization/barbarism binary.[64] Colonialism has long worked through racist hierarchies, as scholars like Aimé Césaire (1950) and Frantz Fanon (1963) in the Black radical tradition demonstrate. In the unmistakable tone of scientific racism, writers for the Brazilian magazine *Paraguay Ilustrado!* speculated about an inferior Paraguayan race prone to criminality but also a "passive obedience" befitting a people in the sights of imperialist conquest.[65] One cartoon of two Paraguayan military recruits is captioned, "Original types of two Paraguayan volunteers.... [E]ach soldier is a rarity worthy of a zoological collection."[66] Scientific racism thus helped the Brazilian monarchy justify conquest and the mass land grab that followed Paraguay's defeat, as the aftermath of Latin America's bloodiest war set the conditions for dependent political-economic relations that continue to define the region.

These racialized imaginaries live on in attendant forms of criminalization. The Brazilian researcher Roberta Brandalise describes what she calls the hegemonic representation of Paraguay within Brazilian media as pivoting on a so-called cultural predisposition to illegality, counterfeiting, and corruption.[67] These notions of racialized alterity authorize a mocking attitude toward Paraguay across the Brazilian media. In a fight between contestants on the reality show *Big Brother Brazil 9*, for instance, Newton calls Ana a "Paraguayan blonde" to ridicule her dyed hair.[68] In 2009 the popular Brazilian newspaper *Globo* ran with this stereotype in a headline: "Paraguayans Say They Love to Pirate."[69] A Paraguayan-American Chamber of Commerce survey found that half of Paraguayans agreed that "counterfeiting is an acceptable way to make a living," while 80 percent did not object to the purchase of pirated products like DVDs. Lamenting Paraguayan attitudes as a "tragedy for the country's economy," the Paraguayan-American Chamber of Commerce followed the official

FIGURE 7. A Brazilian magazine in 1865 disparages Paraguayans with the language of scientific racism: "Original types of two Paraguayan volunteers. . . . [E]ach soldier is a rarity worthy of a zoological collection"; courtesy of Biblioteca Nacional Digital, Brazil

U.S. free-trade position, aiming to protect U.S. business interests by criminalizing counterfeiting and steadfastly ignoring the negative impacts on popular economies of these policies.[70] Ordinary Brazilians sometimes share this view of Paraguayans: in Brandalise's (2017, 8) interviews in Foz do Iguaçu, Brazil, one resident noted that "[Paraguayans] don't care at all what kind of work they do."

Brazilian media coverage similarly blames Paraguayans for the failure of a project to formalize *sacoleiros* called the RTU (discussed further in chapter 4). One news report lauded Brazilian motivation to adhere to RTU protocols—compared to a Paraguayan attitude of legal flexibility—by highlighting a Brazilian vendor: "With or without information, Mr. Isac proudly always follows the law."[71] Another article quoted a Brazilian industry association president who predicted that RTU would fail because irregularity "is the law in Ciudad del Este," implying that legal flexibility is restricted to Paraguay.[72]

These discourses of disconnection imagine counterfeiting and rule-breaking as a Paraguayan phenomenon, ignoring or downplaying the material connections that link Ciudad del Este to people and places in Brazil and beyond. These representations generalize a subset of rule-breaking frontier commercial relationships into a national Paraguayan character. The racist discourses proposing a Paraguayan cultural predisposition to illegalities justifies the fantasy that legal flexibilities are confined to the Paraguayan side of the border.

Many in Ciudad del Este contest the persuasive power of these discourses of disconnection. Pérez, the trade advocate, insists that "Paraguay is *not* a country of contraband," explaining that Brazilian consumer demand provides the incentive for counterfeit goods produced in China to be sold in the city, which Brazilians (more than Paraguayans) transport through semiclandestine trade routes.[73] Some Brazilians living in Foz do Iguaçu likewise saw this frontier complexity: "It's not just Paraguayans who are involved with counterfeits. It's easy to blame our neighbors, but we too are responsible, and, what's more, even here in Foz there is a lot of prejudice against Paraguayans."[74] Pérez, the trade advocate, went further, insisting that all frontiers, not just Paraguayan ones, are spaces of freewheeling capitalism: "Frontiers are not convents. There are no nuns here."[75] In working against discourses of disconnection, many in Ciudad del Este see the city instead through a perspective that acknowledges how the gray spaces of global capitalism are relationally produced.

NEOCOLONIAL SPATIAL IMAGINARIES

Paraguay looks different from the vantage point of U.S. foreign policymakers. Amid post-9/11 paranoia, the U.S. security apparatus portrayed the Tri-

Border Area as an "ungoverned space," asserting that such areas act as "sanctuaries" for "terrorist support activities."[76] Verónica Giménez Béliveau calls this discourse the myth of a land without law, noting that it rests on unproven links between Muslim communities in both Ciudad del Este and Foz do Iguaçu and terrorist financing networks.[77] This hyperbolic imagination of the city emerged alongside the rise of disciplinary intellectual property discourses aimed at criminalizing counterfeits. In the 1990s the English-language media drew attention to this bustling trade of counterfeit products. The *New York Times* reported that Ciudad del Este was the "latest battleground" between transnational corporations defending profits in the emerging terrain of intellectual property and "legions of third world entrepreneurs."[78] Following the lead of free-trade proponents like the WTO, these publications took the official line that piracy is a criminal problem, a "global scourge," according to George W. Bush.[79] In the 2000s transnational corporations, global organizations like the WTO, and the USTR promoted the view that piracy is the crime of the twenty-first century, as harmful as drug trafficking or organized crime.[80]

This increased media coverage of pirated products in markets around the world tended toward sensationalism, as researchers of the yellow capitalism (*capitalismo amarillo*) initiative argue.[81] Reporting on Ciudad del Este in English trafficked in stereotypes of the city as lawless, describing the trade route as "deadly" and the street market as a place that "feels shifty."[82] A 1988 *New York Times* article described Paraguay as a "parallel ersatz galaxy," conjuring a separate world of inferior substitutes while retaining the colonial hubris to define the norm against which other places are compared.[83] Journalist Jeffrey Robinson went further in his assessment of the rise of global organized crime, calling Ciudad del Este "the anus of the earth," a foul center marked by the dirtiest of dealings.[84] Robinson, like the USTR, showed little concern for the popular economy that coexisted with the elite smuggling circuit or how Paraguay's subordinated insertion into the global economy and the history of U.S. backing for authoritarianism set the stage for contraband as a theory of development (discussed further in chapter 3). This increasing media attention also reinforced the inaccurate view that outlaw economies exist outside state power.

Within the post-9/11 U.S. security paradigm, which reenvisioned global space as a theater of endless war, Ciudad del Este was cited as an exemplar "ungoverned space." The presence of Arab communities in the region sending remittances to the Middle East spurred a series of sensationalist media reports in popular outlets like the *New Yorker* and *Vanity Fair*, hypothesizing that contraband profits flowed to groups like Hizballah.[85] These speculations then became sources in U.S. security state assessments of the dangerous character of the Tri-Border Area, even as evidence of actual links to "terror" was scant.[86] Writing for the Federal Research Division at the Library of Congress, Rex Hudson (2003, 1) imagined the "large Arab community" as "highly conducive to the establishment of sleeper cells of Islamic terrorists," an openly Islamophobic assertion. Almost exclusively, Hudson cited media sources: regional newspapers, long-form English-language stories in outlets like *Vanity Fair*, intelligence community news translation services, and the anti-Communist magazine *Jane's Intelligence Review*.[87] Hudson's report was then widely cited as proof of the terrorist presence. This world of hyperbolic and largely unsubstantiated reports became a self-referential common sense. The myth of the land without law sanctioned the neocolonial hubris among U.S. reformers claiming vast authorities of intervention paired with little concern or knowledge of everyday life in this border town, especially the struggles of the most marginalized.

These spatial imaginaries took on a life of their own, appearing in USAID documents, embassy cables, and even a graphic novel. In 2014 Oni Press published the graphic novel *Ciudad*, a brutal thriller set in Ciudad del Este.[88] Amplifying Ciudad del Este's reputation as a lawless place, the novel used the city as a blank slate for an exoticized rendering of an "unregulated border" run by a "Lebanese power structure" controlling an economic "machine—a network of profiteers, ranging from sophisticated counterfeiters to violent street gangs."[89] Erasing history, culture, context, and global interconnection, *Ciudad* is an unrecognizable distortion of Ciudad del Este. The city is only lawlessness, seediness, and violence. The reductive rendering of urban life in this place is a form of epistemic violence.

U.S.-led efforts targeted Ciudad del Este as a site for reform through the Threshold Project, a U.S.$30 million USAID project launched in 2006. The Threshold Project sought to formalize trade and reduce corruption along the border by investing in training and computerized systems for tracking commodities and capital flows across the border. In a small trove of leaked U.S. Embassy cables, officials described Ciudad del Este as an exceptionally troublesome place. They called the city a "hotbed of illicit activities" and "a haven for contraband, piracy, and other illegal activity."[90] In this "critical city," they worried, corrupt police officials offered "protection not only for drug traffickers, but for terrorist fundraisers, IPR [intellectual property rights] pirates and other organized crime kingpins."[91]

The spatial imagination of the Threshold Project opposed corruption to both modernity and state presence. Leaked U.S. Embassy cables note that "corruption in Paraguay's political and economic system undermines its efforts to modernize" because of "bloated but weak state institutions."[92] Claiming expansive power to shape policy and economic practice around the world, embassy officials called U.S. intervention a "powerful medicine" and proposed U.S. funding and oversight as forces supportive of Paraguayan efforts to "reform and modernize."[93] This stance ignores the antidemocratic history of U.S. involvement in Latin America. It is also remarkably silent about the distributional impacts of cracking down on popular elements of the border trade. This occidentalist spatial imagination continues to invoke neocolonial hierarchies that divide the world into categories of advanced and underdeveloped, modern and backward, carving interconnected systems into discrete bits and slotting them into spots on a ladder of development. It misses the productive power of places like Ciudad del Este.

Blanqueamiento

In the context of these state and popular representations of the region, Paraguayans issue their own popular critiques of elite illegalities. In Ciudad del Este anticorruption protests are aimed at the powerful Zacarías family, which ran the municipality of Ciudad del Este for almost two decades. With calls of *¡Intervención ya!* (Audit now), protesters demanded outside accounting of the municipality's books, which had long been shielded from legally mandated oversight by a shadow institution, the Tribunal de Cuentas, described in chapter 3. On the national level, in March 2017 protesters torched the headquarters of the ruling Colorado Party as President Horacio Cartes pushed constitutional changes in his bid to seek national reelection, a contentious move in a country with a legacy of authoritarian power grabs.[94] One protest sign sporting Cartes's image read, "I want reelection to keep looting the country," reflecting a widespread assessment of Cartes's corruption. Indeed, Cartes's rap sheet is long and includes contraband, currency fraud, and money laundering.[95] The CIA's Heart of Stone investigation named Cartes as the "head" of a money-laundering ring operated through his Banco Amambay, chartered in a tax haven in the Cook Islands near New Zealand.[96] During and after his presidential term, Cartes's contraband cigarettes produced in frontier factories flooded the Brazilian market, moving through clandestine ports in and around Ciudad del Este (a process discussed further in chapter 2). Yet in addition to his dirty dealings, Cartes is also a celebrated business tycoon. *Forbes* wrote a glowing assessment of his presidency, congratulating him for "ushering in a new era of Paraguayan economic success."[97] Indeed, Cartes embodies the alchemy by which transgression transmutes into legitimized political authority.

Paraguayans use the term *blanqueamiento,* or "whitening," to speak of political moves to whitewash the crimes of the powerful. Cartes, for instance, served jail time for currency fraud but then had his record expunged by the supreme court. U.S. Embassy officials warned against a controversial pick to head the Paraguayan agency responsible for monitoring money laundering because he had "a direct personal role as Central Bank president in whitewashing ('blanquear') funds for so-called pillar of the community Horacio Cartes and his Banco Amambay."[98] Indeed, terms like *blanqueo de dinero* (money laundering) and *blanqueo de divisas* (currency laundering) are common across the region, signaling the widespread extent of these practices and the traction of racialized metaphors used to describe them. Back in Ciudad del Este, when the Zacarías family was ousted from the municipality in 2018 after serial corruption scandals, political pacts protected the husband-and-wife duo by stalling cases in the courts. The Zacarías family kept eleven properties in the Brazilian beach town of Itapema, properties that were widely reported to have been purchased through ill-gotten wealth (*plata mal habida,* as it is called in the local grammar of critique). These relationships of protection and judicially backed plausible deniability are open secrets: they are discussed in newspaper articles, on the streets, and in leaked U.S. Embassy cables.[99]

With these open secrets, what matters is a confident performance of authority alongside the political capacity to secure protection from prosecution. Cartes denies that his frontier cigarette factories are linked to contraband: "Contraband is a customs problem. We do not do any contraband. We have a totally clean conscience."[100] When pressed by reporters about the regional circulation of his Tabesa cigarettes, Cartes deflected. When a reporter asked, "Are you aware that in Brazil and Argentina, where you are not allowed to export, Tabesa products are for sale?" Cartes responded, "Yes, of course," implicitly acknowledging that his products move via illegalities. He then blamed customs, claiming that his responsibility ends at the point of sale. The reporter pressed him: "But [Tabesa] produces more than is consumed [in Paraguay]." Cartes responded, "No, I believe that what is made is consumed. Otherwise, we would not be producing." Thus, he obliquely denied what he had just affirmed. The brazenness of Cartes's transgression alongside his claim to a clean conscience suggests a deep-seated sense of entitlement to profit outside the law. His posttruth claims to innocence illustrate both a logic and a practice of impunity. Coherence is not the point. In what follows I assess how these raced and classed performances of (im)plausible deniability hide accumulation by transgression.

Elite illegalities are often described using the language of corruption. Sapana Doshi and Malini Ranganathan (2018, 438) show that talk of corruption is slippery, available for use by different political projects promoting very different worldviews, arrangements of power, and distributions of wealth.[101] Given this polysemy, how different social groups talk about corruption matters. The category of corruption talk draws from Teresa Caldeira's (2001) influential work on the talk of crime and aims to capture the co-constitution of the discursive and symbolic with the material and structural.[102] This framing emphasizes that corruption talk is a contested field rather than a neutral concept identifying a stable external object. The talk of corruption is, in fact, inseparable from ethical judgments about the distribution of social wealth. Here I consider two forms of corruption talk: a propoor social critique and the hegemonic, liberal epistemology of corruption. The book's conclusion focuses on a third variant, corruption talk as a reactionary anti-Left project spectacularly on display in the corruption trials and media spectacles that took down the Brazilian Workers' Party and stewarded the rise of Jair Bolsonaro, a right-wing authoritarian. Here I discuss how corruption talk mediates the formation of various publics, as Malini Ranganathan, David Pike, and Sapana Doshi (2023) also show.

In my conversations with street vendors, they often talked of corruption, with cutting critiques of social hierarchies. They analyzed the political pacts protecting elite illegalities, observing that the transgressions of the poor were harshly punished. In both Brazil and Paraguay, the popular saying "for friends anything; for enemies, the law" encapsulates the powerful commonsense notion that following the rules is a weakness, a condition only required of those without social status or powerful connections. The saying clarifies the expectation that elites will break the rules as a sign of their power, as part of what James Holston (2009, 20), in his history of Brazilian democracy, calls "a habit of wealth." Elites expect and are often afforded impunity for their transgressions. I encountered a specialized vocabulary ridiculing the privileges of elite power: their rule-breaking proclivities, greed-based ethics, and the overlap between outlaw capital and state actors. Terms like *esquemas* (schemes), *negociados* (shady deals), and *mechanismos* (mechanisms) connote deals cut with the explicit or tacit support of state officials and involve the transgression of legal codes. This local vocabulary describes the on-the-ground logics of accumulation by transgression as experienced by ordinary Paraguayans while doubling as an implicit social critique of these logics. These critics named the systemic and classed character of rule-breaking and dealmaking, as well as the reality that prisons and punishment are for the poor.

Mainstream assessments of corruption rely on the dominant mental mapping of separate political and economic spheres inherited from liberalism and Eurocentric state theory.[103] These assumptions are behind the World Bank's definition of corruption as "the abuse of *public* office for *private* gain" (emphasis added).[104] Emboldened by Enlightenment categories and their confident claims to universal relevance unbranded by the specificity of place, context, or culture, these received conceptual divisions lend themselves to misunderstandings about the co-constitution of the state with private and economic forms of power.

This liberal epistemology of corruption gained power through a global anticorruption industry that relied on the disciplinary assumptions of neoclassical economics and ignored other social science research.[105] It also relied on internationally circulating legal-institutional models, located moral authority in U.S.-based think tanks, and claimed scientific validity through country-based rankings of perceptions of corruption, a circular measure that influenced the very domain it claimed to objectively assess.[106] These theories of corruption promote individualist remedies seeking to punish bad actors rather than rework systems, overlooking the legalized forms of taking, dispossession, and exploitation that comprise the normalized relations of racial capitalism. This liberal epistemology of corruption also has its own spatial imaginary. Its predictable imaginative geography locates corruption in the Global South, whitewashing the extensive role of corporate power, private interest, and dark money in the Global North. This imaginative geography is on display in Transparency International's corruption map, which codes most countries in the Global South as highly corrupt, while most countries in the Global North are rated as "clean."

This imagination of corruption is also "fundamentally antagonistic towards the state," assuming that the market is virtuous and meritocratic.[107] The antistate bias of corruption talk is historically produced and contingent. In the United States Progressive era populists used the talk of corruption to challenge monopoly power, while in India today poor people's movements use it to challenge structural inequality and decry elite land grabs.[108] On the other hand, in Brazil the Tenentismo movement in the 1920s called for moral renewal as a critique against corruption and impunity among the powerful agrarian elite.[109] While contesting some abuses of power, this anticorruption alliance between Brazilian elites and the urban middle class assessed political action by poor people as manipulated by corrupt populists.

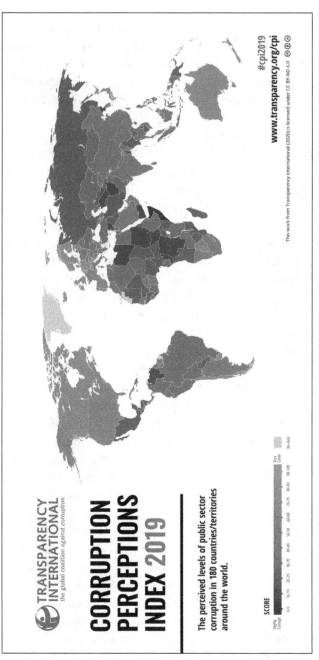

FIGURE 8. A widely circulated Transparency International map locates corruption in the Global South; courtesy of Transparency International

Against the notion of separate spheres inherent in the liberal epistemology of corruption, outlaw capital reveals the *doublings* of political and economic power. I borrow this frame from Joshua Barkan's (2013) work on corporate power and the state of exception.[110] Using law to act outside of it, the state is both inside and outside the law, occupying a "zone of indifference" more blurred than a "simple topographical opposition (inside/outside)" (Agamben 2005, 23). Extending Giorgio Agamben, Barkan (2013, 4) argues that corporate and state power are "ontologically linked" in both their historical co-becoming and their similar forms of political reason via the state of exception.[111] Thus, instead of separate economic and political spheres, state and corporate-economic power are coevolved, doubled, "conjoined but also in conflict," each animating the other's conditions of possibility.[112] Likewise, the relations between outlaw capital and state power are doublings, not distinct domains. Of course, the transgression of law is different from its suspension. Yet both suspension and transgression of the law enable action in a blurred zone of indifference that is more accessible to the powerful than to the marginalized. Transgression looks ad hoc, like individual bad apples breaking the rules, but it is systemic. Conceptualizing this systematicity is part of the power of the concept of outlaw capital. Outlaw capital, as a doubling of political and economic power, therefore pushes back against the reductive frame of separate political and economic spheres. The liberal anticorruption epistemology authorizes some blurrings of the political and economic, like the legalization of dark money in elections and policymaking—think *Citizens United*—or the suspension of law underwriting Guantánamo's brutalities. Other doublings are declared corruption, like the transgressive dealmaking that enables a large portion of the city's border trade. The point is not to celebrate contraband but rather to situate outlaw capital as an important dynamic internal to global capitalism in order to contest its inequalities and the antidemocratic forms of governance it generates.

The transgressive doublings of outlaw capital require obscuration. I suggest that this obscuration is worked out through dealmaking and race-class performances of propriety. Deals were central to Horacio Cartes's business empire and the longevity of Javier Zacarías Irún's political career.[113] In colloquial use, Paraguayans use *blanqueamiento* to critique political pacts like these that create protection and impunity.[114] *Blanqueamiento* names how wealth and whiteness serve as a means of claiming legitimacy and impunity.[115] The social standing of these men buttresses their claims to legitimacy: they occupy positions of power and are favorably assessed by media outlets like *Forbes* and *The Economist*.[116] Indeed, successful performances of legitimacy are unsurprisingly worked out through social hierarchies of race, class, and gender.[117] Thus, *blanqueamiento* names a kind of blindness through which we look away from the transgressions of outlaw capitalists or interpret them as legitimate precisely because their bodies themselves index the commonsense category of the successful businessman.

Blanqueamiento is thus a vernacular critique of elite illegalities in the context of racial capitalism. Rationalities of what Aileen Moreton-Robinson (2015) calls the "white possessive" naturalize settler possession of Indigenous land while exonerating the innumerable ethical and legal transgressions that enable ownership.[118] In settler societies, Indigenous dispossession is foundational: it is the condition of possibility for the nation-state, shaping both forms of property and personhood. The ontology and epistemology of the white possessive includes a sense of entitlement to own, to take, to exclude, and to dispossess. Whiteness is thus an unselfconscious taking rendered as the natural order of things. This is a collective power and a social project that hides its thievery through masquerades of meritocracy and advancement allocated to individuals rather than social groups. Whiteness is thus also a racial cartel, a profit-seeking alliance bound by legal trespass.[119]

This points again to a certain doubleness: whiteness shapes the landscape of legality and the terrain of rights in the political-economic interest of the dominant group, a time-honored tradition of race-class power. Yet at the same time, whiteness also secures protection for ill-gotten wealth and legal trespass, as any water protector decrying the U.S. government's violation of its own treaties with sovereign Indigenous nations will tell you. Outlaw capital is one form of entitled taking. *Blanqueamiento* is the means by which outlaw capitalists enact legitimacy for their transgressive forms of possession. Forms of property of course differ historically, and I am not suggesting that outlaw capital reproduces the grotesque logic of Black enslavability and mass Indigenous dispossession. I am suggesting that extending this vernacular critique of *blanqueamiento* through the lens of whiteness as property focuses our attention on how elites naturalize transgressive forms of possession.

Conclusion

Geographies of uneven development produce some places, like Ciudad del Este, as freewheeling spaces of frontier capitalism, as useful extralegal trading hubs. We should be open to learning from these places. These places help us see that accumulation by transgression is a central mode of accumulation by extra-economic means. While accumulation by transgression is not generative of surplus value, it is still internal to capitalism. Spatial and racial imaginaries blame cultures of corruption for the transgressions in the border economy while eliding their historical and relational production. National, regional, and colonial-global spatial imaginaries work differently, but all conspire to construct Ciudad del Este as an aberration that is irrelevant to efforts to understand global capitalist change. These discourses of disconnection gain traction because they resonate with Eurocentric myths of progress that read modernity as equivalent to Western forms of economy, urban form, and governance. Within Paraguay, elites in the capital city, like Elisa and Colmán Gutiérrez, express anxiety about the city's reputation for lawlessness, seeking to recast elite illicit *esquemas* as remnants of the past or as somehow apart from the relations that make up the so-called real national community. Outside Paraguay, race mediates these regional and neocolonial discourses of disconnection. The Brazilian media mobilizes notions of Paraguayan alterity to enact distance from the contraband economy, even as countless points of material interconnection suture the two countries together. This useful discursive maneuver helps justify the fantasy that rule-breaking is a Paraguayan problem. Islamophobia shapes U.S. discourses of the city, as does the long history of U.S. interventionism that claims all of Central and South America as "our backyard," a spatial imaginary of paternal authority, one that promises protection but dishes out violence. Brazilian and U.S. discourses, then, construct Paraguayans as inferior others through different racial logics, even as they share a perspective of backward or defective cultures of corruption.

In local parlance, *blanqueamiento* names the political pacts for protection that confer impunity on elites based on class position and proximity to whiteness. It offers a subversive perspective on elite illegalities, naming them as the norm. Yet the *blanqueamiento* critique often identifies elite illegalities as individual moral failings rather than the social relations of racial capitalism in which whiteness as property includes forms of accumulation by transgression. Extending *blanqueamiento*, then, emphasizes whiteness as a racial cartel protecting transgressive forms of property and ill-gotten wealth.

CHAPTER 2

Contraband Urbanism

When I arrived in Ciudad del Este in 2015, piles of rubble stretched along blocks of the street market, the ruins of vendors' stalls, *casillas* (permanent vending stalls with roofs), shops, and a few brick-and-mortar galleries cleared to make way for a formalization project called the Pilot Plan. Anticorruption activists, business owners, and some, but not all, street vendors fought hard against the demolitions, battling the Pilot Plan in the courtroom and on the streets and forming a new group I call the Citizens' Coalition. In 2001 the Zacarías administration proposed the Pilot Plan as a temporary solution, provisionally upgrading vendors' workspaces along the central artery that slopes downhill to the International Friendship Bridge until the municipality could construct a shared space for vendors on the Nine Hectares. However, fifteen years into the Pilot Plan, the municipality had abandoned efforts to relocate street vendors and instead steamrolled through a new vision for the Pilot Plan as permanent. The municipal criteria determining which vendors would benefit were opaque and caused worry for many.

Through the early weeks of August 2014, coalition members believed they could stop the demolitions.[1] Powerful lawyers argued their case, obtaining a legal stay and several protection orders from the courts. Protests punctuated the lead-up to the demolitions. The Zacarías alliance fractured when a linchpin taxi drivers' union defected to the other side. Hundreds of taxi drivers shut down streets, blocked the bridge, and brought trade to a screeching halt.[2] Vendors stayed put in their stalls and shops: by showing up each day to work and storing their wares in stalls slated for demolition, they expressed faith in their cause and defended their workplaces with their presence. But on a mid-August evening, municipal crews wearing bulletproof vests showed up with bulldozers. Facing the imminent destruction of their stalls, vendors frantically sought to save their merchandise from confiscation or burial. Completing the demo-

FIGURE 9. A makeshift taxi stand in the rubble of the Fourth Stage demolitions; photo by author, 2015

FIGURE 10. The vending stalls in the Pilot Plan have standardized sizes and tin roofs, conveying the look of legality; courtesy of the Municipality of Ciudad del Este, 2007

litions required several more months of lawsuits and an operation backed by three hundred armed police officers, including members of the Special Operations Force. When the dust settled, somewhere between one thousand and two thousand vendors and *casilleros* and a few bigger shop owners had lost their establishments.[3]

The Citizens' Coalition included Kelembu, a self-made frontier salesman, regular candidate for mayor, and fierce critic of Clan Zí, shorthand for the political alliance led by the husband-and-wife duo Javier Zacarías and Sandra McLeod de Zacarías, who, between the two of them, held the position of mayor from 2001 to 2019. Kelembu—meaning "ugly" or "low quality" in Guaraní—was a stage name, a means to mock local politics by performing a caricature of a simple-minded, Guaraní-speaking campesino unaccustomed to the ways of city life. In his series of DIY videos, Kelembu critiqued local corruption by making fun of its material consequences. In a 2015 viral video, Kelembu and his sidekick enjoyed an afternoon swim in a water-filled pothole in the city center. Indeed, much of Ciudad del Este lacks basic services like potable water, reliable bus service, and paved roads.

Kelembu invited me to tour these physical manifestations of the local state's incapacity (*mal desempeño*, or "bad performance," as he called it).[4] After we toured the ruins of vendors' stalls, *casillas*, and shops in the fourth stage of the Pilot Plan, we passed a *contrabandista*, a bored-looking teenager in a white T-shirt and flashy sneakers, as he watched over a small mountain of boxes piled under the shadow of shopping mall construction. Kelembu showed me shoddy street paving and a walking path around the Lake of the Republic. At each stop, Kelembu quantified the gap between the municipality's reported expenditure and his own cost estimate, a difference he argued proved overinvoicing (*sobrefacturación*), a revenue stream lining the pockets of the Zacarías administration and their allies in the merchant bloc. Like a detective at a crime scene, Kelembu sought evidence in urban form of what the municipality hid by evading supposedly mandatory national audits. His videos underscored the frustrations of frontier life marked by the disjuncture between the profit potential of the border trade and the experience of working in an underserviced, divided city.

Indeed, the city's shoddy infrastructure circulates commodity flows worth several billion dollars.[5] Squads of cash-carrying armored vehicles navigate roads with swimming-hole-sized potholes. This is because the merchant bloc built Ciudad del Este as a sieve for these money flows rather than as a catchment. As if magnetized, money is pulled across the border or out of the country. Off-the-books Brazilian sales staff spend their earnings where they live, in

Foz do Iguaçu, as do many middle- and upper-class businesspeople residing across the Friendship Bridge. Paraguay's corporate tax rate—among the lowest in the hemisphere—and institutionalized customs fraud keep state coffers chronically low. An elaborate network of shell companies and offshore banks hide the profits of dubious import-export schemes. Parts of this story are old: rutted pathways along which money is spirited away from the so-called developing to the developed world or piled up in the bank accounts of the already rich. This chapter focuses on a newer phenomenon: the social production of space in a city built for contraband.

Ciudad del Este moves a lot of commodities cheaply because of the kinds of relations, connections, and mobilities enabled in and through particular city spaces. Indeed, outlaw capital produces its own space: its logics mark the built environment, offering clues to the practices that built it. *Contraband urbanism* describes the spatial forms of a hub city in extralegal trading circuits. My concept also describes a suite of political strategies and ways of knowing innovated by the merchant bloc and aimed at displacing the contradictions of exclusionary economies and state-supported forms of lawbreaking. Indeed, the built forms of Ciudad del Este materialize struggles over the boundaries of authorized economic practice, struggles that determine who will benefit from the border economy and who will be excluded or expelled.

The template of global urbanism seeks an orderly, bourgeois commercial aesthetic rooted in an urban epistemology associating work with private, enclosed spaces. The informal trade city produces urban spaces aimed at circulating goods as cheaply as possible with legal compliance in spatioeconomic practices as a second-order concern. Indeed, the popular economy relies on publicity and open built forms to gain access to the border trade. Thus, popular spatialities conflict with the kinds of spaces promoted by global urbanism. Its superficial forms of urban knowledge assert that we can infer legality and legitimacy from visual cues and a restricted aesthetics. This chapter challenges the assessment that compliance can be read off of urban form, instead arguing that the spatial form sometimes hides social processes. The modes of obfuscation are symbolic, social, and spatial. Ironically, the merchant bloc wants it both ways—to maintain the city's trade volume and profitability but through a limited repertoire of urban forms that align aesthetically with the so-called modern city. The frame of the social production of space for outlaw capital helps direct our attention to this structuring tension.

In this chapter, I analyze key urban forms and their animating epistemologies. After proposing a theoretical framework for analyzing the social production of space for outlaw economies, I explore four forms: clandestine ports, city center streets, street vendors stalls, and shopping malls. This sequence starts with the most unbuilt and open forms (extralegal riverside ports), leading to the most built-up, enclosed, and surveilled forms (flashy riverfront malls). Each expresses a different tangle of extralegality. For each, I offer a conceptual lens that decodes the relations between the spatial and the social. Clandestine ports are hidden by *blindaje*, a practice of differential visibility necessary to hide accumulation by transgression. Official logics attempt to order streets through an *antipoor epistemology* that is reluctant to contend with streets as sites of work. The municipal plan to formalize street vendors' stalls demonstrates the space-times of what Oren Yiftachel (2009, 90) calls "permanent temporariness," while fancy malls cover over their legal transgressions by *looking legal*. Turning an urban lens on extralegal economies shows how globalized capitalism produces cities like Ciudad del Este.

Outlaw Capital and Urban Development

"I thought it would be more urban," a friend commented to me when he arrived to visit in 2011 during my first research trip. Ciudad del Este did not fit his expectations of an urban center. Like my friend, urban scholarship struggles to locate Ciudad del Este in its typologies. From the vantage point of mainstream academic canons of development and urbanization, this city does not fit. Ciudad del Este is a node in global trade networks, but it is not a command-and-control center as described by researchers of global cities. The city is shaped by extralegal spatioeconomic practices, yet it cannot be thought through the rubrics of an informal city shaped by the politics of informal settlements. Instead, as I have argued, Ciudad del Este is a key spatial expression of outlaw capital: vast commodity flows shape the city and require urban infrastructure oriented toward enabling commerce, both registered and off the books. Transgressive trade economies, in their popular and elite expressions, require specific kinds of spaces from which to organize various transactions, like clandestine ports, shopping malls, and street vendor stalls. From these sites, vendors, entrepreneurs, traffickers, and customs agents all enact globalization, connecting this small South American border town to world-spanning circuits of capital and commodities. Indeed, the merchant bloc promotes the extralegal economy by making urban spaces for commerce, contraband, and their heady intermingling.

The concept of *contraband urbanism* explains the social production of space in this border city through its attention to both the built environment and the forms of urban knowledge that claim to know the city or, perhaps as often, that fail to know it.[6] My choice of the term *urbanism* is intentional, as it connects to intellectual lineages concerned with urban life, social struggle, and the production of space. Indisputably, circuits of capital shape cities and urban life. Furthermore, different forms of capital produce distinct urban forms and spatial arrangements. Finance, industrial, and petro capital shape built environments. Respectively, these forms of capital demand and produce places like New York's financial districts, export processing zones in the Pearl River Delta, and sacrifice zones like the Alberta Tar Sands. To this incomplete list, I add outlaw capital. Of course, as we learn from comparative and postcolonial urban scholars, globalized capital articulates with other regimes of power like nationalism and (settler) colonialism as forces shaping the urban.

Urbanism also captures epistemological struggles over how to see, understand, and act on cities. Far from intervening in the urban from a position of exteriority, urban planning—as an academic discipline interwoven with repertoires of practice—contributes to constituting this field of contested knowledge. Some ways of knowing the city are bound up in the reproduction of capital or the maintenance of other structures of violence, while other ways contest these exclusionary urban visions.[7] *Global urbanism* is a hegemonic form of depoliticized, market-oriented urban development bound up with neoliberal logics of competition, optimization, privatization, and the like, kneeling at the altar of economic growth.[8] The premises of global urbanism are often unquestioned by decision-makers as they align with their commonsense understanding of economic growth and urbanization. From this vantage point, the city is a "growth machine," urban space is a commodity, and the role of planners is to attract investments and maximize the exchange value of land.[9] Cities, through this lens, are bounded, competing units traveling along pregiven development paths. Reformers then seek to make their particular urban unit competitive in a marketplace of cities. To do so, they turn to global urbanism's proposals for the competitive city.

These proposals pull from a limited stockpile of urban forms offered as best practices: think San Francisco's private tech campuses, Rio's Olympic stadiums built atop cleared *favelas*, East Asian export processing zones, or Minnesota's Mall of America. Indeed, across Latin America, urban development projects increasingly promote shopping malls as "models of how cities and citizenship should work," as Arlene Dávila (2016, viii) demonstrates. This interurban referencing is a form a "worlding," according to Ananya Roy and Aihwa Ong (2012), practices of connecting to elsewhere, becoming global, and enacting modernity. Some forms, of course, like state-subsidized housing in Shanghai, rarely get taken up as a model. Around the conference tables where empowered actors debate urban futures, the question of how the urban poor can make a living in these competitive global cities is often but a haunting.

Dominant ways of knowing cities are, too often, forms of unknowing, patterns of misapprehension, collective amnesia, and socially sanctioned ignorance. Analyzing this, Henri Lefebvre described urbanism's ideological "blind field" (2003, 23) as a set of overlapping "illusions" that "claim . . . to be a system" (153). Too often, Lefebvre insists, urban practitioners are willfully oblivious to the ways they produce space for capital, as a commodity, and as a "class strategy" (2003, 157) rather than for use, need, or desire. Representations of space used in urban planning—like maps, plans, or censuses of authorized street vendors—rely on and produce grids of visibility, sketching the domains that can be seen and thought while also bounding those that are hard to see or even unthinkable.

Lefebvre anticipated the commodification of space and urban life along with the rise of secondary circuits of capital made through property rather than production (what he called the primary circuit of capital).[10] Urbanization, he argued, now displaces industrialization in the reproduction of capitalism. City space and even urban life are now acted on as commodities and sites of investment and speculation. This is half of what Lefebvre calls the "urban revolution." The other half insists that everyday urban life and its social reproduction are key arenas of struggle, thus expanding politics beyond the factory floor. Everyday life expresses contradictory dynamics: it is "colonized by capitalism," including, I suggest, its outlaw forms.[11] It is also the ground of transformation, of radical possibility, containing the seeds of other, more emancipatory ways of being, building, and becoming (Lefebvre 2002).

Lefebvre further argued that via "extended urbanization," the spatiosocial dynamics of the urban extend over vast geographies, influencing spaces not usually thought of as the city. As he says, the urban zone—the built environments of the stereotypical city—explodes into a vast "urban fabric," spaces shaped by "the dominance of the city over the country" (2003, 4), even as their forms do not align with dominant notions of cityness. The spaces and functions once imagined as belonging in a bounded city are now geographically dispersed, disassembled, and recomposed by extended urbanization. Extended urbanization includes many spatial forms, from the urbanization of remote places like the Amazonian city of Manaus, to the financialization of everyday urban life in a Chilean mining boomtown, to Toronto's exurban, not-quite-suburban "in-between zones."[12] Ciudad del Este exemplifies a peripheral space in the extended urban fabric that is both integrated into and productive of urban systems, what Juan Miguel Kanai and Rafael da Silva Oliveira (2014,

62) call "functionally-articulated-yet-marginalized." Its inequality-producing dynamics diverge from informal settlements in periurban zones, a spatial form that tends to stand in for all peripheries. Outlaw capital requires and produces spaces that facilitate its own reproduction, even as its spoils are contested. Ultimately, the thrust of urban space in Ciudad del Este is its production as a class strategy. While Lefebvre did not attend to politics and spaces of outlaw capital in his theory of the urban revolution, this chapter examines this dynamic.

Ports

Clandestine ports are key to this trade network. Hundreds of ports dot both shores of the Paraná River and the upstream Itaipú Lake. Estimates of the number of ports jumped to 250 in 2019, up from 120 five years prior.[13] Defying expectations of what globalized spaces look like, these unassuming patches of riverbank process millions of dollars' worth of inventory without cranes or container ships. Rare public photos taken by a journalist show piles of boxes on a cleared patch of shore surrounding a skinny, slide-like wooden ramp sloping steeply into the water, where a small dinghy with a single outboard motor stands ready to take merchandise a football field's distance to a sibling port on the Brazilian bank of the Paraná. On the Paraguayan side, clandestine ports operate in three poor neighborhoods: Remansito, San Rafael, and San Miguel, just north and south of the Friendship Bridge. Commerce spreads to upstream towns dominated by contraband, like the twin cities of Saltos de Guaíra, Paraguay, and Guaíra, Brazil.

Clandestine ports represent a transformation in contraband logistics. After the city's founding in 1954, traders relied on small planes and private landing strips, transporting luxury goods like whiskey from Miami.[14] Highway 2 and the International Friendship Bridge transformed the material basis of the border trade, and soon the bridge became the central trade artery. As I discuss in the next chapter, these transport infrastructures unexpectedly decentralized access to smuggling. Post-9/11, securing borders and cracking down on traffickers took on new regional importance, driving another round of transformation. In response, traders turned to the river, clearing patches of the steep Paraná riverbank for makeshift landing zones.

From my vantage point as a foreign researcher, clandestine ports were hard to see, even as they were open secrets. The local term *blindaje* helps explain the practices of power that protect the ports from certain publics. Residents use *blindaje* to describe arrangements between judges and politicians, prom-

FIGURE 11. A clandestine port along the Paraná River; courtesy of Andrés Colmán Gutiérrez

ises exchanging impunity for kickbacks. *Blindaje* is also a military term for a protective screen. Its double sense connotes both protection and an impediment to visibility. *Blindaje* zones clandestine ports as off-limits from certain kinds of publics, including journalists and foreign researchers. *Blindaje* also protects the clandestine ports obscuring the illegalities that move cigarettes from the ex-president's factories to Brazilian and Argentine consumers along both the Paraguayan and Brazilian riverine border. The former president's factories produce twenty billion cigarettes yearly, 2 percent of which are smoked by Paraguayans.[15] Cartes disavows connections to the contraband networks that move his merchandise, as discussed in chapter 1. Along these clandestine trade routes, risk concentrates in the moments—and in the spaces—of illegal border crossing. Traffickers called *cigarreros*—the ones of the cigarettes—navigate these risks as they ferry boats across the river. These transportation workers are often poor and treated as if they are disposable. This complex division of labor concentrates risks onto specialized traffickers and allows Cartes to displace responsibility for trespass onto others.

The patches of riverbank along the Paraná are also networked to other, technology-intensive ports. Tracing these expansive underground transit networks, investigative reporters described how a notorious Brazilian *contrabandista,* operating from Paraguay, "cut deals with tobacco traders in Arizona and smoke shop owners in Indian reservations in Washington state to smuggle millions of Paraguayan-made contraband cigarettes through the ports of Miami, Norfolk, and Baltimore."[16] Massive tax evasion reduces the cost of Cartes's cigarettes, such that rule-breaking is the source of his profit. This is accumulation by transgression, and it requires obfuscation: methods to hide the litany of legal trespasses behind these practices of profiteering. In 2018 media outlets detailed deals between the Itaipú Dam officials, the Paraguayan navy, and the Department of Forests and Environmental Affairs protecting clandestine ports on land administered by Itaipú Binacional.[17] Between 2013 and 2018 state agencies did not carry out a single enforcement operation in the protection zone administered by Itaipú Binacional. Political pacts for protection outlived Cartes's presidential term, surviving even the contentious Colorado Party power struggles between Cartes's political movement and his rival and successor to the presidency, Mario Abdo Benítez. *Blindaje* works to obscure these deals.

Moreover, social norms of access regulate spaces of smuggling, including mechanisms that effectively zoned the ports as off-limits. My social network helped me meet poor hawkers, community leaders, business tycoons, senators, and even President Cartes. However, this network lost effectivity as it neared the riverfront neighborhoods. Even with introductions facilitated by a community leader to a port worker and a lawyer for small-scale traffickers, I had trouble accessing the ports. Yet the ports are open secrets. Small-scale *contrabandistas* provisioning a produce market in Ciudad del Este with cheaper Brazilian goods even had their own labor association and a lawyer to represent them.

Blindaje produced cartographies of both access and prohibition. When I chatted with a taxi driver about a riverfront neighborhood, he commented casually to me, "Oh, *you* can't go there." He emphasized the "you," suggesting that the spatial restriction was not universal but rather connected to me and, I suspect, due to my embodied outsiderness. This small act of *blindaje* emerged from, yet also produced, a conditional map of no-go zones. Likewise, a journalist recounted covering an enforcement operation at a port. As his car wound down the dirt road, residents gathered to block the path, cursing, brandishing sticks, and yelling, "Leave us poor people alone!" This small uprising defended the popular extralegal economy. Yet these port workers and contraband runners are also enrolled in *blindaje*, protecting the spaces of smuggling that generate fortunes for rich men. Thus, I argue, *blindaje* is also a spatial practice.

These narratives of spatial exclusion and danger imagine certain places as threatening, spaces produced by and productive of criminal poverty. One riverfront neighborhood, Remansito, appears in Caroline Schuster's (2015) ethnography of gender and microcredit in Ciudad del Este. Going against the common perception that women, as mothers, are reliably good investments, a women's lending collective in Remansito aggressively refused to repay their loans. The NGO microcredit counselor in charge of the group commented, "The neighborhood made the women hard" (Schuster 2015, 141). The discourse of "hard women" echoes the territorial stigma associated with the neighborhood.[18] Early in my fieldwork, my Guaraní language teacher Ignacio and I walked through Remansito's incoherent slapdash of houses: shacks set alongside minimansions hidden behind fifteen-foot walls, where traffickers were rumored to live. Ignacio recruited a resident to show us the river, a means to gain access to a space otherwise effectively off-limits to nonresidents. Our impromptu guide led us down a dirt path between close-set shacks, asking permission to pass through the side yard of a skeptical woman sweeping up leaves and trash. The path turned into stone stairs, paralleled by a single line of light bulbs leading back to the house. Our guide led us to a small strip of shore, a few yards of exposed earth amid a dense tangle of bushes, from which we watched a small skiff crossing the river. I did not yet appreciate the import of this unremarkable landing, a key space in global contraband routes. Ironically, once I did, I was not able to make my way back to the ports.

On our way back from the river, we chatted with the young woman in her yard. The dirt floor of her small home and the broom made of sorghum leaves signaled poverty. Her responses to Ignacio's questions where short, foreclosing conversation. When Ignacio asked if she worked, she replied brusquely, "I study." Ignacio, however, did not believe her. He later commented, "She doesn't have the look of a student; a prostitute is more likely." He continued, painting broad brushstrokes of criminality across the neighborhood. Ignacio's casual assertion tainted the woman as transgressive, echoing the microcredit counselor's analysis that spaces of smuggling produce hard women. These narratives of spatial danger stigmatize both the neighborhood and poor residents. Territorial stigma gains power through collective imaginations of safe spaces and proper subjects. Hard women challenge norms of feminine friendliness as they also index a string of shared meanings about the spaces of poverty. Collective maps demarcate riverfront neighborhoods as dangerous and protect key spaces of commerce by helping to cloak ports from inquisitive eyes and uncomfortable questions.

While hidden, the ports still become visible in journalistic or official accounts that find evidence through a lack of effective enforcement, that is, in absences. One article described the aftereffects of a state enforcement action:

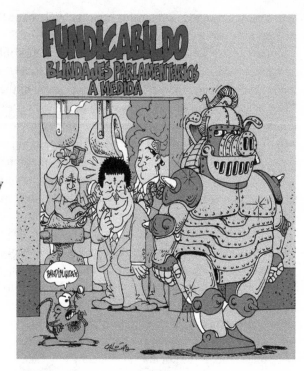

FIGURE 12. A political cartoon by Caló depicts an ironworks advertising "Blindajes for parliamentarians, forged to fit" while a rat comments, "Blindaje for bandits" as ex-president Cartes looks on; courtesy of Caló

"More than a month after the mega-operation that 'discovered' four clandestine ports stocked with merchandise ready to be brought into Brazilian territory, the prosecutors in charge, Marca and Erario, have been unable to charge even a single person. They have not even determined the names of the homeowners, which held the ferries that bring the merchandise into the neighboring country in an illegal manner."[19] The unnamed journalist described what they could see: lackadaisical prosecutors and no charges. Yet the journalist could not see the owners of the boats or those responsible for the merchandise, because the prosecutors did not seek their names. Bracketing the word "discovered" in quotes, the journalist suggested that the verb did not accurately describe the relationship between enforcement officials and the find. Instead, the journalist implied that officials already knew about the ports. Similarly, in 2016 the USTR also noted the problem of ineffective enforcement, including "long lag times in obtaining warrants and low prosecution rates."[20] The 2015 USTR report "applauds" the Cartes administration for its commitment to "transform Ciudad del Este into a legitimate marketplace" even as the 2017 report commented that "effective seizures at Ciudad del Este are inadequate and in decline."[21] Standards of journalistic sourcing, like mainstream corruption frameworks, require evidence linking particular individuals to specific acts based on notions of individual culpability. *Blindaje* is a technology of transgression that works by obscuring these linkages. It produces predictable patterns of protection, providing immunity for politically connected elites.

The popular imagination of *blindaje* critiques political practices of elite impunity more generally. The cartoonist Caló, for example, depicts a factory producing armor sized to fit politicians to protect them from prosecution. A character comments, "*Blindaje* for bandits," as a metal worker forges a suit of armor for Cartes. The term *blindaje* was used even by those suspected of being implicated. Responding to another congressional attempt to audit the municipality's budget, Mayor Sandra McLeod de Zacarías used the language of *blindaje* to deny that her administration benefited from these forms of protection.[22] While the specific connections between judges, prosecutors, and municipal officials remain masked, the mayor's comment reaffirmed *blindaje*'s political potency in collective imaginaries of how politics works. As a vernacular means of critique, *blindaje* names the networks of obfuscation enabling impunity as a commonplace practice of governance.

Streets

Streets, in addition to ports, are key sites of commerce in Ciudad del Este. Commerce is concentrated in about eight square blocks radiating outward from the foot of the International Friendship Bridge along Highway 2, which connects Asunción to Brazil. Highway 2 is flanked by two streets, Avenida San Blas and Avenida Monseñor Rodríguez, each divided from the highway by a broad median. This streetscape space hosted small brick-and-mortar galleries and a maze of street vendor stalls until the municipality demolished them over the course of a decade, replacing them with the Pilot Plan's standardized vending stalls. Constructions by street vendors range from a stool next to a cooler full of icy drinks to semipermanent, fully enclosed constructions with display cases, on-site storage, and roll-up metal doors to protect merchandise overnight. Likewise, itinerant hawkers ply their wares from the street. Some carry them in backpacks, while fruit vendors push carts so large they sometimes cause traffic jams. Taxis, mototaxis, and vans vie for street space to park and recruit riders. Access to street space is managed through thirty-four associations of taxi drivers.[23] While intricately organized by formal organizations and informal codes, this street commerce is often described as chaotic, disorganized, and unplanned.

Struggles over streets and sidewalks offer a window into competing urban epistemologies, that is, ways of knowing and acting on the city. During the 2013 launch of a public-private partnership simply called the Development Plan (Plan de Desarrollo del Este), the city's leadership convened a planning commission meeting to address troubling declines in the border trade.[24] The assembled group of business leaders, local officials, and a representative from the Ministry of Industry and Commerce sought to maintain the profitability of the reexportation economy while addressing the city's international reputation as a site of lawlessness. They also sought to address the difficult task of formalization, a project that participants described as "restructuring the city" (*reconversión de la ciudad*). *Reconversión* was equal parts imaginative, spatial, and economic. Governor Lucho Zacarías opened the meeting, saying, "We want a new Ciudad del Este," proposing a radical break from the present city. Yet the governor also emphasized protecting the border trade by saying that "the calling of Ciudad del Este is commercial." Meeting participants wrestled with what should be preserved and what should be transformed. Without naming the paradox, participants debated how to both build a modern-looking city and maintain the cheap, informalized spaces and logistics systems that turned Ciudad del Este into a trading hub.

The proposals drew from the grab bag of global urbanism: formalizing or evicting street vendors, establishing public-private partnerships for commercial riverfront development, and consolidating SEZs. Local businessmen focused on the built form: one prominent businessman passionately argued that upgrading urban infrastructure for "modern commerce" would necessarily "eliminate contraband and informality," two related vices, he insisted, antithetical to the modern city. For him, "the new Ciudad del Este" required a particular aesthetic and spatial form, one that would end the haphazard aesthetic of self-built vending stalls. In this vision, streets and sidewalks should be for circulating consumers rather than working vendors.

Other visions relied on the strategic use of special customs lists to reduce tariffs for high-volume consumer goods. The national Ministry of Industry and Commerce representative, Nomei Haudenschild, highlighted the city's comparative advantages, including its strategic location in continental commodity flows and the commercial "know-how" of importer-exporters (she used the English word).[25] In asking what tax level "we have to have so that there isn't undervaluation," she proposed using importer-exporters' willingness to pay to set the tax rate. Haudenschild thus legitimated frontier businessmen's knowledge of global factories, "friendly" customs officials, and clandestine ports. This framing of trading know-how as a comparative advantage valorizes the knowledge gained through contraband. To promote city competitiveness and attract foreign investors, Haudenschild further endorsed rereg-ulation to legalize contraband, envisioning the city as an economic unit com-peting against other urban units.

How would these new urban plans conceive of streets and street vendors? At the planning commission meeting, some businessmen called for the mu-nicipality to "clean the streets" of vendors, a straightforward call for mass ex-pulsion. This view was echoed across a dozen interviews with municipal offi-cials who described their plans to create "order" and to "clean up" the streets by "reclaiming" them from street vendors. "Who creates this disorder? They [vendors] do. Because of them there is no urbanistic relationship," one mu-nicipal official said to me.[26] Seeking to transform Ciudad del Este into a com-petitive city legible through the rubrics of global urbanism, these officials pro-posed streets for cars and sidewalks for pedestrians, both oriented toward circulation for consumption.

Even though the meeting expressly sought to address street vending, ven-dors' associations were not present. Some vendors promoted a radically dif-ferent view of the city, one that insisted that streets and sidewalks were sites of work. However, street vendors' associations took different positions on the best pathways toward tenure security. Some advocated for relocation to a shared commercial space on the Nine Hectares, while others sought more se-cure claims to their existing vending spots. Both groups used the popular ver-nacular of *acquired rights* to claim street and sidewalk spaces, arguing that longevity of tenure and livelihood need justified their claims to space. Some claimants even used this idea of acquired rights to insist that family need trumped legal compliance as a measure of legitimate occupancy. Chapter 4 describes street vendor politics in detail.

Among these competing visions of the new Ciudad del Este were those who sought to relocate vendors to the Nine Hectares. Cinthia Ayala, for example, a lawyer with the Citizens' Coalition and a community leader, envisioned streets clear of shoppers and vendors as entrepreneurs:

> They need some time to adapt, but they have to formalize. They must learn how to invoice sales, register their claims, pay their taxes. By becoming for-malized, vendors can make something of themselves [*convertirse en alguien*]. This implies education. This implies time. . . . My only intention is that things become formalized so that we can reclaim the streets of Ciudad del Este. This was the reason for the expropriation of the Nine Hectares. For this. Anything else is illegal. . . . With formalization, Ciudad del Este can become a real city like all the other cities.[27]

Ayala emphasized legal compliance as a precondition for becoming a "real city" and a core attribute of good economic subjects. Yet her work as a key lawyer in the anticorruption suits of the Citizens' Coalition meant that she was well versed in the litany of transgressions underwriting shopping mall development on the Nine Hectares, the very spot slated for vendor relocation. As such, she understood rule-breaking and even informality as a cross-class phenomenon, but she still faithfully invested law with the power to order space and economy. She wagered that formalization would transform vendors so that they could "become someone," that is, become acceptable economic subjects with the attitudes, orientations, and spatial practices of the microentrepreneur. Thus, she saw vendors as subjects in need of reform and hoped that streets clear of vendors would pave the way for Ciudad del Este to become a "real city." Yet the ubiquity of informalized street vending throughout Latin America meant that the blueprints for this imagined real city must come from elsewhere.

Planners in Ciudad del Este defended the legitimacy of the Development Plan by signaling that the municipality was moving away from the "planning by deal" that had built much of the city. When the municipality hired the Brazilian engineer Cássio Taniguchi to spearhead the Development Plan, Taniguchi distinguished himself from those advocating mass evictions by proposing limited zones for street vending.[28] He sought to incorporate some vendors into a more orderly urban aesthetic of an open-air shopping district. As an advocate for the importance of technical aspects of urban planning, Taniguchi worked with aerial images and AutoCAD plans as classic Lefebvrian representations of space used by state planners. Yet the planning process angered working vendors, who were not invited to participate and largely treated as a problem to be solved. In reflecting on the way that Taniguchi's perspective mapped the city from above rather than engaging with everyday life as it actually existed, one architect commented that the plan was "totally disconnected from life on the ground."[29]

Even as meeting participants complained about rule-breaking street vendors, other illegalities were also taking place in the streets. Local reporters had just uncovered an elaborate extortion scheme involving the local transit police in which they impounded cars and required bribes to release them. The scheme reportedly even had quotas for individual officers.[30] I experienced this scheme firsthand when a stern cop pulled me over for an illegal left turn, glaring as he commented, "This is very serious."[31] He ordered me to follow him to the transit police headquarters, which was run by a man with fascist tendencies who once told me that the solution to poverty required "sterilizing Indi-ans."[32] The police impounded my Toyota Platz. After a long wait, a young officer summoned me to a metal table in an empty room for a lecture on traffic safety and the rule of law. I folded my arms across my chest and tried to harden my eyes. The ticket was expensive, amounting to 20 percent of the monthly minimum wage.[33] I cast about for stratagems and came up with nothing. I opened my wallet, took out all the cash, but came up short. "I'm just a student," I said. "I don't have much money." "OK, this will do," the officer replied as he wrote something down in a ledger. "You can go." I walked away without a ticket or a receipt, feeling defeated, to collect my car. When I recounted this to a friend, he lamented, "Oh, you should have called Don Braulio! He could have gotten you out of the fine," explaining that everybody knows that the transit police "fundraise" (*recuadar*) for Javier Zacarías and suggesting I should have leveraged my connection to an important street vendor leader and Zacarías ally. "They got the foreigner's price out of you," he observed. "It's too bad you didn't think to call Don Braulio."

At the planning commission meeting, Governor Lucho Zacarías referred to the transit police extortion scheme even as he painted a rosy picture of the city's commercial future. He framed the city's challenge as an image problem compounded by inadequate urban infrastructure, both of which hurt the city's commerce:

> We live off of our neighbors, our friends, the shopping tourists. [That's why we need to] make Ciudad del Este more calm. I've spoken with the transit police about the issue of extortion, and they are not going to do illegal things. We need to leave off this. We want a healthy, comfortable city with running water and amenities. We need to do "marketing," pro–Ciudad del Este advertising, and then we must offer what we promise. Now, the police are bad for our marketing campaign. . . . One month without breaking the balls of the tourists [demanding bribes], and the Brazilians will come back.[34]

When the governor acknowledged the transit police bribery scandal as "illegal things" that broke "the balls of the tourists," he described extortion as a minor problem, one he claimed to have fixed with a man-to-man chat, saying, "I've spoken with them." Nomei Haudenschild similarly downplayed extortion and elite illegalities, acknowledging "a small bit of bad" in the city "but a lot of good." Both proposed an urban branding campaign to address the paradoxical challenge of maintaining the border trade while upgrading urban space and expelling some street illegalities. Both sought specific spaces of commerce aligned with the global urbanist aesthetic that came to underwrite the proposal to formalize street vendor stalls and promote mall development on the riverfront.

To many business owners, decision makers, and the nonpoor, the popular economies of the urban majority look unruly and inherently problematic. This perspective, which diagnoses street markets as problem places and vendors as objects of reform, resonates with a common discursive frame that construes the urban poor and rural migrants as culturally disposed to creating spatial disorder and uncleanliness.[35] I think of this orientation as an antipoor epistemology because it construes the livelihoods of the poor as problematic while turning away from or even celebrating the overconsumption, entitlement, and illegalities of the rich. This antipoor epistemology refuses to conceive of streets and sidewalks as sites of work. As a result, street vendors are understood as problems to be tolerated or targeted for reform.

Stalls

In these discussions of vendors' place in urban futures, municipal authorities focused on the regulation and formalization of vendors' stalls. The municipality promised to order the city center through a project called the Pilot Plan, a pathway for some vendors to regularize their claims to street and sidewalk spaces in areas they already occupied. Promising a spatial solution to the haphazard aesthetic of the street market, which was marked by vendors' self-built infrastructure, the Pilot Plan also proposed a pathway to regularize the noncompliant occupations of vendors. Theoretically, vendors in the Pilot Plan occupy numbered, standardized stalls, pay a small "precarious use tax," and follow municipal codes. The Pilot Plan's new standardized stalls consist of a table for vendors to display merchandise over a small storage space, covered by a corrugated tin roof. The standardized, state-owned stalls would impose spatial order, proponents argued, visually marking the transition to a formal city by banishing vendors' self-built *puestos* (vending spots).

While planners claimed to express concern about vendors' irregular occupations, in practice municipal officials only intermittently and obliquely prioritized legal compliance. Instead, for decades, the municipality managed vendors through a mix of repression, patronage, and forbearance, that is, the nonenforcement of law. In this, Ciudad del Este reflects dynamics common in cities across Latin America and beyond.[36] The city's first mayors, appointed by Stroessner, extended provisional permission to political allies and poor internal migrants as a populist strategy of party building and a pragmatic re-

FIGURE 13. A municipal official enforcing use of space codes in vendors' self-built stalls; photo by author, 2013

sponse to the influx of displaced campesinos. The first census, conducted in 1987, designated vendors as either "authorized" or "without authorization."[37] Yet authorized status did not mean legal compliance. Instead, it indicated that a Colorado Party member had approved the occupation of the space. In an early move toward regularization, various municipal ordinances delineated authorization procedures, including restricting vending to certain categories of citizens, like town residents and military veterans, and establishing spatial requirements, like allowable dimensions for vending infrastructure. As the constitution forbids the use of public space for private commercial gain, except in special cases and via fee payments, in the 1990s, as the country remade itself after the fall of Stroessner, the municipality began collecting a "precarious use tax" from vendors.[38] This tax was first collected daily and then monthly. Yet this regularized status did not equate to clear, legally backed rights to urban space. Vendors certainly saw their *puestos* as theirs. However, municipal officials claimed the right of eviction based on their interpretation of the precarious use laws.[39] One street vendor explained that by paying the precarious use tax, vendors became "less informal." In this vendor's experience, informality is a spectrum, and formal status is an ephemeral condition more than an attainable end state.[40]

The resulting microgeography of eviction risk was confusing and changeable. Indeed, as Fernando Rabossi (2011b, 88) shows in his ethnography of the street market, actual practices of occupancy and authorization were an "intertwining of rules and uncertainties." Vendors routinely claimed space organized through block associations or improved their vending infrastructure without seeking municipal permission. Municipal officials ignored their own codes and regulations. Vendors could sell for years or decades and then suddenly face eviction. The municipal criteria for eviction were opaque, based in shifting urban plans, backroom negotiations between municipal officials and individual vendors or association leaders, and deals cut by business owners seeking to rid sidewalks in front of their storefronts of vendors.

The Pilot Plan divided vendors politically, spatially, and aesthetically. For some vendors, the Pilot Plan represented progress and improved working conditions. Others worried that municipal officials would distribute spots in the upgrades only to their supporters and feared future evictions.[41] Indeed, the Pilot Plan only included vendors along the central artery of San Blas Avenue, excluding about half of street vendors. For this reason, many fought for inclusive development on the Nine Hectares, especially for those working outside the Pilot Plan zone. While political divisions had always existed, the Pilot Plan introduced a new pivot.

Indeed, the plan was politically contentious from the beginning. The municipality under Mayor Javier Zacarías proposed the Pilot Plan in 1994 as a stopgap measure, a means to improve working conditions for vendors and give the city a new look before relocating vendors to the Nine Hectares, as stipulated in the terms of the expropriation.[42] The surprise 2006 construction of Shopping del Este on a corner of the Nine Hectares signaled that the municipality had different plans. By my fieldwork in 2011, the municipality envisioned the Pilot Plan as a permanent project and considered the question of relocation settled.[43] While the largest street vendors' association, the Federation, had fought for expropriation, it ultimately abandoned its claims to the Nine Hectares and allied with the municipality based on promises that its members would have spots in the Pilot Plan. But other vendors' associations and transparency activists continued to fight for relocation. Critics suspect that the Federation leadership cut deals with Javier Zacarías, selling out its constituency. Federation leadership, in contrast, argued that vendors lacked the power to contest the urban growth machine, that the streets of Ciudad del Este would never be clear of vendors, and that relocation would only expose its members to more competition from new arrivals.

Spatially, the Pilot Plan introduced a new gradient of insecurity for some vendors. It split the city into a corridor of "upgraded" space flanked by eight square blocks of approximately twenty-five hundred vendors. Inside and outside the Pilot Plan zone, vendors were subject to the same official processes of registering and regularizing their claims to space.[44] Yet in practice the Pilot Plan was a zone of relative tenure security. It divided vendors along a new axis, disincentivizing vendors inside the Pilot Plan zone from joining efforts to mobilize collectively to defend against eviction. The infrastructure improvements of the Pilot Plan benefited some but also created spatial divisions and gradations of tenure security that ultimately undercut the collective power of street vendors.

These spatial dynamics articulate with a temporality of deferment. Collectively, street vendors have waited since 1994 for the municipality to build permanent relocation facilities for them on the Nine Hectares. More recently, the municipality rolled out the project in four stages over more than a decade. Each stage redrew the boundaries of inclusion, raising again questions of who would be included and who would be cast out. Each stage was another opportunity for negotiation and dealmaking. Interminable negotiations seeded uncertainty while fostering division among vendors about the best political strategies. Prior to the construction of each stage of the Pilot Plan, the municipality supposedly registered all vendors in a municipal census in order to ensure their fair distribution. However, as I detail in chapter 4, the census generated confusion among street vendors, dangling the possibility of inclusion alongside the threat of exclusion. These temporal dynamics of governing kept vendors suspended in a state of constant negotiation and mobilization.

Aesthetically, the Pilot Plan sorts vendors into visually distinct categories, differentiating those benefiting from state-funded upgrades from those selling from self-built infrastructure. Unlike the self-built, incremental constructions of street vendors, the Pilot Plan communicates spatial order through visual standardization, as vendors within the Pilot Plan gain additional security because their stalls look legal. The match between the visuality of upgrades and the hope of the global urbanist project is a key resource, given the provisional nature of tenure security. The architectural design and building materials of the upgrades, however, are relatively insubstantial. The tin can construction, as critics described it, looked as though it was built in order to be torn down.[45] Indeed, this temporary materiality matches the original intent of the Pilot Plan. Raul Muñoz, then a leader with the Federation, explained that he refused to sign the 1994 deal with the municipality precisely because of the Pilot Plan's flimsy infrastructure, which replaced not only ad hoc stalls but also some brick-and-mortar buildings.

The Pilot Plan invoked spatial imaginaries that divided up places, people, and activities to then slot them into pregiven categories: formal or informal, legal or illegal, modern or underdeveloped. The aesthetics of the upgrades and indeed even the term *upgrades* invoke a transition from the disordered and antimodern to the orderly and global. In this rubric of visuality, unreformed street vending figures as an antecedent to the modern city. Following D. Asher Ghertner (2015, 4), the desire for the modern-looking urban form constitutes a type of "rule by aesthetics" in which legality matters less than the appearance of legality, a visual register that, I argue, works through the antipoor epistemology. Looking legal is thus a rubric of visuality that interprets the built forms of global urbanism as preferable by default, giving short shrift to the spatial needs of the popular economy. Some vendors, although certainly not all, internalized this aesthetic hierarchy and thereby participated in making effective this mode of governance, as this "vision of social order [is] imprinted on their sensibilities, inscribed in their senses" (125).

Indeed, the built form of the Pilot Plan invoked the promise of a modern city with orderly spaces of commerce and an aesthetic unmarred by the self-built stalls of vendors. Yet the spatial form hides social processes, as the ordered visuality of the upgrades mystifies the dynamics that intensify insecurity for many vendors. Negotiability paved the pathways of construction and distribution in the Pilot Plan upgrades. Furthermore, the municipality manages street vendors through the spatial dynamics of "permanent temporariness," to borrow Oren Yiftachel's (2009, 90) phrase. Permanent temporariness captures how the ubiquity and permanence of informalized worlds of the poor conflict with official attempts to manage them as problems to be solved or eliminated. The tension between the terms *permanent* and *temporary* reflects the tension between official desires for reformation or elimination and the tenacity of practices like street vending. Informalized work persists—in spite of endless and varied reforms—precisely because it meets the needs that capitalism and neoliberalizing states leave unaddressed.

The Pilot Plan ultimately reworked rather than banished informality. The political maneuvering transforming the Pilot Plan into a permanent project signaled the extent to which the municipality perceives the need to manage street vendors as permanently temporary. Both their infrastructure and their tenure status remain revocable. The political impacts of this mode of governance intensified uncertainty about vendors' place in the city. The aesthetic dynamics of looking legal allowed the municipality to claim movement toward the formal city. Yet at the same time, through various dimensions, the space-times of the Pilot Plan enrolled vendors as incompletely belonging to the economic life of the city, as subordinated beneficiaries rather than rights-bearing citizens. The politics of this inclusion are more fully explored in chapter 4.

Malls

Since the mid-2000s, the merchant bloc has promoted shopping mall development along the Paraná riverfront on the Nine Hectares as a cornerstone planning strategy. After a controversy over the construction of Shopping del Este on the Nine Hectares in 2006—land promised to street vendors—Shopping Box was built in 2013 and Shopping Paris in 2015. Shopping Paris sports two half Eiffel Towers protruding from the mall's front face, and eight-foot statues of the Queen's Guard flank the entrance. The design clumsily recycles core symbols of modern Europe, spurring an internet commentator to call it "a monument to kitsch."[46] Yet the developers used the gimmick without irony. Indeed, the mirrored facade of Shopping Paris reflects the desires of the merchant bloc to belong to a particular kind of "world-class" city.

Before this building blitz, only the Monalisa shopping gallery successfully invoked a global aesthetics of consumption. While shoppers pass a jostle of hawkers crowding the Monalisa's entrance, an entrance watched over by armed guards, once inside, shoppers encounter young Brazilian women who staff six floors of brand-name makeup, clothes, and gourmet food. The gallery, run by an established family of Lebanese traders, links the city to global commodity flows. It also allows shoppers to perform their status as modern citizens by purchasing a real Guess watch or some real Chanel perfume. Most shopping galleries, in contrast, refer to the global with the place-names of elsewhere (Shopping China, Shopping Mina India, Auto-Service Santo Domingo), although the built forms themselves fail to invoke the global mall aesthetic. The Jebai Center, another established gallery, is obviously noncompliant: pirated electrical connections spiderweb the building, and the gallery is routinely shut down for failing inspections, only to be reopened when, rumor has it, the owner pays off the municipality.[47] Inside, fluorescent lights buzz above cracked linoleum corridors in front of seven hundred glass-fronted shops specializing in electronics, perfume, or toiletries. Each is rented by a businessperson and staffed by young, low-paid sales staff. In one section, vendors repair or unblock cell phones from small stands surrounded by cardboard boxes of random plugs and phone parts. The crowds of buyers thin on the top two floors, where armed guards watch offices and warehouse space. On these floors, a ceaseless rasping sound echoes as groups of young men

FIGURE 14. Vendors in front of the Mona Lisa Shopping Gallery; photo by author, 2013

cover boxes of merchandise with layers of packing tape in preparation for their nighttime river crossing.

Yet the spatial form of the mall conceals as much as it reveals, hiding the very social processes of extralegality that create and sustain it. While Shopping Paris looks legal and invokes a globalized modernity, developers broke multiple rules, laws, and codes to build malls on the Nine Hectares, a story I tell more fully in the next chapter. The sneakers and video games purchased at these malls often move through smuggling circuits, including clandestine ports. It was an open secret that taxi drivers delivered merchandise to the ports, although drivers rarely discussed their work logistics with outsiders like myself. Over a lunch hosted by a community leader, one driver described trips to the ports as he lamented the decline in trade and the hit to his income. Street vendors described merchandise as crossing the border "by bridge" or "by water," signaling the ordinariness of both routes out of Paraguayan territory.[48] A powerful spatial imaginary distinguishes these malls from clandestine ports and vendor stalls, affiliating shopping malls with progress while situating stalls and clandestine ports as problems. Yet these forms are intertwined.

Still, for advocates of the Development Plan, Shopping del Este and the Monalisa gallery represent the desirable horizon of urban development, while the Jebai Center, ringed with street vendors, epitomizes the urban problems requiring reform. Development, from this perspective, meant a transition from the Jebai Center to Shopping Paris, visions they promoted by posting architectural renderings of their proposed flashy malls on their Facebook page. With a built form that looks legal, malls promised to solve the disorderly street livelihoods of the poor. When Cartes was president, he headlined a gala organized to fundraise for the Development Plan where he spoke about making the city "comfortable for capital" and extolled the virtues of the private sector as primary steward of development. Taniguchi presented his crisp urban plans, promising to promote urban, economic, and social growth by transforming the city into a tourist destination close to the massive Iguazú waterfalls and strategically located among global trading circuits.[49] Taniguchi's plans proposed special vending zones and limits on licenses. A construction company executive sitting next to me at the fundraising gala, in contrast, proposed a dramatic change: "It's simple. The vendors have got to go." This short sentence proposed the callous destruction of lifeworlds of vending in order to attain the aesthetic of the modern city. Taniguchi's proposal allows that vendors have a limited role in urban life, but for both Taniguchi and the construction executive, vendors' livelihoods conflicted with a core tenet of global urbanism: sidewalks are for circulating shoppers, not working vendors, a view justified by the antipoor epistemology.

This urban form of the mall is a cornerstone of global urbanism. In part, the shopping mall frame casting its shadow over the young *contrabandista* at the beginning of this chapter portended what David Harvey (2001) calls a spatial fix, a means to capture value in the built environment and sop up over-accumulated capital. Malls enable ground rents, that is, profits from property leases. Urban scholars argue that rent gaps organize real estate investments and incentivize gentrification as developers seek out places where the difference between current rents and future, postredevelopment rents are the greatest.[50] Indeed, as Arlene Dávila (2016, 10) argues, in Latin America the mall is a "settling institution." Like plantations, malls are tools for gaining control of space and profit, a means to link landholding to transnational capital circuits and generate revenue streams for landowners. In the early 2000s undeveloped riverfront land certainly represented a huge rent gap, singing a siren song of future profits. Mall investors sought to capture some of the value in the secondary circuit of capital, although malls also enabled accumulation by transgression when the goods purchased there moved through smuggling circuits. This profit potential tempted international investors and later led to mall financing from politically connected contraband kingpins.[51]

But exchange value, rent gaps, and under-the-table kickbacks to smooth construction pathways are only part of the story. Shopping malls index widely held aspirations, cross-class desires to participate in global modernity through consumption—to live in places that look like "real cities," as Ayala said. Malls help many make these worlding bids. Thus, malls are talismans and fetishes invested with powers to promote economic development, provide jobs, offer (privatized) community space, and push cities in the Global South toward a Eurocentric modernity. The mall is an effective fetish because it so successfully mobilizes the commonsense associations between modernity and legality.

Across Latin America, planners have come to imagine the mall as "an effective solution to the problem of informality" because the mall mobilizes the look of legality.[52] In Ciudad del Este, the merchant bloc uses the mall to make an aesthetic claim to legality and formality. Malls align with a global urbanist common sense that determines what globally integrated and economically productive spaces should look like. Malls also represent the securitization of space through increased control and surveillance capacity. Indeed, part of the promise of the mall is precisely how it scuttles the street livelihoods of the poor. Theirs are the spatial forms that must be destroyed to build the so-called formal city, one from which city officials and elites can aspire to a particular kind of globality. And so the aesthetics of global urbanism work as a form of governance. Ultimately, contraband urbanism is the spatial form of an elite class project.

Conclusion

Elite and street illegalities together, interwoven in place, built Ciudad del Este as a key node in networks of commerce and contraband. Over decades, diaspora businessmen, rural Paraguayan migrants, and Brazilian traders materialized this commercial hub on the margins of the so-called periphery. They did so with their daily labors, situated knowledges, and dealmaking prowess, suturing together disparate places and building a highly functional distribution network for circulating commodities cheaply through global space. This city is integrated into globalized capital circuits through these interwoven extralegalities.

Seeing Ciudad del Este through the lens of the social production of space challenges assessments that read illegality off of urban form. While obviously transgressive, clandestine ports are one spatial form of contraband urbanism; however, they intertwine with formal-looking, less scandalous spaces like high-end shopping malls. Frontier malls mobilize the look of legality, yet as we will see in the next chapter, the merchant bloc built them through dealmaking and legal trickery. Likewise, the upgrading of street vendor stalls in a bid to formalize vending did not banish negotiability and tenure insecurity. Animated by an antipoor epistemology, formalization instead introduced political, spatial, and aesthetic divisions among vendors, undercutting their collective power.

Furthermore, commodity flows connect malls, streets, stalls, and ports, yet a powerful imaginative practice uses spatial heuristics to allocate authorization by visual cues rather than legal compliance. At the scale of the city, spatial imaginaries bound illegality to poor riverfront neighborhoods, street vendor stalls, and clandestine ports, ignoring how these spaces connect to frontier malls. Just as these linkages enable commerce at the city scale, interconnected places fuel global commerce. Discourses of disconnection split these places apart. Urbanism's blind field makes it hard to see how celebrated spaces of production, like SEZs, rely on and produce spaces of extralegal commerce like Ciudad del Este. This is a useful blindness. Outlaw capital remakes peripheral spaces and then casts these places out of thought, constructing them as irrelevant to today's big questions, like Latin America's left turn, its subsequent rebound to the right, and the links between outlaw capital and political power.

By making urban theory from Ciudad del Este, we can more honestly account for the centrality of outlaw capital in building cities, enabling specific practices of state power, and shaping the far horizon of the politically possible. Conceptually, outlaw capital helps us see how global capitalism produces zones of transgression, spaces where relations of profitable dealmaking are both channeled and hidden. The merchant bloc capitalizes on Ciudad del Este as a nodal city with place-based advantages both in its location along global trading routes and in its concentration of outlaw capital. These too are forms of urban agglomeration and centrality, in this case oriented toward exploiting the circulatory capacity of a city built for contraband. Thus, the urban fabric includes places like Ciudad del Este where accumulation by transgression shapes urbanization.

This provincializes the urban revolution, highlighting the links between theory, place, and positionality. Like all theories, Lefebvre's ideas are situated, imprinted by the biases of his time, place, and social location. As a Frenchman responding to the 1968 Paris rebellions, Lefebvre developed his concept of the urban revolution from the heart of Europe during a riotous moment. Unsurprisingly, he missed key urban dynamics constitutive of southern urbanisms: streets as sites of work, disorder as a strategy of state power, and the transgressive as constitutive of capitalist urbanization. Indeed, the lessons from Ciudad del Este are at once particular and general. The intensity of elite illegalities is perhaps unusual, yet we can generalize the finding that global capitalism produces places for contraband—that transgressive regimes of circulation concentrate in particular, stigmatized spaces. Global capital produces similar places in border zones around the world. The banishment of these spaces from theories of the urban is paradoxically part of their power. Thus *contraband urbanism* as an analytic pushes theories of uneven development to include the processes producing places for outlaw capital.

Schemes and State Power

One afternoon over lunch in a cafeteria, the political organizer Raul Muñoz inveighed against Shopping del Este. I welcomed the opportunity to discuss the mall and its relationship to the Nine Hectares, that key land parcel that epitomized deep divisions in the city about urban futures. Over the previous three years, I had struggled to piece together a coherent history of the land parcel, as stories about its development conflicted wildly. Street vendors joked about "land with wheels" (*tierra con ruedas*) and "walking land" (*tierra que camina*), a jab at the municipality's claim that the land under Shopping del Este did not infringe on the Nine Hectares and was therefore free from its social interest development restrictions. Indeed, the stories of municipal officials and those of vendors and transparency activists occupied incommensurate universes of meaning. I had a hard time accessing case documents through official channels, but my personal archive grew quickly as activist vendors and anticorruption lawyers passed me file folders full of photocopied land titles, court cases, municipal ordinances, construction contracts, newspaper clippings, organizational statutes, and agreements called *convenios* between vendors and the municipality. Soon I had a foot-high stack of papers, but they offered little clarity. Conflicts over the best uses of land are of course common, but these disagreements were also about the boundaries and spatial location of the Nine Hectares.

My archive included a photocopy of the 1990 expropriation, a document that recorded a major win for street vendors' associations. Mere months after Stroessner's fall, the national legislature expropriated the Nine Hectares and promised to build a municipal commercial space for vendors. Proponents of relocating vendors to the Nine Hectares pitched it as a win-win scenario: it would formalize vendors and free up streets and sidewalks from vendors' occupations. Given the valuable spatial location of the Nine Hectares—abutting the International Friendship Bridge and at the heart of the trade circuit—the

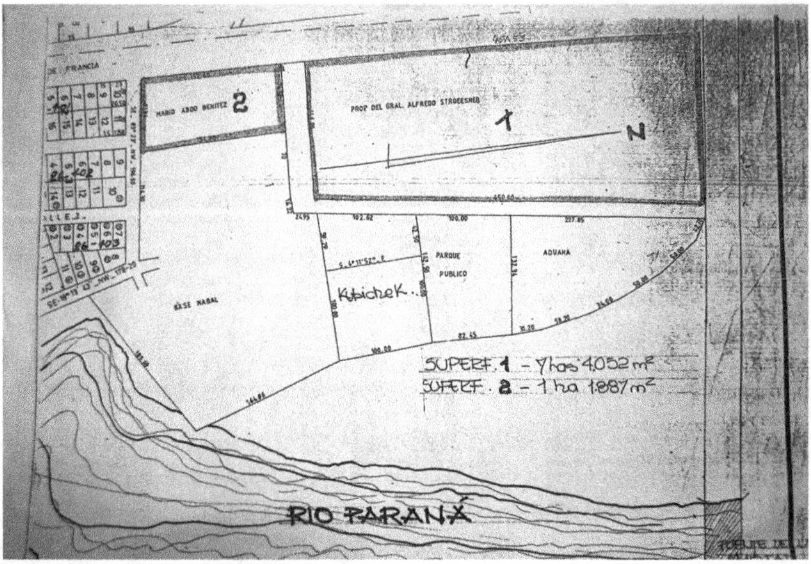

FIGURE 15. An undated map of the Nine Hectares (parcels 1 and 2) and Kubitschek's land circulated among vendors and transparency activists, challenging the municipality's claims that Shopping del Este was built on Kubitschek's land and not the Nine Hectares; author's archives

proposal suggested that urban development under democratization might benefit ordinary Paraguayan street vendors. It would also "bring some order to our streets" and symbolically repudiate the unrestrained greed of the Stroessner regime, as one senator commented during Senate proceedings.[1] Indeed, the Nine Hectares epitomized "ill-gotten land" (*tierra malhabida*), shady land transfers used by the Stroessner regime to cement political alliances.[2] The Nine Hectares joined two of these ill-gotten parcels: a land parcel Stroessner gifted to his loyal personal secretary, Mario Abdo Benítez, and a second parcel he gave to himself. Stroessner also gifted a nearby third parcel to the Brazilian president Juscelino Kubitschek de Oliveira (1956–61), a parcel that would later become part of the controversy.

Yet after this major win for street vendors' associations, for decades the land lay fallow as protests and legal battles stymied construction. Suddenly, in 2006 the sleek mall Shopping del Este sprang up in a prime location next to the International Friendship Bridge and San Blas Avenue. Livid, vendors and transparency activists insisted that Shopping del Este was thoroughly illegal, built on the Nine Hectares in violation of its social interest stipulations. Raul Muñoz explained his take on the convoluted history of the Nine Hectares and the shady "deals" (*negociados*) underwriting the construction of Shopping del

Este by joking that a hurricane picked up Kubitschek's land and dropped it on top of the Nine Hectares. As a gifted orator, Muñoz performed even for his audience of one. "Only in Paraguay are there storms as strong as this!" he exclaimed. "We have a mild, tropical country, with the very best weather, yet there was this violent storm! The land spun around, and we lost part of the Nine Hectares."[3]

In 2006 a claimant produced a title to Kubitschek's property, suing the municipality and launching a series of surprises. According to her documents, Kubitschek's land overlay a corner of Stroessner's gift to himself. The municipality, which was the steward of the Nine Hectares postexpropriation, ceded the land rather than fighting in court. The claimant worked for the municipality as a *limpiadora* (cleaning lady). As the anticorruption lawyer Cinthia Ayala explained the case to me, her voice rose as she commented, "She lives in a shack in [a poor neighborhood]! Just how is it possible she suddenly is a shareholder in Shopping del Este?! What's more, when the land moved, it shrank!"[4]

The case forced a new set of documents into the court's records with a contradictory reading of the Nine Hectares boundaries. In the new papers, the land under Shopping del Este avoided the Nine Hectares' social interest restrictions, even as the old reading of the land's location remained on record, showing Kubitschek's land suspiciously south of the Nine Hectares. The merchant bloc threw their weight behind the interpretation that placed the land underneath Shopping del Este outside of the Nine Hectares. Judge Mario Aguayo Rodríguez, a political ally of then mayor Javier Zacarías, backed this interpretation. In the throes of these confusions over the boundaries of the Nine Hectares, the relative power of competing alliances determined the site's effective edges. Paraguayans describe these alliances as *esquemas* (schemes), lucrative, opaque relationships between politicians, regional judges, and economic practices.

Anticorruption activists often fixate on the truth of the Nine Hectares' boundaries, understanding truth as external to power. But interpretations of so-called formal or legal constructions are always power-laden and cultural.[5] Courts do not uncover an objective, external truth but rather stabilize a given reading over competing interpretations, often with bias toward the already powerful. Some land occupations are understood as more legitimate than others. Malls are more able to index modernity than the self-built stalls of street vendors. The Nine Hectares was also central to the brazen legal maneuvering that unhooked the municipality from national oversight for almost two decades, a story that unfolds over the course of this chapter.

With the metaphor of the municipal storm, Muñoz analyzed municipal practices of power put to work in the interests of the merchant bloc. He helped me see how the local government produced confusion as a strategy of governance. Like a hurricane, municipal planning practice can feel like a violent, unpredictable, external force, upending temporarily settled spatial orders. Lefebvre (2017, 143) asserts that state power "will always choose order." Yet in this case, the merchant bloc used confusion as a productive strategy of rule: spatial confusion and legal trickery are not evidence of state incapacity but strategic modes of governing. While Muñoz suggested that rule by storm was a distinctly Paraguayan phenomenon, the laundry list of elite illegalities laundered licit is a core dynamic building urban environments in many contexts.[6]

This chapter tells the story of the merchant bloc's contentious rise as a force in national politics and global trade. Against shallow explanations of state absence, I argue that outlaw capital has long affiliated with Paraguayan state power. Indeed, state projects set the conditions for the city's rise as a major contraband hub, and the high modernism of Paraguay's authoritarian period helped make the city a gray zone of profitable confusions. After offering a theoretical framework of frontier and territorial development, I show how state-led projects eventually transformed eastern Paraguay from a zone of extraction into a hub of global trade. I tell this story through three entangled political-economic logics: extraction, colonization, and cultivated wildness, each of which develops historically even as they cannot be reduced to a neat historical sequence.

Frontier Territorial Development

History is alive. It is a force that shapes present possibilities. Understanding the surprising rise of Ciudad del Este thus requires a historical framework of territorial and frontier development. Thinking spatially about history matters, because the passing of time does not displace prior practices of power. Practices of power settle into sedimentary layers, which are partially available as mutable resources in the present, enabling particular modes of power, resistance, negotiation, and subject-making, what Donald Moore (2005, 6) calls "landscapes of rule." Paraguay's landscapes of rule sediment authoritarianism and state-sponsored dealmaking, practices of power that are reworked rather than overcome, even as they are always contested. The renowned Paraguayan author Augusto Antonio Roa Bastos (1987, 217) captured this, calling his country's difficult past "a reality that raved and ranted and spat shafts of history into the faces of the survivors."

Frontiers are particular kinds of places, accentuating three sometimes contradictory dynamics.[7] First, frontiers challenge the extension and effectivity of state power. As places that are far from the administrative logics and political controls of capital cities, frontiers challenge state sovereignty. Multiple forms of political authority often intermingle, as "informal sovereigns," including paramilitary organizations, drug traffickers, or contraband kingpins, wield considerable power.[8] Frontiers, however, are not sites of state absence. Instead, they are places where alternative, nonstate sources of political authority often vie for advantage. Second, frontiers are often zones of contestation between different political-economic orders, especially as capital restlessly infiltrates spaces organized by other economic logics. Finally, frontiers are places of productive confusions, mixing the illegal and the legal. Anthropologist Anna Lowenhaupt Tsing (2005, 27) argues that frontiers *"create* wildness" by confusing practices often thought of as opposed, like "law and theft, governance and violence, use and destruction."

Frontiers are also, of course, colonial formations, only existing because of the long project of Euro-American imperialism, which extends the nation-state form worldwide. Colonialism depends on imagining a threatening or savage outside in order to justify violence as necessary to defend something called "civilization." These imperial ideologies of racial superiority require an imagination of temporal progression through which the agents of progress "civilize" Indigenous and non-European cultures that occupy what Anne McClintock (1995, 65) critiques as historyless "anachronistic time." These progress narratives rest on the dispossession of Indigenous communities, as well as on their elimination and erasure.[9] Indeed, across the hemisphere, nation-states established themselves "without . . . and against the Indian," as Peruvian Marxist José Carlos Mariátegui argued (1970, 83), an epistemic violence that was rooted in conflicts over land.[10] The problematic of the frontier question is thus also a land question. In the United States, Frederick Jackson Turner (1893) famously linked American democracy to westward expansion. Settlement on newly stolen land was a safety valve for the labor surplus and an explicit strategy to transform poor immigrants into bootstrapping settlers. Thus, Turner argued, the frontier infused American democracy with an individualistic, libertarian, and lawless pioneer ethos. The midcentury colonization of eastern Paraguay also constructed a racialized imaginary of national belonging.

Frontier territorial development was also shaped by tensions between state and local capacities. Especially after the fall of Stroessner, the merchant bloc played a key role in frontier territorial development. As an analytic, the idea of the merchant bloc is inspired by Clyde Woods's work on the enduring hegemony of the plantation bloc in the U.S. South. Woods (1998, 81) describes the plantation bloc as a "coordinated regional ethnoclass alliance" that has a monopoly on "resources, power, historical explanation, and social action." This definition emphasizes the capacities of regional blocs to shape the dominant ethos and epistemology of a moment as part of a political-economic strategy. Yet the power of regional blocs is always contested and perpetually incomplete. The merchant bloc is thus an alliance of traders, local and national politicians, and regional judges committed to protecting their interests in the border trade through political-economic strategy, institutional innovation, and ideological power.

Zones of Extraction

Historian Andrew Nickson (2005, 223; see also 1981) has described eastern Paraguay as an "abandoned zone," a place absent of state projects until the 1950s. I offer a different story, tracking a much longer history of the coproduction of state power and outlaw capital. With independence from Spanish rule in 1811, Paraguay pursued debt-free development and economic self-sufficiency, a national development that sharply diverged from regional trends. Self-proclaimed Supreme Dictator José Gaspar Rodríguez de Francia ruled from 1814 to 1840, embodying a fierce spirit of nationalism and egalitarian redistribution backed by tendencies toward absolutist power.[11] Francia forcibly nationalized vast tracts of land, confiscated the property and assets of foreigners, and founded successful homeland ranches for national food production.[12] Francia's rule turned into the state socialism of Carlos Antonio López and later the reckless anti-imperialism of his son, Francisco Solano López. The López father-son duo sought modernization via European expertise, reversing Francia's ban on immigration. Yet Paraguayan economic policy remained defiantly protectionist and proceeded without external debt financing.

The War of the Triple Alliance (1864–70) derailed Paraguayan development. Solano López, remembered as either a mad tyrant or a valiant anti-imperialist, envisioned a regional alliance capable of contending with Brazil and Argentina, continental powerhouses with imperial ambitions.[13] When the Empire of Brazil invaded Uruguay, Solano López retaliated, seizing the Brazilian town of Corumbá. The confrontation set Paraguay against the combined forces of Brazil, Argentina, and Uruguay. In Latin America's bloodiest war, as many as 70 percent of Paraguay's adult men died.[14] Some historians describe the war as genocide.[15] Only the valiant grit of a determined people—or a reckless patriotism that sent children to doomed battlefields—saved Paraguay from being divided between Brazil and Argentina.[16] As it was, Paraguay lost 54,054 square miles of land.[17] The trauma still haunts the national consciousness with a deep sense of loss and outrage at stolen national greatness.

The postwar truce required that Paraguay pay the costs of the war incurred by Argentina, Brazil, and Uruguay. To raise money, state planners sold off vast tracts of land to English and Argentine speculators. After subsequent default in 1885, restructured loans were backed by land warrants that included huge swaths of eastern Paraguay.[18] These land deals depended on politically connected gentlemen in the capital city who imagined and then materialized eastern Paraguay as a space of international capital speculation made possible through the mass privatization of land. The process required imagining forests as convertible into bonds, which, in turn, enabled state planners to act as if living forests and Indigenous homelands could be rendered into chits of fluctuating value based on the speculative whims of distant gamblers. Thus, dispossession "configures possession," as Jodi A. Byrd and coauthors (2018, 3) argue.

Expanding capitalism's frontier, mass land privatization and liberalization turned the region's rich North Atlantic rainforest into an "enclave for extraction."[19] This political-economic logic would dominate through the mid-century. By the late 1800s, a few rich absentee landlords and an elite class of *patrones* controlled huge landholdings called *latifundios* producing yerba mate, tannin, and hearts of palm. The holdings of the yerba mate producer Industria Paraguaya exceeded 2.6 million hectares, an area greater than the U.S. state of Wyoming.[20] Latifundios depended on indentured servants. An 1871 state decree wrote these brutal labor terms into law, binding workers—dismissively called peons—to employers. Workers needed permission from *patrones* to leave the plantations. Those who abandoned their jobs faced prison time and could be charged for the expenses. The anarchist essayist Rafael Barrett (1910, 35) described these working conditions as "slavery, torment and murder."

While indentured servitude was outlawed in 1901, state inspectors and regional judges continued to enable "dissimulated" slavery.[21] Isolation masked ties between national statesmen and indentured servitude in the yerba mate plantations as the lack of roads through dense forests made the region difficult to access. Historian Fidel Miranda Silva (2007, 73) suggests that after privatization, politicians "forgot on purpose" about the region, a convenient spatial amnesia that enabled profiteering. Foreshadowing contemporary *es-quemas*, Barrett detailed the close ties between national politicians and plantation owners:

> [In Alto Paraná, you will find] a judge bought by the Industrial [Paraguaya], The Mate, or landowners of Alto Paraná. Local authorities are bought through a monthly bonus, as an accountant of the *Industrial Paraguaya* confirmed for me. The judge and the boss eat, then, from the same plate. Often, they are simultaneously national authorities and enabled *yerbateros* [plantation owners]. So Mr. B.A.—a relative of the current President of the Republic—is also political head of San Estanislao and paymaster of the *Industrial [Paraguaya]*. Mr. M.—also a relative of the President—is a judge in the fiefdom of the Señores Casados and also in their employment. The Señores Casado exploit the tannin trees through slavery—[locals] still remember the murder of five laborers who tried to escape in a boat. No need, then, to wait for the State to reestablish slavery. It is through slavery that profit is made and justice is sold retail. (1910, 37–38, my translation)

Shady deals and relational networks of complicity between national statesmen and plantation owners enabled indentured servitude even after it was outlawed in 1901. Regional businessmen took advantage of their murky status as "simultaneously national authorities and enabled *yerbateros*," or as relatives of the president, like the untouchable *patrones* in the Casado family. The metaphor "eating from the same plate" describes kickback schemes between the judiciary and *patrones*, what we can think of as an early *esquema*. Marking out lines of complicity, I imagine that these payments were accompanied by handshakes and entitled nods sealing the fate of the five escaped laborers. I imagine their murderers sleeping easy, knowing there would be no investigation while *patrones* continued denying workers their most basic rights: the right to leave employment, the right to not be killed.

Thus, active state support in the late 1800s transformed eastern Paraguay into a zone of extraction and land speculation. These regional formations would be reworked by an emerging authoritarian regime's modernizing and settling ambitions, as we will soon see. During the *yerbales* era, physical geography helped hide these death-dealing networks of profit and state power. As regional forms of political-economic authority, these *esquemas* had their own spatiality: distant enclaves connected to centers of power by networks of empowered men. Rafael Barrett traveled for days up the Paraná River, suffering from gout and malaria, to witness and record the trials of life on the *yerbales*. The plight of most plantation workers echoed unrecorded in the tannin trees.

Politicians claimed plausible deniability, forgetting about the region on purpose. Then, as today, the opacity of *esquemas* and their links to state power
support rule-breaking profiteering.

Midcentury Colonization

State planners would soon seek a more forceful national presence in eastern
Paraguay and begin planning for colonization. Eastern Paraguay is the an-
cestral home of many Indigenous groups, including the Ava Guaraní, Mbya
Guaraní, Aché, and Pai Tavytera. Through the middle of the century, vast forests and plentiful land offered some protection for Indigenous communities
from colonial violence. The majority of Paraguayans lived in the three depart-
ments ringing the capital city, most as subsistence farmers, and the 1950 census counted fewer than ten thousand inhabitants in the department that today
encompasses Ciudad del Este.[22] As elsewhere across the Americas, colonization involved both Indigenous resistance and colonial violence.

In 1954 the agrarian nationalist Colorado Party took power in a coup led by
General Alfredo Stroessner and soon found a clarifying vision in frontier settlement and land reform.[23] The Stroessner regime's project of state-led colonization sought to establish a presence in the region through the modernization
project called the March East (Marcha al Este), which included infrastructure,
the Itaipú Dam, land for smallholders, and a frontier town that would become
Ciudad del Este, then called Puerto Presidente Stroessner. When Stroessner took power, there were few indications that he would become one of the
longest-ruling dictators in the hemisphere, his thirty-four-year rule surpassed
only by Fidel Castro. "Settling" the frontier played an important role in consolidating the power of the Colorado Party and expanding state presence in
eastern Paraguay. Indeed, the long rule of the Colorado Party was ultimately
an arduous achievement, requiring constant work.

Colonization of eastern Paraguay was a racial project.[24] State planners
imagined eastern Paraguay as empty and wild, awaiting the civilizing touch of
the nation-state. Silva (2007, 296) wrote that "roads did not even exist. Nobody
dared to come and live in these parts, where the most savage and ravenous
wild beasts stalked the exuberant virgin green jungles of Alto Paraná." Imagining the region as empty justifies colonization, and Silva's comment that "nobody dared . . . live in these parts" ignores Indigenous presence by constructing these communities as outside the terms of the body politic. Indeed, officials
excluded Indigenous groups from census counts until 1980. The image of the
jungle conveys a Hobbesian state of nature, a presocial place devoid of culture.

Sexualizing the jungle as "virgin" relies on a colonial-masculinist imaginary, which envisions Western cultures bringing civilization to spaces outside modernity through the penetration of reason and progress. These frontier imaginaries have material consequences. Settlers, ranch hands, and *latifundistas* violently pushed Indigenous communities off of newly desirable land or into deculturization camps.[25] This settler violence was physical and epistemic, as it depended on devaluing the personhood and lifeways of these communities.

At midcentury, narratives of nationalism and modernization swept the continent, and the Colorado Party linked them to colonization projects that proposed to "tame" the frontier. Responding to dwindling supplies of arable land for smallholders in central Paraguay, land reform also drove population expansion eastward.[26] Despite the redistributive potential, land reform concentrated holdings upward.[27] This enclosure movement was later accelerated by industrial agriculture. These forces dispossessed hundreds of thousands of peasants, casting them out to cities like Ciudad del Este and Asunción. However, land reform enabled the Colorado Party to perform a populist promise, that of bringing peasants into the nation through landownership.[28] Indeed, state planners explicitly modeled colonization projects on the expansion of the U.S. frontier.[29]

With the March East, Stroessner reoriented toward Brazil, proposing a frontier city and a road connecting Asunción to Port of Santos, Brazil, and a bridge connecting the two countries over the Paraná River. An overland route to Brazilian ports would enable access to foreign markets unmediated by Argentina's capricious control of trade along the River Plate. A presidential decree outlined the rationale for Puerto Presidente Stroessner as building the urban infrastructure necessary for regional economic integration, envisioning Puerto Presidente Stroessner as "a site concentrating regional possibilities" and as a material means to "unite with Brazil."[30] Even as state planners sought regional integration with Brazil, they resented Brazil's expansionist doctrine of flexible borders, or "living frontiers" (*fronteras vivas*).[31] As infrastructure eased access to eastern Paraguay, Brazilian pioneers settled Paraguayan land. This mass migration later birthed a new social identity called *brasiguayos*: immigrants and their descendants who are nationalized Paraguayans but who retain strong cultural ties to Brazil. Today, this Brazilianization of land contributes to the industrialization of farming and the dispossession of Paraguayan peasants.[32]

The frontier town appeared first in state documents and only later in built form. A 1957 presidential decree founded the frontier town as Puerto Presidente Stroessner, announcing the city's role as a cornerstone of Stronista statecraft.[33] Another presidential decree appointed members of the administrative commission to organize urbanization, land sales, and economic development.[34] In one of its first acts, the administrative commission recruited the businessman Elias Saba to spearhead urban planning, crowning the private sector as the appropriate steward of urban development.[35] Officials also feared that left-wing social movements were organizing in the unprotected east, and so Stroessner charged his confidant, Edgar Ynsfrán, the minister of the interior, with overseeing city planning and administration as part of the administrative commission. Ynsfrán's position within the national security apparatus linked the projects of town settlement with state violence. Indeed, in the tradition of autocrats the world over, Stroessner quelled dissent through organized state violence.[36] Repression was justified by virulent anti-Communism and backed by extensive U.S. support.[37]

Yet for a decade, urban construction proceeded slowly in the president's port town.[38] Regularly, the appointed surveyor set up an outdoor table at the bridge construction site, selling land between eight and ten o'clock in the morning. There was, however, little interest in the president's port town, and the surveyor's land trade was slow. State presence was largely ceremonial. In 1958 Ynsfrán's exploratory crew of surveyors and military men boated up the Paraná River but struggled to find the spot where the bridge would one day be built. They set Stroessner's 1957 decree in a concrete landmark. The iconic photograph of men in military uniforms grouped around the monument symbolized the close ties between frontier city building and the authoritarian regime. This flurry of activity was as much about performing the Paraguayan state at its edges as it was about deploying the technical capacities of the regime to site a planned city.

Land was key to city building, as it also helped Stroessner cement alliances that were held together by networks of patronage that blurred the distinction between state and party.[39] Soon after the city's founding, Stroessner gave hundreds of hectares of land on the settlement's outskirts to allies in the military.[40] The government likewise expropriated huge swaths of land for urban development.[41] Stroessner also gave away three key land parcels on choice riverfront property near what would become the International Friendship Bridge, as discussed in the vignette that opened the chapter.[42] State planners executed some of the land transfers illegally or gave away land claimed by others, producing a confusing geography in which land parcels often had multiple claimants. Paraguayans call these transfers "ill-gotten land" (*tierra malhabida*) as a critique of these legal and ethical transgressions. Against a Lockean workmanship model of property rights—itself implicated in dispossession—Stroessner's gifts/thefts worked through the logic of the gentlemanly transfer, a means to cement bonds of political loyalty between men through the speculative promise of land value increases and the performative power of documents.[43]

Planners drew on masculinist notions of authority as they sought to steward the so-called unruliness of the region into more profitable forms. In his memoir, Ynsfrán (1990) titled the chapter on city founding "Intuimos el porvenir" (We intuited the future). Describing his aerial view from a plane window during a reconnaissance flight over the region, Ynsfrán claimed exceptional foresight in choosing the most propitious location for the city, a capacity for sight and vision characteristic of men like himself who were charged with the civilizational project of settling the frontier. This sort of "state seeing" is a claim to a particular kind of masculinist power (see also chapter 4).

Yet forces exceeding the envisioning capacities of state technocrats compelled the location of the city. In 1955, the year before Ynsfrán's security reconnaissance flight over the region, a commission of Brazilian and Paraguayan officials set terms for Brazilian financing of Highway 2. Roads materialize a state presence in frontier regions across Latin America, even as road projects are often financed through a mix of state, private sector, and international sources.[44] The commission planned to connect Asunción to the Brazilian coast by way of the small Brazilian town of Foz do Iguaçu, settled in the 1880s. A year later, a bilateral agreement laid out plans and financing for the International Friendship Bridge, sited on the Brazilian side at Foz do Iguaçu. Thus, contrary to Ynsfrán's claims of technocratic visioning, the propitious siting of Puerto Presidente Stroessner responded to the exigencies of Brazilian frontier settlement patterns and diplomacy. As state planners imagined colonization and state-led modernization as antidotes to the frontier's challenge to state power, infrastructure and city building helped materialize a state presence in the region. Urban development practice included an elevated role for private-sector action in urban development and illiberal, patriarchal styles of governing the city.

Boomtown

While Puerto Presidente Stroessner began as a sleepy river port town, the city soon grew into itself through trade and contraband. The rise of a new economic order based in arbitrage, however, did not displace prior economic logics. Instead, new ways of capturing value overlay the extractive logics of the prior era. State infrastructure projects, especially Highway 2 and the International Friendship Bridge, transformed the material basis of the border trade.

Infrastructure decentralized access to smuggling, as traders could cross the bridge on foot rather than fly over dense forests between private landing strips. Brazilian buyers—*compristas* and *sacoleiros*—appropriated state infrastructure for their own ends as the bridge opened up trade to more people. Against expectations, the extension of state projects into the frontier region contributed to producing Ciudad del Este as a gray space and hub of extralegal trade.

As the city grew, urban development followed the familiar spatial pattern of young cities across Latin America: expanding residential neighborhoods surrounding an urban core. Yet commerce, not manufacturing jobs, drew migrants. During the 1970s and 1980s, annual population growth rates spiked to 15 percent as rumors of the city's profit potential drew migrants from Paraguay's countryside, as well as diaspora entrepreneurs from China, Taiwan, Korea, and Lebanon. One Lebanese importer-exporter recounted to me how he arrived in the city just sixteen years old and alone: "I heard Paraguay was a good place to make money."[45]

Construction of the mammoth binational Itaipú Dam, the world's largest hydroelectric dam, also shaped the city.[46] State projects funded homes and neighborhoods for dam engineers and laborers, while internal migrants built their own modest homes on unclaimed land along the river. Inaugurated in 1967, the dam helped the regime to present itself as a modernizing force.[47] The dam, signifying "man's" power over nature, also represented the taming of the wild frontier.

With the city, like with the dam, state planners sought infrastructural proof of a modern state. They based Puerto Presidente Stroessner's master plan on Brasília, the exemplar modernist city. Modernist urbanism promoted urban design and planning as a means to reshape social relations through top-down interventions into space.[48] This ethos promised to shepherd society beyond traditional, communal roots toward supposedly more rational orders. In Puerto Presidente Stroessner, modernism stitched together urban spaces and state jobs through state-owned housing stock and other amenities for Itaipú engineers, administrators, and construction crews. Planners built neighborhoods segregated by economic function, with engineers and technicians living in upscale neighborhoods in Area 1 and Area 2. Construction workers lived in Area 8, located in nearby Hernandarias.

The modernist urban planning rationality hit different limits in Brasília and Puerto Presidente Stroessner. In Brasília, the top-down administration of urban space mixed with desires to produce a more egalitarian society. Yet urban development plans excluded the construction workers who built the city, overlooking the housing needs and daily lives of the working class. These workers built their own settlements on the peripheries, which became crucibles for new forms of insurgent citizenship.[49] In Puerto Presidente Stroessner, town planners anticipated accommodating the Itaipú labor force. State planners, however, did not respond to the second major frontier state project even as they facilitated it: the border trade. Planners thus built a city for the Itaipú workforce rather than the global trading hub that Puerto Presidente Stroessner would become.

State planners also imagined power as a hypermasculine capacity exemplified by men like Carlos Barreto Sarubbi, the first appointed mayor of Puerto Presidente Stroessner (he held office from 1975 to 1986). As I prepared for an interview with Barreto, a friend called him a dinosaur, critiquing the old patriarchal order that Barreto represented as an out-of-date throwback. Just as she predicted, when I arrived for the interview he touched the back of my head during the greeting kiss on each check, a gesture of masculine dominance. Sporting the white linen suit of a landed patriarch, Barreto confidently recounted his populist vision for state-sponsored land distribution from a 1970s-style hotel he owned:

> It fell upon me to be mayor, and so it was my responsibility to settle people. . . . The people who came here were poor, humble people. They didn't come with money, they came with hope of finding work. . . . I would give them their place, their lot. I did the land parceling. I sold [the land] for a symbolic price, something like 30,000 guaranies back then, and they had to pay 2,000 guaranies monthly. . . . Poor people didn't have enough to pay for their land, just like today, and so the government has to help these people.[50]

As a traditional Latin American strongman (caudillo), Barreto presented himself as the caretaker of "the people," with whom he empathized. At the same time, Barreto's paternalistic style of caretaking naturalized the skewed power relationship between the ruler and the ruled. Using the first-person-singular pronoun ("I did the land parceling"), Barreto blurred the lines between public office and himself as an individual man. We shall see that these paternalistic modes of power can flip quickly to violence.

Indeed, Barreto also orchestrated regional contraband networks, administering Runway Hernandarias, "352 hectares dedicated to contraband and drug trafficking."[51] The Melgarejo family, original owners of the 352 hectares, accused Barreto of ordering the murder of José Melgarejo and usurping the land. Barreto's men met national commissioners charged with inspecting Runway Hernandarias with gunfire in order to prevent oversight. Barreto's power survived Stroessner's fall, symbolizing the coextension of outlaw capital with state power. In the 1990s Barreto accepted appointment as the head of the Contraband Control Commission of Ciudad del Este "without even blushing," as historian Aníbal Miranda commented.[52] Like the plantation bloc, Barreto's style of governing relies on a "mythic paternalism" that claims to offer social uplift when instead it promotes a class project of enrichment, in this case through contraband.[53] Calling Barreto a dinosaur locates these patriarchal practices of power and the coextension of state power with outlaw economies in the past. Yet, as I argue, these illiberal claims to power are modern through and through.

Critiquing the well-worn pathways linking contraband and political power, a fiery speaker at an opposition rally lamented "contraband as philosophy," wielding the phrase like a bludgeon meant to smash any pretense of Stroessner's claims to legitimacy.[54] Yet both Stroessner and contraband resiliently resisted reform. What is this philosophy of contraband? Famously, Stroessner called contraband "the price of peace," intimating that he doled out access to contraband routes among loyalists to stabilize his restive alliance. Indeed, Stroessner's early hold on the presidency was by no means secure. Between the 1947 Civil War and Stroessner's rise to power in 1954, seven presidents assumed office. Some researchers have therefore depicted an instrumental patronage machine or straightforward exchange relationships: trades of loyalty for jobs or contracts or "opportunities for graft, smuggling, and illicit trade," as Gustavo Setrini (2010, 18) notes.[55]

I suggest that contraband is more than a medium of instrumental alliance building: it is a theory of development through outlaw capital. As we learn from Woods (1998, 26), all power blocs require a "system of representation," practical economic knowledge with a worldview and ethos to explain and legitimate their relations, including violent ones. The border trade complicates the explanatory task because the legal framework supposedly regulating it is so at odds with the activities of everyday life. Thus, contraband knowledge includes strategies to deny the undeniable, smokescreens to hide the elephant, even as she trumpets and stamps. To document Stroessner-era contraband, I turned to a compilation of state security documents colloquially known as the Archives of Terror: two tons of state documents detailing thirty-five years of U.S.-backed state repression and violence by regional authoritarian regimes during the Cold War.[56] Though it is always officially denied, "semi-official smuggling," as one commentator called it, nonetheless casts shadows across the archives.[57]

One document recorded the report of a rural informant charged with spying on his neighbors. His report described the flight patterns of "phantom planes" and "an air strip strategically prepared for night landings" operated by a military colonel.[58] In a 1976 document, Police Inspector Celso Cantero described a fight about a box of machetes on a bus from Puerto Presidente Stroessner that were destined to be props in a military parade celebrating Stroessner.[59] A local police officer refused to recognize the "authorizing letter" granting transit permission for the box of machetes, even though the letter was signed by Chief of Investigations Pastor Coronel (who was also a notoriously brutal torturer).[60] These authorizing letters helped Stroessner maintain centralized control over contraband networks.[61] During the scuffle, the dissident police officer yelled, "Absolutely all the contraband that arrives from Brazil is Pastor Coronel's!" A 1983 report detailed a priest handing out mimeographed flyers with questions in Guaraní to a small meeting of "supposed SEMINARIANS." In the discussion, the informant continued, "They critique the activities of the Government, and the Chief of Investigations; saying that the presents distributed in the area are not of good origin because they are the fruit of contraband. They also said the head Priest is very authoritarian and demands contributions in cash."[62] These traces demonstrate the tight ties between state power and outlaw capital, as well as the extent to which contraband became part of the Paraguayan political imaginary.

The archives indeed corroborated what I learned in interviews: that Stroessner maintained centralized control over contraband *esquemas*.[63] The *Book of Gold*, a volume commemorating the Union of Customs Brokers, sketched out these contraband logistics: "In the city of Puerto Presidente Stroessner, there also existed 'Godfathers' [*"Los Padrinos"*] who exercised control over the biggest [import-export] businessmen. . . . Thus the shipments of these businessmen also were centralized under an elite group of Power. From there, those who wanted to work in this profession necessarily needed to have the permission of these 'powerful men.' . . . [T]he important work of Customs Brokers was monopolized by these small groups, who obeyed and collected for 'the crown.'"[64] In calling Stroessner "the crown," Silva describes a centralized command structure pivoting on presidential authority that is linked to godfathers who collected rents. As in the days of the *patrones* running *yerbales*, contraband relied on politically connected men and a system of parallel, nonlegal norms to govern the border trade. This illiberal philosophy of political power justifies impunity and violence for select, empowered men.

Outlaw capital also needs cloaking mechanisms. An anonymous author recorded in an opposition newspaper in the Archives of Terror described the mysterious ways contraband generated great wealth: "For a large sector of Paraguay and for many years . . . semiofficial smuggling . . . was a survival strategy for some, but for others it became the philosopher's stone that turned everything into gold. But with the passage of time, contraband became more than a commercial specialization in the country. And it was not exactly clandestine. Contraband created a mercantile conscience—or rather an unconsciousness—that today has boomeranged back, hurting the weak Paraguayan economy."[65] This mercantile unconsciousness suggests the presence of businesses that capture rather than create value by negotiating profits and distributing rents. Foreshadowing the critique of national economists thirty years later, the anonymous author argues that contraband hurts the Paraguayan economy by competing with national manufacturing and agriculture and therefore stifling economic growth. This notion of the mercantile unconsciousness implies a split between productive capitalist activity and unproductive rent-seeking, a division that I suggest fails to capture the coproduction of these worlds. Yet here, the metaphor of the philosopher's stone goes further, suggesting mysterious processes conjuring value out of thin air. The philosopher's stone transmutes, changing one thing to another through unknown ways and worlds. Its mysterious power is hard to see; the pathways to fantastic wealth and the powers turning rocks to gold are shadowy, opaque, occult. So too with contraband: visible effects, hidden processes. Like the occult economies analyzed by anthropologists Jean Comaroff and John Comaroff (1999)—witchcraft, pyramid schemes, the sale of body parts—contraband schemes generate wealth seemingly from nowhere. As schemes that flourish in neoliberalism's "promiscuous mix of scarcity and deregulation," they "put the *con* in *economics*."[66] Contraband likewise offers this promise of profiting without production. In both cases, the con is on the inside.

In this boomtown period, the Paraguayan state innovated a peculiar amalgam of authoritarian state power and the free reign of capital, including its outlaw forms. Contraband as a theory of development requires obfuscation to hide the networks of men orchestrating contraband from government offices. Early on, Stroessner maintained centralized control over large-scale contraband even as state-led infrastructure eventually decentralized access to smuggling. Throughout, illiberal practices of power infused both city building and economic life.

Liberated Territory

In 1989 a military coup ousted Stroessner. The dictator's fall threw into question the management of contraband, which was hitherto centrally organized under Stroessner. In the following tumultuous decades, local alliances fought for control over border profits and the local state apparatus. The merchant bloc emerged from these struggles, ultimately developing a successful strategy to uncouple municipal administration from national oversight. Decentralization downscaled *esquemas* to the regional and local level and helped create the conditions for the merchant bloc's gambit to unhook local governance from national oversight.[67]

How did the merchant bloc successfully unhook the municipality from national oversight and public review? Transparency activists often blamed Clan Zí, shorthand for the political alliance led by Javier and Sandra Zacarías, who, between the two of them, held the position of mayor from 2001 to 2019. In many of my conversations, critics imagined the power of Clan Zí as nearly total, painting Zacarías as a patriarch orchestrating a massive *esquema* that enfolded powerful judges, politicians, and businessmen and was backed by factions of street vendors, taxi drivers, and municipal employees. With a tone of lament, one vendor reflected, "It's truly impressive how Zacarías organizes his structure [of power]; it's impossible to go against him."[68] A lawyer commented, "In this city, the will of Javier Zacarías dominates; there is no rule of law. This is a liberated territory under the rule of Clan Zí."[69] Evoking autonomous zones, the phrase "liberated territory" suggests that Clan Zí not only evades national oversight but also frees the city from state rule.

Emilio Sosa, a vendors' association president, disagreed as he analyzed viral audio recordings of Zacarías bullying a police chief and threatening to revoke the licenses of taxi drivers who refused to fall in line, even though as ex-mayor he had no official position within the city government. "Part of the trick of governing is making people believe in his power," Sosa said, arguing that Zacarías's masculinist performances helped to create the political authority that he claimed.[70] Sosa stressed that Zacarías is important to this story but also that he is just a man. Strongman theories of power do not explain the rise of the merchant bloc and the successful unhooking of Ciudad del Este from national oversight. Only with history and an attention to the coproduction of extralegality and state power can we clearly see the forces producing Ciudad del Este as liberated territory. "Frontiers *create* wildness so that some—and not others—may reap its rewards," as Tsing (2005, 27, emphasis added) argues.

In this next period of what I call "useful wildness," the dominant frontier logic shifted as the emerging merchant bloc generated and capitalized on the city's useful confusions and profitable grayness. All along the trade route, economic activities diverged from what was supposed to happen according to the law. While many broke the rules, the powerful had more access to the sociolegal processes that constructed the boundaries of effective legitimacy. The stakes of frontier struggles were often about drawing and redrawing these lines of effective legitimacy.

Stroessner's fall reworked the terms of these struggles. In towns throughout the country, citizens toppled statues of the dictator, and mayors expunged Stroessner's name from streets, plazas, and towns. Politicians grappled with ways to avoid future concentrations of presidential power. The 1992 constitution thus promoted political and fiscal decentralization, as lawmakers sought to limit the power of the executive branch. For the first time, citizens directly elected mayors and municipal councils (*juntas municipales*), replacing presidential appointments.[71] The constitution also established the post of regional governor at the department level. Municipal governments gained new authorities over urban planning and policy. The new constitution also directed royalties from Itaipú electricity sales to municipalities, providing a stable source of funds for local budgets. Municipal elections and new revenue streams opened up the local state as a new arena of contestation.

Paraguay joined other Latin American countries in experiments in decentralization as U.S.-backed authoritarian regimes fell. Indeed, organizations like the World Bank pushed decentralization as part of a suite of neoliberal reforms, arguing that moving government closer to the people would generate responsiveness. However, governing at any scale requires practices of power, and the local scale does not necessarily lead to more democratic forms of governance.[72] Indeed, as this section shows, this period of reconstruction forged a new relationship between the frontier and the center of administrative power in the capital city, even as decentralization did not yield democratization.

The economic slump of 2001 hit the city hard. Through the 1990s, the purchasing power of the Brazilian currency fell steadily, limiting the buying power of *sacoleiros*. Accentuating the regional downturn, Brazil intensified border controls, dropped the quota of tax-free merchandise it allowed *sacoleiros* to declare to U.S.$150, and threatened to shut down the International Friendship Bridge for repairs. A broad coalition of vendors, business owners, and city council members formed the Coordinadora Paranaense de Ciudadanos en Acción (Working Group for Citizen Action of Alto Paraná, CPCA) to push for the "commercial reactivation of Ciudad del Este."[73] They wanted more border trade profits to stay in the city.

CPCA had two adversaries: Brazil's border policies and out-of-touch national policy from Asunción. The group's first demand was the "recovery" (*recuperación*) of sales jobs for Paraguayans, positions often filled by unauthorized Brazilian workers. CPCA also sought better representation of the city's interests in negotiations with Brazil about the tax-free quota and bridge repair timeline. A businessman commented, "Please just stop sending us people from the capital city who come here to do their foolishness [*macanadas*] and then leave us easterners with the blame. And above all, they need to stop dropping their pants for the Brazilians and learn how to negotiate."[74] With sexualized language, he suggested that negotiators from Asunción were unmanly and ill prepared.

Animosity toward out-of-touch national bureaucrats helped build support for the emerging merchant bloc. Javier Zacarías, a representative in the House of Delegates and a rising star in local politics, rallied support by invoking the distance between frontier life and residents of the capital city known as Asunceños: "Our elected officials need to leave their air-conditioned offices, take off their ties, and come here to touch the reality of our people!"[75] This contrast between public workers wearing ties in air-conditioned offices and the sweaty realities of everyday life in the street market came to signal an embodied class difference and the chasm between the frontier and the capital city.

Zacarías's call for national politicians to show up and the businessman's desire that they stay away both mobilize the same sentiment: frontier life is different. It cannot be understood without being lived. Outsiders, underappreciating the rough realities of the frontier, only offer ill-suited policy proposals and inept international negotiation teams. Thus, CPCA also demanded administrative decentralization, that is, regional offices of national ministries employing local residents. A writer for the popular gossip column "Puenteguýpe" voiced the discontent of local prosecutors with their Asunceño colleagues with irony: "The 'superprosecutors' of Asunción don't even greet their coworkers. . . . But prosecutors from the capital city are load$ more $killful [*mucho$ má$ capace$*], and that's why they deserve the trust of the attorney general."[76] This reporter suggests that Asunceños are snobbish, uninvested in Ciudad del Este, and seeking the under-the-table opportunities to line their pockets available to those with assignments in a city zoned for transgression.

The government under President Luis González Macchi refused to negotiate with CPCA. In response, CPCA called a mass protest early in September 2001 by organizing thirteen road blockades. By nine o'clock in the morning protesters and taxi drivers had shut down the International Friendship Bridge, Highway 2, and other major access points into the city. On the second day, they burned an effigy of the president, and a CPCA representative commented, "The attitude of the national government reveals their clear indifference toward our problems."[77] Students joined. High schools and universities suspended classes. Supermarkets, gas stations, and banks shut their doors, while public busses stopped service. The central government sent representatives to the negotiating table, including a local priest, but talks stalled. On the third day, CPCA members chased the unpopular governor, widely viewed as corrupt, out of the talks. He had to be whisked away in a military helicopter. By day 4 business owners estimated U.S.$23 million in economic losses. Even so, businesses began supporting the cause, taking out newspaper ads: "Electro Paraná SRL is honored to be part of the people of Alto Paraná, who, with historical heroism, have taken to the streets to make themselves heard."[78] The national government began making concessions.

After both sides signed an agreement, CPCA committed to lifting the blockade. To address the recovery of the Paraguayan labor force, the group scheduled inspections targeting unauthorized Brazilian sales staff to start the following week. The enforcement team included members of CPCA on the supposition that locals would be less susceptible to bribes. Paraguay agreed to pay for bridge maintenance instead of Brazil in order to postpone the work. The Macchi government rejected the desired duty-free zone but formed a committee to investigate a possible future free zone.[79] Challenging contraband *esquemas* proved difficult: Did the CPCA want to clean up the border trade or wrest control away from Asunción so that local alliances could control trade? Voicing this key question, one columnist commented, "I sincerely hope this is more than 'regionalizing el padrinazgo,'" referring to the systems of sponsorship and protection that make up *esquemas*.[80] With a campaign slogan declaring, "Alto Paraná para alto paranenses" (Alto Parana is for those who live here), Zacarías won the mayoralty months later. His first acts in office set the tone for his governing style: he built a wrought-iron fence around the municipality and fired unionized public employees.

Out of this turmoil, the merchant bloc orchestrated a spatialized power grab, worked out through conflicts over the Nine Hectares. The 1990 expropriation of the Nine Hectares was a major win for vendors.[81] It signaled, perhaps, that post-Stroessner leadership might promote urban projects beneficial to ordinary Paraguayans. Yet speakers at a 2015 political rally challenging Clan Zí tapped into a felt sense of dashed hopes. The crowd yelled "¡Cierto!" (True!) as a campaigner mixed Spanish and Guaraní: "It's an outrage that the Nine Hectares were *sold* to a handful of foreigners when they were expropriated so that *Paraguayans* would have a place in Ciudad del Este! We will not forget the theft of this land!"[82] Many political-economic theories predict this outcome: relentless urban growth machines seeking out rent gaps to exploit. But in the messiness of that conjuncture, in the rubble of Stroessner's social order, the future was not yet written.[83] The crisis was more than unmoored economic dynamics pushing toward predicable outcomes—it created openings for different factions to put forward particular visions of the good city.

Once Zacarías took power, his administration quickly allied with the largest street vendors' association, the Federación de los Trabajadores de la Vía Pública (the Federation).[84] The Federation promised to support vendors' claims on the Nine Hectares, but the temporary alliance gathered factions with starkly different visions of urban development and the social interest. Anticorruption activists, on the one hand, sought to reclaim ill-gotten land, recuperate public space occupied by vendors, and move toward a modern urban aesthetic. Vendors, in contrast, insisted on their right to occupy city space to earn what they called their "daily bread" (el pan de cada día).

The tensions between spatial order and livelihood rights haunted the coalition. By the time the Zacarías administration took power, there had already been conflicts and delays over construction for vendors on the Nine Hectares. Soon after expropriation, the municipality leased the land to a foreign construction firm to build a retail complex called Shopping Aspen. Project negotiations included some, but not all, vendors' associations. Vendors worried about who would be included in the new development and who would not. Vendors supporting relocation fractured around the terms of the construction contract, especially proposals to include some higher-end commercial spaces. One coalition of vendors opposed Shopping Aspen and organized a long occupation of the Nine Hectares.[85] The Federation, however, protested the protest, a conflict that divided the movement.[86] Eventually, the construction company slated to build Shopping Aspen withdrew, having grown tired of the conflicts and, if the rumors are true, the bribes demanded by Paraguayan officials as part of the costs of doing business.

During these construction delays for Shopping Aspen, other interests began eyeing the land. Seeking to guarantee that development would benefit vendors, street vendors' associations and other groups helped pass an amplification of the expropriation specifying that the totality of the Nine Hectares must be used to relocate vendors.[87] Both the original expropriation law and its expansion (with Law 533/95) defined the social interest as the relocation of vendors from public streets to a shared commercial space. The municipality under Zacarías soon rebelled against this dictate from the central government by contesting the amplification in court. Municipal lawyers argued that the amplification impinged on municipal autonomy, a new legal figure in the 1992 constitution. Municipal autonomy gave some rule-making and taxing powers to local jurisdictions. Municipal lawyers went further, asserting that municipal autonomy gave the local government vast discretionary powers and that the national government lacked the authority to constrain local visions of development by specifying land uses. In a confused 2–3 ruling, the Supreme Court decided that Law 533/95 unlawfully restricted municipal autonomy by concluding that congressional powers of expropriation require the definition of a social interest but that local governments can negate this interest.

The decision revealed antipoor biases. Justice Oscar Paciello Candia, voting with the majority, blamed the city's "social problems" on vendors' weak work ethic: "The solution is not to concede to whoever shouts the loudest or turns to de facto tactics to secure real or imaginary rights. . . . This only destroys public squares and green spaces without benefit for anyone, not even for the affected people themselves, who, generally, are under the sway of manipulations with secret ends. The solution . . . is the adoption of a more responsible attitude toward life through strengthening the work ethic . . . and the organized participation in the social product of work."[88] Candia dismissed vendors' claims to urban space as illegal usurpations, even as just five years prior, senators legalized the elite illegalities behind Stroessner's gift/thefts. During Senate proceedings, the land surveyor described Stroessner's suspicious payment for the land, recorded as 10,000 guaranies (U.S.$80), and speculated that Stroessner refused to pay even that tiny sum.[89] While one senator commented on Stroessner's greed, the lawmakers, without discussion, agreed to compensate title holders of the Nine Hectares—Stroessner's family members—at market rate. In a powerful illustration of blanqueamiento, the question of property rights for the holders of ill-gotten land slipped by like quicksilver, unasked.[90]

The decision also laid the groundwork for new political technologies of rule. The municipality began using an expansive interpretation of municipal autonomy to carve out a space of action beyond national oversight. Tracing the "social uses of the law" shows how municipal autonomy gained traction as it was made real in practice.[91] Using municipal autonomy, the Zacarías administration evaded a legal mandate to contribute to the health-care plans of municipal employees and indefinitely postponed compliance with a court ruling to reinstate unionized public employees fired in 2001. The municipality also withheld a census of vendors from the government agency funding infrastructure upgrades and refused to comply with a court order to return a group of street vendors to their vending spaces after an unlawful eviction, in both cases, claiming municipal autonomy.[92]

Some (although certainly not all) ordinary workers took up this notion that the municipality could draw its own boundaries of legality. A vendors' block association president explained to me his understanding of municipal powers of eviction: "Autonomous means that the municipality can decide right now to kick you out of your vending space, to speak directly." Even when vendors regularize their claims, the block president asserted, municipal officials could stop accepting payment of a small tax (the precarious use tax), rendering the vendor, he said, "immediately illegal."[93] Thus, municipal autonomy as a practical technology of rule was made real from the bottom up, not just the top down. As a claim to unaccountable power, municipal autonomy draws on authoritarian logics, a mutable resource with a long regional history that the municipal officials put to work in the present.

The municipality also created a shadow institution to evade mandatory audits of its accounts.[94] The constitution requires the Office of the National Comptroller (Controlaría General de la República) to audit all municipal budgets. In 2003 the Zacarías administration convinced a judge to issue a restraining order against the National Comptroller, forbidding that office from evaluating the municipality's books and establishing a parallel governmental body, the Tribunal de Cuentas (Audit Court). The Tribunal de Cuentas evaluates the municipality's filings in closed-door proceedings, producing a single sheet of paper approving or rejecting the municipal filing. More than a decade later, this single sheet flashed on-screen in a municipal lobby while I waited for an interview. Red block text stamped across the top read, "Approved by the Tribunal de Cuentas."[95] This shadow institution enabled a kind of plausible deniability, especially useful as transparency activists brought multiple legal and legislative challenges seeking to pry open municipal accounts and substantiate their suspicions that the Zacarías administration was diverting public funds to private pockets, what they called "caja dos" (cash register two).

Municipal autonomy and the Tribunal de Cuentas pushed the limits of municipal prerogative. Like the judge and the boss eating from the same plate in Rafael Barrett's description from the late 1800s, today's *esquemas* work through relationships between judges and moneyed frontier interests. But more is at stake than corrupt, bad-apple judges. Regional judges in *esquemas* helped the Zacarías administration create an exceptional regulatory zone, that is, liberated territory. Municipal autonomy and shadow institutions like the Tribunal de Cuentas composed part of the rule-by-storm style of governing described in the opening of the chapter, through which urban planning proceeds by opaque negotiation and dealmaking.

The Zacarías coalition was, at the same time, a provisional arrangement requiring constant political work to maintain. For fifteen years, the municipality successfully concealed its budgets, even amid intensifying mobilizations for transparency. Yet in February 2019 the House of Delegates moved to remove Mayor Sandra McLeod de Zacarías from office after the Supreme Court reversed course and backed an audit by the National Comptroller. Their investigation revealed thirty budget irregularities and missing funds totaling U.S.$23 million, confirming suspicions of fungible public revenue streams flowing into the private bank accounts and campaign coffers of Clan Zí. A journalist recalled the scene after the decision was announced, saying to me that residents "celebrated in the streets like it was the World Cup."[96] This could represent the fall of the Zacaríases' political alliance, even as transforming the underlying *esquemas* remains another task altogether.

Conclusion

Outlaw capital generates profits through transgression without producing surplus value. Yet it is not an aberrant distortion of some pure or universal logic of capital. Outlaw capital is rather one expression of a variegated complex, an assemblage of practices and supporting epistemologies made and remade from the ground up. In Paraguay, state officials stewarded contraband as a development strategy, producing social relations that generate and legitimate vast inequalities in wealth and social power even as contraband helped to create one of the largest popular trade circuits in the world. Against easy explanations of state absence, this chapter examined the consolidation of contraband as an engine of urban development involving frontier politicians and regional judges alongside traders and *contrabandistas*. State modernization projects like road building and city founding unexpectedly decentralized access to the border trade, birthed the popular economy, and transformed elite-led, large-scale contraband schemes. State planners founded the frontier town and the Itaipú dam to establish a state presence in the hinterland. While these projects provided the authoritarian state with infrastructural proof of its modernizing capacities, the expansion of a state presence into the borderlands paradoxically accentuated the dynamics of created wildness.

Ciudad del Este's rise as a commercial hub emerged from a long regional history of political, economic, and spatial experimentation, working through all three registers of the frontier. Over a century and a half, frontier profit-making shifted from land speculation and plantation economies to state-sponsored commerce and contraband. While the dominant frontier logics shift, elites have profited from rule-breaking throughout. From the city's founding, the economic life of the frontier boomtown was trade, which overlaid rather than displaced older logics of extraction and land speculation. In the decades after Stroessner's fall, the merchant bloc gained power, creating new political technologies and institutional forms that decoupled local governance from national oversight, building the city as a space of useful confusions where legal and illegal economic practices intertwine.

Ciudad del Este is therefore a useful place to ask after the state-making dynamics of outlaw capital. Outlaw economies and state power are not mutually opposed terms but practices—always situated and contested—that come into being in and through one another. Outlaw capital thrives in the created wildness of the frontier *because of state projects*. Lamenting an absent state overlooks the many ways that state practices set the conditions for this commercial city to become a key node in world-spanning trade circuits.

CHAPTER 4

Urban Livelihood Rights

Throughout the Zacarías era, disagreements swirled around competing plans to relocate vendors to the Nine Hectares or to upgrade and regularize their street occupations through the Pilot Plan. Without abandoning claims on the Nine Hectares, members of Emilio Sosa's La Colectiva also organized to secure spots within the Pilot Plan's zone of increased tenure security. On paper, the Pilot Plan promised certainty, a means for vendors to secure their claims to space outside the old politics of negotiation and quiet encroachment. In practice, however, formalization reconfigured rather than banished uncertainty. As the municipality staged the rollout of the Pilot Plan in four segments over more than a decade, the prolonged implementation timeline translated into an extended horizon of worry for vendors. Each stage required removing thousands of ad hoc stalls and pushing vendors out of their old spaces onto the street as they waited for construction crews to finish the upgrades. Before each round of demolitions, municipal authorities recorded vendors' claims in a census, promising to distribute upgraded space accordingly. But the role of the municipal census was not clear. Rumors swirled about the backroom price of securing a spot in the census, and vendors' associations organized competing lists of their membership rolls. Members of La Colectiva shared semiformalized status with registered claims to space. However, most were located outside the zone of the Pilot Plan upgrades and lacked the additional security gained by looking legal in standardized vending stalls.

As I listened in on a meeting of La Colectiva in a stuffy back room on the periphery of the market, Sosa proposed several strategies, including a self-census. Introducing the proposal, Sosa commented, "It's for our certainty."[1] A self-census would serve multiple purposes, he explained. First, it would help members assert claims to specific vending spaces in negotiations over inclusion as the final stage of the Pilot Plan unfolded. Further, if the municipality tried to

FIGURE 16. Self-built vending stalls; photo by author, 2013

relocate any new vendors in the midst of La Colectiva members' spaces, members would have a way to show that those people did not belong. Sosa stressed that his proposal would be public and follow official municipal procedures.

Calling it the "third front," Sosa differentiated his strategy from other approaches, including the Federation's clientelistic strategies, the confrontational tactics of protesters, and the embodied politics of the most marginalized women vendors. The logic of the self-census rejected legitimation through political loyalty, the primary strategy of the Federation. Sosa critiqued this logic by mimicking the language that a Federation leader might use with their members: "Japaga 2000i jasegurahagua nande puesto" (Let's just pay U.S.$2,000 and secure our spot). With uncertainty and fear pushing vendors to engage the municipality on their terms of negotiability, Sosa named fear as a motivator of action, and the woman next to me repeated to herself, "Yes, fear and anxiety," as others cried out in agreement.

The assembled vendors also voted to send a letter demanding that the municipality provide official notification—as required by law—before relocations or temporary evictions. Sosa said, "We deserve official notice, and the municipality, as a public institution, has an obligation to give us this respect." This letter sought to nudge municipal officials away from capricious, hard-to-predict practices of governance. If his members learned to advocate for their right to dignified work, Sosa wagered that local officials would need to respond differently. Thus, this new brand of claims making was a pedagogical project aimed at both his association members and the local government. He thus sought to cultivate new sorts of political subjects, subjects ready to claim rights rather than activate dependencies with municipal officials.

While La Colectiva was an important force during my fieldwork in 2013, by my return visit in 2015, Sosa's project had stalled. Several affiliate organizations had peeled away, casting their lots with the Federation. On different occasions, three association presidents recounted to me their decisions to leave La Colectiva and join the Federation. Two presidents made the decision after meetings with the municipal official in charge of inspections, Santiago Torres, in which he plainly laid out the stakes through a populist discourse of friends and enemies: "You are either with us or against us."[2] Sosa sought to counter this political vision by saying, "We aren't opposed to them [municipal officials]; we just want them to do their job well. We aren't going to let them evict our people as if we are nothing."[3]

The uncertainty surrounding the Pilot Plan shaped the political strategies of vendors. I chatted with one of Sosa's former associates, Samuel, in front of his stall, stacked high with fake leather jackets. He recounted his decision to leave La Colectiva regretfully and somewhat warily. The friendliness that characterized our earlier conversations had been replaced with unease. Samuel admired Sosa yet felt he had no choice but to leave Sosa's organization, given his assessment that Torres interpreted affiliation with La Colectiva as casting one's lot with the municipality's opposition. Inclusion in the final stage of the Pilot Plan hung in the balance, and Samuel wagered that the distribution of upgraded vending stalls would flow toward those with demonstrable political loyalties to the current municipal administration.

Amid considerable uncertainty, vendors like Sosa responded creatively to defend their livelihoods. These resourceful responses both contested and reinforced social hierarchies. At the same time, I argue that vendor politics sometimes offers ethical urban epistemologies that contest the exclusionary models offered by global urbanism. Vendors insist that their work is dignified and use various strategies to claim spatial rights. If their work transgresses municipal ordinances as they sell from public streets and sidewalks, they assert that their livelihood needs justify their rule-breaking. The most marginalized Guaraní-speaking women also invoke a shared condition of vulnerability and need as the condition of urban belonging, not legal compliance or individual rights.

To interpret these claims, I start by situating the street market as an urban commons and discuss the fraught politics of representation by which I recount these stories across considerable difference. The next section examines how the constrained agency of street vendors is shaped by uncertainty as a mode of governance. The following two sections explore insurgent street vendor politics. I trace an urban epistemology rooted in the use value of urban space and in an ethic that prioritizes livelihood rights.

Ethics and Our Urban Imagination

Workers in popular economies contest the distribution of social wealth, making claims on urban spaces to capture value. In deeply unequal cities, popular economies are a central means of redistributing wealth among marginalized people. This critical reading of popular economies disputes dominant ways of knowing valuable work, people, and places and works against antipoor epistemologies that systemically overlook the forms of value—economic and otherwise—produced and distributed by popular economies. This frame also helps center places like Ciudad del Este's street market as an urban commons, a place built from below to capture and circulate wealth among the poor and working classes. It makes clear that illegalities are a terrain of class conflict.

The collective project of creating an urban commons exists in tension with individual vendors seeking profit for themselves and their families. Street vending is decisively entrepreneurial, structured by logics of individual profit, competition, and the promotion of the consumer society. Vendors, fearful of competition, sometimes try to keep new entrants out. Indeed, the first associations of street vendors in Ciudad del Este sought—unsuccessfully—to restrict the right to vend to their members.[4] Like "actually existing commons," the market is organized through social hierarchies of race, gender, and class, just like other social spaces.[5] Yet, as discussed in the next chapter, vendors also mobilize an ethic of contingent solidarity. Verónica Gago (2017, 12) captures this ethic when she argues that La Salada, a huge market outside Buenos Aires, is home to both "diverse notions of freedom" and new forms of submission and self-exploitation. This framing emphasizes that popular economies are both oppositional to and entwined with the social reproduction of capitalist life. Further, workers in popular economies often confront trade-offs between struggling against exploitation and dispossession.[6]

Street vendors cannot be easily categorized as subjects of resistance. Against the desires of critical researchers like myself, they do not directly contest the logics of capital and sometimes police the boundaries of inclusion in the street market. Indeed, vendors *desire* inclusion in urban development.[7] At the same time, there is always an ungovernable excess. Informalized worlds of work are *in* and *of* working-class and poor communities, materialized by resourcefulness and creativity. Negotiating both disinvestment and state programs of poverty management as a matter of survival gives vendors an important vantage point from which to critique both processes. Vendors exist at some social distance from elite centers of power in marginal spaces that are nurtured by different sorts of rationalities. Gago (2017, 9) describes this rationality as oriented by "vital strategies," restless, life-seeking Spinozan capacities. Informalized workers are entrepreneurs of themselves, embodying optimizing, self-interested orientations fostered by the neoliberal milieu. These practices coexist alongside more communitarian ones. Thus the political terrain is the social fabric of daily life rather than electoral politics or campaigns to institute new, more egalitarian social structures.

Street vendor politics are thus multiple, intertwining individual and collective strategies to claim space for urban livelihood. Very broadly speaking, in different moments, vendors have used confrontational protest, clientelistic (vote-bank) politics, and individual negotiation. Social position shapes vendor strategies. Unsurprisingly, established vendors with secure claims to space rely on politics different from those of itinerant hawkers, who often face criminalization. Across social positions, vendors use diverse tactics, including making discursive claims about the value of their work, mobilizing collectively against eviction, organizing into vendors' associations, attempting to regularize their claims, paying off municipal officials, leveraging political connections to municipal bureaucrats, strategically promising their votes to politicians, making themselves visible through projects like Sosa's self-census, and finding ways to squat spaces from which to sell.

Vendor politics are shaped by local political regimes and strategies of governance. As we saw in chapter 2, street vending is governed by perpetual negotiation mediated by an antipoor epistemology, a deeply ingrained common sense that denigrates the lifeworlds of the poor. These attitudes shape the spatial management of the street market. Across Latin America, public space is a key site of work. Legal codes delineating authorized uses of streets and city spaces wildly mismatch the ways that vendors actually claim and defend space from which to sell. Instead of legal compliance, intricate social norms adjudicate who has access to what urban spaces.[8] Moreover, street vendors are managed through intense negotiability over the use of urban space.[9] Responding to this social reality, I join critical urbanists who reject the formal/informal binary, instead arguing that informalization and formalization are power-laden social *processes* allocating land, resources, speculation opportunities, vulnerability, and exposure to violence.[10] In this context, law is an unreliable compass to guide action. Instead, dynamics of provisional recognition, perpetual deferral, persistent threat of eviction, and grudging toleration shape the management of street vending. These dynamics create uncertainty for vendors seeking to chart a path toward more stable claims to urban space for livelihood.[11]

Representing the claims of street vendors is no small task. I interpret street vendors' claims across chasms of power, language, class, and culture. Postcolonial literary scholar Gayatri Chakravorty Spivak (2013) insists that these projects of translation are always incomplete; they cannot but fail to capture the textures, contingencies, and dramas of ontologically distinct others. Furthermore, the politics of representation is always fraught. Scholars like myself can only interpret the stories of others through our own embodied epistemologies, themselves shaped by our positionality and the uneven political economy of knowledge production, which values some voices and has a hard time hearing others.[12] Indeed, representing others across race-class differences is also about learning to represent ourselves, to see the ways that we too are shaped by and complicit in reproducing the very structures and epistemologies of oppression that we may contest.

Thus, it is my own desire for more humane urbanisms that orients my telling of the stories that follow. For Faranak Miraftab (2016; Miraftab et al. 2019), humane urbanisms break epistemologically and ontologically with dominant forms of planning practice to move toward justice, reparation, and material equality through direct democracy and bottom-up direct action. They require centering insurgent politics, counterhegemonic actions that "destabilize the normalized order of things," while also, following the Zapatistas (see Zapatista Comité Clandestino Revolucionario Indígena 1996), promoting a world where many worlds fit.[13] This framework is inspired by a long tradition of radical scholarship that insists on going beyond interpreting the world, seeking instead to change it. Sociologist Boaventura de Sousa Santos (2018, 15) suggests that bridging the gap between today and a more just tomorrow requires a "sociology of emergences." This is about excavating already existing, counterhegemonic practices of everyday life to uncover and amplify the embers of different ways of thinking, being, and becoming, modes that move toward liberation, justice, and a redistribution of social resources. Thus, I choose to lift up these insurgent stories because learning to re-present the stories of street vendors in this way has shaped my own political imagination and pushed me to be more ethical within unethical systems that position me with a certain (constrained) power and perhaps even some credibility to present these stories, which are not my own.

Street vendor claims to the city are insurgent when they move our political imaginations toward justice and freedom, when they destabilize elite representations of what cities are for, and when they expose capitalism's contradictions. I suggest that vendors can offer a useful urban epistemology that prioritizes livelihood rights over profitability, use value over exchange value.[14] By claiming streets as sites of work, vendors challenge dominant notions of global urbanism, which conceive of streets and sidewalks as sites of circulation rather than livelihood. Furthermore, vendors ground their claims in ethics and need rather than legal compliance in a further challenge to global urbanism.

I argue here that the most marginalized women vendors use an affective, embodied politics. In interpreting this politics, I draw from the affective turn in the social sciences, which analyzes how bodily life and felt experience shape social action.[15] In doing so, the affective turn contests tendencies within political theory to overvalue rationality and construct an untenable binary opposing reason and emotion. Rather than drawing from a psychological view of emotions—emotion as interior to and as the property of individuals—I follow feminist theories of affect as political, relational, and transpersonal.[16] Political emotions are historically specific and culturally mediated. Further, affect circulates, mobilizing relations of power.[17] These feminist approaches acknowledge a divided subject with fissures between desire and interest without reducing such disjunctures to false consciousness.[18]

The power to generate emotional fields is, of course, unevenly distributed. As Lauren Berlant (2011, 24) argues, emotional attachments to "compromised conditions of possibility" are key to reproducing late capitalism and implicated in its uneven distribution of vulnerability. Globalized neoliberalism requires economic *and* emotional investments, especially as we careen through intensifying crises. The geographies of these investments are as variegated as capitalism itself. In San Francisco, passionate attachments to precarious start-up labor stabilize neoliberal economic forms.[19] Haitian survivors of state violence perform their suffering to gain redress as "trauma portfolios" become currency in an economy of humanitarian aid that commodifies women's suffering.[20] As a lucrative site of private-sector disaster profiteering, post-Katrina recovery in Louisiana depends on unpaid volunteer labor mobilized through an "affective surplus."[21] Scholars usually attribute this capacity of "affective orchestration" to capital or states.[22] In Ciudad del Este, the most marginalized women vendors seek to mobilize affect by displaying their embodied vulnerabilities. They aim to cultivate useful emotional states in municipal officials to sidestep eviction. As practices of constrained agency, these tactics underscore the contingencies of urban politics, illuminate everyday practices of power, and point to different sorts of political subjects.

Uncertainty as a Mode of Governing

I arrived at dawn to meet Ña Gabriela and a dozen of her colleagues, anticipating a confrontation.[23] (*Ña* is an honorific in Guaraní similar to *doña* in Spanish.) For many years, these vendors sold tennis shoes, fake leather jackets, and inflatable water toys under brightly colored umbrellas with the de facto authorization of the municipality. But a municipal official had ordered their evictions during the Thirty-Day Plan, a June 2013 campaign to enforce use-of-space rules in the street market. Emphasizing urban aesthetics, the mayor, Sandra McLeod de Zacarías, argued that a more orderly street market would attract shopping tourists and jumpstart the slumping border trade. She publicly promised no evictions, but the reality on the street was different. Breaking legal protocol, the municipality did not give these vendors written notice, only a verbal eviction order that foreshadowed a period of uncertainty and upheaval. "Shouldn't they have given us notification?" asked a middle-aged vendor, his kind eyes looking weary. Another fumed, "Sandra came *here* and *said* that under her administration they wouldn't kick us out. Now they don't need us, and so it's ciao?!"

By defying the eviction order and showing up to work, these vendors staked claims to city space and urban livelihood. When the first municipal official in charge of compliance, called a *fiscal*, arrived, he looked at the assembly with consternation. "You shouldn't do this," he scolded, pulling out his personal cell phone to place a call to Santiago Torres, the municipal director of inspections.[24] As he reported the vendors' protest, the block association president showed up looking worried as she realized she had lost control of her members. The group was affiliated with the Federation, an umbrella organization aligned with the municipality that had promised their members spaces in the proposed final stage of the Pilot Plan. Surveying the situation with a desperate look, the block president said, "You need to abandon this spot right now if you want to negotiate for a relocation. If you don't leave, I will take you off our membership list!" Ña Gabriela grumbled and looked away. Later she commented, "She takes our monthly dues, and now she abandons us? The Federation has sold us vendors out."[25]

The Thirty-Day Plan unsettled the old equilibrium of grudging toleration, and vendors had a hard time predicting what municipal officials might do. Each morning in June, teams of municipal employees swept through the mar-

FIGURE 17. Spray paint possibly marking out smaller vending spaces during the Thirty-Day Plan; photo by author, 2013

ket, ticketing food vendors, enforcing strict limits on how much space vendors and taxi drivers could occupy, piling unauthorized slot machines into the back of a dump truck, and confiscating the merchandise of unlicensed hawkers. One morning, ominous yellow squares appeared spray-painted on the street, presumably marking reordered vending spaces, which were much smaller than what most currently commanded. Another morning, a group of vendors found their roofs gone. Rumors swirled that it was municipal employees who had stripped and later sold the valuable metal roofs.

The legal status of Ña Gabriela and her colleagues was tenuous and confusing. Many only sporadically paid the precarious use tax—a small monthly fee required to get around restrictions on using public spaces for commercial gain. Tax payment was one step toward becoming "less informal," as one vendor put it, the short phrase conveying the experience of formality as part of a spectrum of shifting intensities rather than a clear, legally backed status.[26] When I asked Ña Gabriela's neighbor if he paid the tax, he snorted, "Well, I give the *fiscales* their 'pocket money' every day to leave me alone. Does that count?"[27] Ña Isabel showed me a receipt from her precarious use tax payment that recorded her name, her vending spot, and her most recent payment from that very month. But legal compliance did not protect Ña Isabel. It seemed the municipality was targeting informalized and more formal vendors alike for eviction.

The vendors held their ground, and, to my surprise, they stayed the day without further incident, strategizing their next move. Then several small street rebellions erupted as crowds of vendors shouted down officials attempting to deliver warnings or eviction notices. Ña Gabriela reflected on these confrontations, "We were ignorant, but now we are awake. We have lost our patience. Now we have all risen up!"[28] New to the role of advocate but accustomed to getting things done, Ña Gabriela started organizing, connecting with other groups of evicted vendors, and warning vendors throughout the market that the municipality wanted "bare sidewalks" (*vereda nandi*). I joined one protest of several hundred vendors marching through the streets as the crowd ran the *fiscales* out of the market. A small group of municipal officials ran ahead, followed by a line of armed Special Operations Force officers protecting the officials. The vendors chanted, "¡Mondaha! ¡Mondaha!" ("thieves" in Guaraní), asserting that the state in fact produced theft instead of controlling or punishing it.[29] Excitement flashed in the eyes of onlookers. Ña Gabriela and her colleagues marched in front with raised fists. Momentarily, vendors reclaimed the streets.

After a few weeks, the street rebellions died down, and the pressure on vendors to negotiate a deal increased. Finally, Torres offered them different spots a few blocks closer to the International Friendship Bridge. I visited Ña Gabriela, curious to learn how she secured these new spots for her group. "It was the only way," Ña Gabriela sighed. In a meeting, Director Torres explained the conditions: he would give her group spots only if Ña Gabriela publicly renounced her protest on a local radio station, affirmed her support for the mayor, and corroborated municipal assertions that there were no evictions. "It was the only way," Ña Gabriela repeated.

By late August, Ña Gabriela and her colleagues had realized that the relocation spots were no good. They were pressed in among established vendors who resented the competition. While the vendors were close to the bridge, pedestrian flows bypassed the group. Sales were poor. Ña Isabel commented, "I have aged ten years in the last two months."[30] By November, Ña Gabriela had left street vending, using her savings to open a corner store. Ña Isabel also struggled, but she lacked savings. Soon, she did not even have the money for the bus fare into the city center. Ña Gabriela reported that Isabel was bedridden with hopelessness. When I called to check in, her voice cracked. "I have a family to feed," she said, her voice trailing off. "I don't know what to do." Isabel sent her eldest son to Chile for work, but he would not be able to send money home for months. When I hung up the phone, I wondered how many others shared Isabel's experience of dispossession through projects of formalization.

Across town, another vendor, Ña Lucia, defiantly reoccupied her spot after she and two dozen of her colleagues were evicted from their *puestos* along Avenida Centenario. Ña Lucia sold medicinal herbs, honey, and peanuts from a six-foot stretch of sidewalk in front of a low, crumbling brick wall on a busy avenue, Avenida Centenario. She explained that she had overcome the fear of the municipal officials who had driven her colleagues away: "I turned myself into a lion. I became a street tiger for my vending space. . . . They can no longer keep tricking us, keeping us on alert in a state of permanent fright [*nderembotavyveima ha ne'ẽveima la ¡chake!*], . . . hiding in the side streets where supposedly no one can see us. Isn't this true? Tell me if I am not speaking the truth."[31] In Guaraní, the exclamation *¡chake!* indicates a warning of impending danger, a figurative "state of permanent fright."[32] Ña Lucia attributes *chake* to municipal strategies of governing, which I interpret as a generalized, affective condition of uncertainty. By invoking lyrical metaphors of her lionlike strength and conjugating its force in the past tense, she asserted her own distance from this state of permanent fright.[33]

Others also described these situations of danger. Obdulio, a longtime vendor and former association president, reflected on how municipal practices of power worked as a kind of "disguised brutality." He continued by saying, "Physically, right, looking physically there isn't brutality, but if we look inwardly, we see it's calamitous, it's even worse [than under Stroessner], because physical wounds are temporary. . . . Now we are worse off, okay; our interior experience makes up our reality."[34] In his analysis, Obdulio suggested that municipal practices work "inwardly" and compared the harms of authoritarian tactics of physical violence under Stroessner to a new era of covert governance strategies aimed toward inner experience. From his vantage point, both modes of governance are, he says, "calamitous."

I met with Director Santiago Torres several times to understand the municipal criteria for allocating spots in the Pilot Plan and the relocations of those evicted as part of the Thirty-Day Plan. He explained that the municipality used a census to record the spatial claims of current vendors, which would enable the fair distribution of valuable vending spots in the Pilot Plan. In theory, the census should have operated as a tool to engender certainty, a classic means of using state power to render space and subjects visible and knowable.[35] Indeed, in interviews, officials invoked this census as a technical instrument cataloging an external object: the spatial distribution of vendors.

Yet Torres tried to dissuade me from pursuing the census. In a disorienting conversation, the status of the census shifted: Torres simultaneously claimed that the census belonged to the municipality and was therefore not available to the public and that it was unavailable because a vendors' association had it. Next, he suggested the census was irrelevant:

> When the fourth stage [of the Pilot Plan] begins, many will be left out because they will not have their documents. And many will say, "But I've been here for sixteen years!" "For fifteen years!" and "Thanks to God, I've been here for twenty-two years!" I know each and every one of them. I know them. I have photographic vision, I do. I see them, and I already know where they are from [in the market] and how long they have been there, because I have already done an X-ray [*radiografía*] of all the streets and each one in their vending space.[36]

Through the language of photographic vision and X-ray, Torres claimed exceptional capacities rooted in his embodied knowledge of each vendor and their history. He posited that his body, not the census, was the appropriate instrument to assess the truth of vendors' claims. This assertion of ultimate discretionary authority was beyond external review. I argue that these practices of power draw from the living legacy of authoritarianism. As we will see later in the chapter, Torres was capable of extending care as well as enacting dispossession through eviction.

While the municipal census did not work as a technical instrument mapping objective claims to space, it still impacted vendors' livelihood possibilities. It held mysterious sway in the final allocation of vending spaces in the Pilot Plan. Part of the power of the census lay precisely in its instability, its capacity to mean different things in different circumstances. Municipal officials used the census as a tool to claim fair allocation of vending upgrades. Yet the unknowability of the census also provided municipal officials with the raw material for promises of inclusion in the Pilot Plan.

The perpetual contingency of their claims rendered vendors dependent on fickle municipal recognition. By maintaining some vendors' claims as tenuous, municipal actors generated political support by either extending or threatening to revoke provisional authorization to street space. Through the enforcement campaign and the Pilot Plan, the municipality actively maintained vendor claims as contingent, always requiring ongoing defense. Thus, local political technologies intensified the lived insecurities of street vendors. Indeed, municipal officials can use street illegalities to diffuse the contentious politics of workers in the popular economy. Here, uncertainty functions at two related registers: as a situation of perpetual tenure insecurity and as an affective field or shared political emotion. This condition results from the municipal management of street vendors and the gaps between laws as written and enforced.[37] At the same time, nonenforcement and negotiability created possibilities for vendors to make claims to space. While uncertainty disciplines them, urban workers can still sometimes leverage it as a "social resource," as Daniel Agbiboa (2016, 936) found in his study of informal transport workers in Lagos. Yet this flexibility is Janus-faced, offering vendors a means to make claims and municipal officials a means to justify evictions.

The unknowability of the census and the gaps between law as written and enforced might be interpreted as a lack of institutional capacity. I argue instead that these processes of ambiguity, uncertainty, and contingent enforcement are part of the directed management of urban space, that is, a technology of government. The census and extended rollout of the Pilot Plan kept vendors suspended in a state of worry, perpetually negotiating for inclusion on terms set by the municipality. They conditioned the claims of vendors and shaped their political subjectivities. Thus, negotiability and dealmaking at the moment of enforcement produce uncertainty as a constitutive dynamic of government rather than as an unintended consequence of governing with insufficient capacity. Even further, the census enacts the state, which has the dual capacity to extend paternal care and wreak havoc through eviction.

These formalization projects are inherently unsettling because by design they upend a given order to introduce a new one. They promise reform and improvement, but these visions are too often imposed from the outside by planners and policymakers who oscillate between promises of reform, grudging toleration, and outright condemnation. Because their projects and worldviews are often marked by an antipoor epistemology, I argue that dispossession runs *through* processes of formalization. In these processes, uncertainty is an affective field constitutive of governing. Municipal plans and practices actively produce uncertainty because the political effects are useful, aimed to-

ward forging political dependencies between street vendors and the municipality. Uncertainty is thus a mode of governance that works without the techniques of calculation that are often assumed to be at the heart of state power.

Defending Dignified Urban Work

Another group of vendors evicted from Avenida Centenario protested their
eviction, gathering daily with signs proclaiming "We want to work!" and wav-
ing Paraguayan flags to craft a media-friendly visual. One morning, Obdulio
addressed the crowd: "In this city, we all eat from the same soup pot! From
this pot, we feed our family. With our work in the streets, we earn our daily
bread [pan de cada día]. This is dignified work! Whether we are hawkers [am-
bulantes] or vendors [casilleros], we are the same! What's different is the per-
secution. Shouldn't the city work for Paraguayans and not just foreigners?"[38]
Ña Lucia also recounted her struggles to defend her space: "I speak the truth.
I've been here for twenty-eight years! I am sitting here in my vending spot [che
puesto], and I am going to keep on sitting here until the mayor pays me my
compensation salary for my vending spot, 1 million guaranies [U.S.$200] for
every year I've been here. The trouble is, in Paraguay there isn't justice. The
thing I hate most is lies; after that, I can't stand injustice."[39]

With the law as an unreliable barometer for sorting legitimate street vendors from illegitimate encroachers, discursive battles helped manage inclusion and exclusion. Vendors argued that both their physical presence and their
livelihood need justified their claims, regardless of whether or not they had
successfully petitioned the municipality to officially recognize and register
their claims. Vendors like Ña Lucia often invoked el pan de cada día, or "the
daily bread," to convey the dignity of working as a vendor to feed one's family. Through stories of hardship, sacrifice, and struggle, vendors underscored
the embodied vulnerabilities of poverty and the dignity of working to sustain
the family, often backed by a Catholic notion of sacred life. Like Obdulio, they
framed their work as dignified. Women emphasized maternal responsibility,
shouting out, "I have five children to feed!" to fend off eviction. These claims
situate street vending as a moral economy, that is, as economic actions that
the poor and working classes tend to view as ethical because they meet urgent
family and community needs.[40]

Vendors also claimed "acquired rights" (derechos adquiridos). Like Ña Lucia's comment, "I've been here for twenty-eight years," vendors often justified
their claims by enumerating the number of years they had worked from a single spot in the street market. The use of the term acquired suggests a right

FIGURE 18. Protesters rallying against the Thirty-Day Plan; photo by author, 2013

gained over time. Indeed, some rights do accrue over time. In rural Paraguay, land reform provides campesinos a pathway to regularize their claims to the land they occupy and work by acquiring the right land reform paperwork to document their claims. Informal housing settlements across Latin America are often legalized after irregular occupation such that residents claim occupancy rights through tenure duration. Settlements that are initially noncompliant become regularized. These rights claims respond to the everyday realities of life in the street market, where only some legal transgressions are punished, and compliance is not a guarantee of tenure security.

References to acquired rights were so common that I searched for their legal backing before discovering that they are in fact unrecognized by law. An interview with a key municipal director, Hugo Domínguez, accentuated my confusion. Domínguez explained who had acquired rights: "These people have been educated, they own a house now and live with dignity. For these reasons [their claims] are respected."[41] Domínguez locates rights to city space in the attainment of the outward signs of upward social mobility, including homeownership, as evidence of formalized status. He invokes respectability, not legal compliance, as the standard for identifying who is authorized. Respectability, the director implied, requires time, a process by which migrants and their children unlearn disorderly rural spatial habits through education and homeownership. This class-based aesthetic delineation of urban belonging constructs the poor as outside urban citizenship.[42] Vendors contest this antipoor epistemology by insisting that their work is dignified and legitimate because it meets urgent livelihood needs.

Acquired rights are also spatial and ethical claims to urban livelihood. Vending requires space and the ability to be physically present in the city. When vendors claim the right to presence in the street market, they are also demanding a right to livelihood. Initially, I conceptualized these claims to spatial rights as linking a particular vendor to a fixed space in the street market. Yet as I traced Ña Lucia's battles with the municipality over her noncompliant occupation, I learned that the location of her *puesto* changed three times between 2011 and 2015. In addition to the spot she called *che puesto*, Ña Lucia sold from a spot temporarily authorized by the municipality alongside a grocery store after the Avenida Centenario evictions. When business was slow in her relocation spot, Ña Lucia occupied a street corner one block down from her first *puesto* after striking a deal with a shop owner. Thus, while vendors' claims to spatial rights are placed, they are not fixed; they belie formalization projects that recognize use rights based on linking individual vendors to specific spots.

There is more to this spatial politics of vendors' claims. As I walked with researcher Sofía Espíndola in the capital city, she pointed out a lone street vendor's cart parked on a broad median and covered by a tarp artfully strung up in the branches of a towering fig tree. She admired the vendor's practical, make-do strategy to build their own place of work and claim a shaded spot in the hot city from which to sell drinks and ice cream to passing cars. She described it as *mbohenda*, a Guaraní verb that means both "to make a place for" and "to seek a solution." Vendors are constantly "looking for solutions" (*buscando soluciones*), a metaphor for the constant strategizing required by the hardships of poverty in cities where official logics resist recognizing sidewalks, streets, and public spaces as sites of work.

Finding solutions, like *mbohenda*, is often a strategy of appropriating space or securing provisional authorization to sell from local authorities. It is also about striking deals to work around official rules that limit where people can sell. It can also mean cultivating useful connections to politicians or powerbrokers, those with the power to bend the rules and make things possible. This logic of finding solutions built Ciudad del Este's under-the-table market for street space—officially public space and therefore nonexchangeable—as vendors rented out or sold their vending spots to family or friends when income needs shifted.

Within Ciudad del Este, *buscando soluciones* is a mode of producing space as vendors incrementally build their own vending infrastructure and claim the necessary space to do so. In cities across the Global South, these extralegal, informal, and incremental practices are a major mode of spatial production in building Brazilian *favelas*, Peruvian *barriadas*, Mexican *colonias*, and many other popular neighborhoods. Teresa Caldeira (2016, 7) describes the "transversal logics" that operate within, alongside, and against official logics as poor people and communities find their own way in cities that too often are hostile to their presence.

With livelihood as its fulcrum, "looking for solutions" does not seek legitimation in law. Instead, vendors argue that livelihood need justifies the legal transgressions their work necessitates. In the face of her eviction order, Ña Lucia was defiant: "I'm staying, and that's the end of it. I'm stronger than they are."[43] She explained how she scared off Torres when he arrived threatening eviction, calling herself *tia'y*, a Guaraní term meaning both "witty" and "vulgar." She continued, "Well, when he comes, I make fun of him. I grab my ground coconut, my ground cilantro, and I say to him, 'Take this, boil it, and drink it; it should give your cheeks a lovely blush.' And then he hides from me [*ha okañy kañy chehegui*]! . . . I am resolved in my decision, I will not leave here, while they haven't paid my compensation salary [*indemnización*] or at the very least got me another spot from which to sell on *this* street." Ña Lucia went further: "I know [municipal] authority has limits. The real authority is God. And we will arrive at his gates without even flip-flops on our feet. I know this truth. I'm just telling you the truth, my dear."

Ña Lucia invoked the limited jurisdiction of the municipality in the face of a God-given moral imperative to tend to family. She also explained the illegitimacy of the eviction order in explicitly gendered terms. Ña Lucia said of Torres, "I don't consider him a real man." Further effacing Torres's masculinity, Ña Lucia explained how she generated fear with her parody of makeup and rouge. In questioning Torres's masculinity, Ña Lucia contested municipal powers of eviction and articulated her urban rights of occupancy and work. At the same time, Ña Lucia's comments reveal how patriarchal forms of political authority are understood as part of the legitimate exercise of power. Eugenia, another vendor evicted from Avenida Centenario, likewise invoked the ethics of livelihood. She called former mayor Javier Zacarías *juru hai'mbe*, a Guaraní curse that literally translates as a "mouth with razor-sharp teeth," figuratively meaning "ravenous." *Juru hai'mbe* dovetails with the common assessment that politicians "eat money," that is, take bribes or appropriate public resources. The

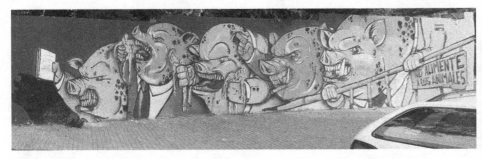

FIGURE 19. A mural by artist Oz Montanía condemning the 2013 parliamentary coup; courtesy of Oz Montanía

metaphor of eating, a universal necessity, suggests that these deals and bribes are widespread, even inherent to state practice. *Juru hai'mbe* is also an ethical analysis of the context of rule-breaking in that it connotes the destructive, unrestrained greed of the rich taking well beyond what they need to sustain life and therefore causing social disintegration. Law breaking by street vendors, in contrast, provides the daily bread: it is necessary and therefore ethical.

A mural condemning the 2013 parliamentary coup echoes this critique of politicians drunk with greed and feeding off the bodies of workers and campesinos. We can critique this mural: the worker and the campesino appear lifeless, without agency. Men dominate the scene of political life, erasing women. Yet its unrelenting critique of elite greed is important. The consequences of inequality are made clear in the politics of early death. Of course, one image cannot represent the complex mechanisms reproducing destitution. Yet this mural, like *juru hai'mbe*, insists we turn our gaze to the brutalities and overconsumptions of the middle and upper classes rather than toward so-called cultures of poverty. When Ña Lucia speaks of injustice, it is this she invokes: crazed wealth alongside dire poverty and all sorts of erasures and justifications about why we should think of this as something other than a crime.

In their struggles to maintain their *puestos*, vendors mobilized a potent urban imaginary for a more humane urbanism. In valuing the use value of urban space, they assert the right to livelihood, to access markets, and to inhabit city spaces to work. Their claims to acquired rights are accompanied by the make-do spatial politics of *mbohenda* as a mode of producing space and strategizing to find solutions. The placed claims of vendors are also spatial rights, even if they fall short of Henri Lefebvre's (1996) right to the city, which calls for the radical democratic distribution of the power to produce city space and shape urban life, a capacity now largely ceded to capital. Yet situating streets and sidewalks as sites of work was a challenge even for Lefebvre's capacious imagination. Lefebvre was able to envision streets as sites of movement, circulation, theater, protest, festival, encounter, commodity exchange, merchandise display, the ordering of social life according to the grid, and the hegemony of the car, but he did not conceive of streets as spaces of livelihood and work.[44] Thus vendors' urban epistemology of use calls us to imagine cities built for urban life and livelihood, not just for (uneven) economic growth. Vendors insist that working to bring home the daily bread is a moral imperative that trumps allegiance to rules about the use of urban space.

Embodied Politics

In this landscape of urban epistemologies, as Santiago Torres asserted extraordinary powers to identify authorized vendors and arbitrarily extend provisional protection, the most marginalized women vendors relied on their own tactics to defend their claims to space and livelihood. A vendor named Magdalena sought to activate Torres's capacities in her campaign to secure a relocation after eviction during the Thirty-Day Plan. Magdalena and her associates had sold a popular cold tea called *tereré* for years from strips of streets between taxis and vendor stalls. However, they lacked documentation of their claims. During the eviction, Santiago Torres promised them relocation without specifying when or where. Magdalena and her associates thus began a campaign of waiting, visiting the municipality each morning at seven o'clock, hoping to catch a municipal official disposed to honor the promise. I sometimes joined Magdalena. As we leaned against a wall of the Division of Urban Development, she shared her plans to manufacture an encounter with the right municipal official, strategizing how to elicit the desired response. She called her insistent waiting *hovyhata*, or "hard-headed," so persistent that the municipality would eventually grant her the relocation.[45] The uncertainty stretched over months. As her debts mounted, Magdalena took out another loan to rent space in an undesirable, low-traffic zone of the street market. But Magdalena worried that without income from *tereré* sales she would be unable to pay for food and school fees for her children.

Emotions played a curious role in extending provisional vending authorizations. I joined Magdalena one morning as she sought information from a stout municipal employee wearing a red suit jacket, the color announcing her affiliation with the ruling Colorado Party. Magdalena recounted her financial hardships, crying as she invoked her responsibilities as a Catholic, God-fearing mother.[46] The employee counseled prayers: "Pray that God will put care in the heart of Santiago Torres." Magdalena retorted, "We have rights!"

and accused the municipal official of treating her like a fool. The employee replied that Magdalena was wrong to invoke rights but then seemed to think better of it as she glanced at me. The official hedged, "We all have rights, but they take time," invoking a temporality of deferment. Shortly after this exchange, Torres called me into his office for an interview. As I pressed Magdalena's case and also asked how he decided who would get a relocation and who would not, he reflected, "Sometimes, someone touches your heart [*te toca el corazón*]." In these cases, he said he would "find a solution" for them. I did not ask him to specify the emotional content of this touching, but I imagine a thin sort of care or perhaps even pity. Whatever its form, it sometimes moved him to use his power to extralegally extend provisional vending authorization.

Throughout the Thirty-Day Plan, I saw this politics of heart touching at work. Once an elderly woman confronted a *fiscal* serving her an eviction order.[47] Her voice cracked with desperation as she invoked her decades-long history of selling cheap lunches. A crowd gathered, watching her wring her hands, narrating the needs of the grandchildren dependent on her small income. A young woman came to her aid in confronting the official, attesting to the longevity of the older woman's tenure and corroborating her frail health. Suddenly, the police commissioner called off the eviction.

Another vendor, Celia, helped me see these politics of the body. I met Celia at a community assembly of those evicted during the Thirty-Day Plan. I sat at a white plastic table with the guests of honor, including lawyers and several vending association presidents. After the official speeches, mostly by men with degrees and salaries, Celia insisted on speaking. She turned toward the news camera:

> I am a jacket vendor, a very honest Paraguayan woman. I've never had to rob anyone, not even an egg. And we each buy [our jackets for sale] through hard work and sweat. And I'm totally exhausted. What am I to do? Must I rob? Will I have to go to jail in order to feed my family? And me, what will I give to my son? My son is five months old, I have him on my breast; I am breastfeeding him. I have to put diapers on him. And what am I going to say to my son? No, I can't change my son's diaper because Mayor Sandra is going to clean up the city.[48]

Text cannot do justice to Celia's performance. Her body shook; her voice rose and quivered while tears fell. Celia demanded an emotional response by calling those present into her emotional field with a mix of intense worry about her children's well-being and outrage at the damage to her livelihood wreaked by eviction. Meeting participants shouted affirmations like "¡Cierto!" (That's right!) as a collective emotional wave rippled through the gathering, circling back and encouraging Celia to continue. After the meeting I asked Celia about her eviction, and I sensed her feeling out how she might engage me in ways useful to her cause. She grabbed my hand and pressed it to her breast, asking me to feel how it was heavy and laden with milk because she was away from her infant son for most of the day. "You see, I am a breastfeeding mother!" Celia's dependencies marked her body as evidence that she was a woman with crucial caretaking responsibilities. If Celia's mothering obligations legitimated her street appropriations, the affective intensity of her testifying served as further proof of her embodied need. In a subsequent meeting, she pressed her hand to her gut as she recalled how the speech for the community assembly just flew out of her body in defense of her children.[49]

In these charged confrontations, women vendors displayed the stresses of poverty and the vulnerability of the body in order to activate an affective response from municipal bureaucrats. Women also invoked responsibilities to dependent children, legitimating claims to space by stressing family vulnerability. I call these interactions "testifying" because of the way that emotional intensity provided proof of embodied need. I also saw officials use strategies to defend their hearts against these emotional politics: crossing their arms over their chests or looking away while delivering eviction notices, eyes hardened against women's affective appeals.

Testifying women worked through, not against, gendered notions of women's social roles and expectations of maternal sacrifice. Rather than challenging gendered hierarchies, testifying women lamented the failures of party, patria, and patriarchy. Celia's first words, "I am a jacket vendor, a very honest Paraguayan woman," indexed both gender and nation as positions that legitimated her speech. As she testified, Celia rooted the dignity of her work in the morality of motherhood and expressed pride in the embodied experience of familial labor. She also named the embodied impact of her labor as exhaustion. Over the following weeks, Celia defiantly reclaimed a square meter of sidewalk from which to sell her jackets, her hip-high plastic bag filled with thick zipped sweatshirts. A friendly taxi driver let her store another bag in his trunk. Daily, she arrived at four o'clock in the morning and sold unmolested until the municipal enforcers began to make their rounds around eight. Then Celia turned to confrontation. She and I laughed as she recounted how she scared away municipal officials by threatening to disrobe, beginning to unbutton her pants, and yelling at municipal officials that they were "on her" so much they must want her body.[50] Celia had to translate her curses for me because I was unfamiliar with the vulgar Guaraní vocabulary of intimate body parts and fluids; these were not words that Paraguayans used around foreign women.

Celia continued to embarrass the officials, challenging municipal pretenses of patriarchal care by accusing them of sliding toward sexual exploitation. She created a scene when a store owner threatened to report her sidewalk occupation. Gesturing to her own compact, brown body, she compared it to the taller, lighter bodies of the young women employed in sales in local shopping galleries, clad in revealing uniforms and perched on high heels. She shouted speculations about the bodies of the store owner's three mistresses, measuring "36-24-36" in breasts, waist, and hips. Celia offered an explicit critique: "Poor women like me have three choices: sales girl, mistress, or street vendor." For her, racialized standards of beauty foreclosed the first. She had no interest in the second, leaving her with the third. In this way, Celia positioned her work as dignified and ethical, itself a political position within the framing of the Thirty-Day Plan, which depicted street vendors as an unclean public nuisance. Celia's boldness won her a few more weeks in her vending space before the municipality succeeded in pushing her out. For her part, Magdalena got tired of waiting for a relocation and returned to her old vending spot. While she did not secure official permission to reoccupy her *puesto*, she had claimed another spot from which to sell when I returned two years later.

Affective politics works because of the contingency of everyday governing practices, a source of worry that is also a condition of possibility for the most marginalized vendors to make claims to urban space for livelihood. These regulatory relationships instantiate vendors like Celia and Magdalena as subjects of a fickle state that rarely bends in their favor but maintains the possibility that it might. Testifying targets the affective field through what Liz Bondi (2005, 442) describes as a malleable "betweenness" and by wagering that another can be influenced through emotional interconnection. Of course, affect is gendered. Men do not testify. These gendered body politics offer small openings to press claims even as they also reinscribe dominant notions of femininity that constrain and regulate women and men. As acts of constrained agency, women's affective tactics are evidence of considerable resourcefulness. Toggling between testifying and aggressive confrontation, their strategies not only worked through norms of maternal responsibility but also transgressed them to provoke useful states of unease in municipal officials. Celia pragmatically testified *and* confronted. Magdalena invoked her rights with one municipal official as she also tried to "touch the heart" of Santiago Torres. These modalities of politics—making rights claims and activating dependencies—are thus not mutually exclusive.

By making claims on the state through frames of need, these women aim to activate dependencies with local power brokers, not to stake claims as rights-bearing individuals.[51] James Ferguson (2013, 224) calls such expressed desires for dependence "pursuits of subordination." Desires for dependence trouble liberalism's philosophical foundation: an assumed universal desire for liberty and the autonomous, rights-bearing individual as the subject of politics. These assumptions restrict politics to liberal frames of citizenship rights and render these women's body politics unintelligible. Yet dependency takes many forms, including the wage relation, even though waged labor masquerades as the standard-bearer of independence.[52] Some forms of dependency have space for dependents to make claims on their leaders; at the same time, these hierarchical relations are often structured through forms of domination. With wageless life as the norm and state supports becoming ever more fragile, we should not be surprised by pursuits of subordination. Our difficult question, then, is how to arrange less exploitative forms of dependence.

The affective lens also shines a spotlight on the political repertoires of the most marginalized vendors. These women display their embodied vulnerabilities and mothering responsibilities to bend the emotional field to their advantage. By framing their work as part of a moral economy, these women insist that meeting basic human needs is an ethic that transcends legal compliance. Rather than claim individual rights, these women orchestrate emotional connections to reactivate dependencies with municipal officials. Indeed, municipal practices enrolled vendors as hopeful subjects of uncertainty, as subordinated beneficiaries rather than rights-bearing citizens, thereby demonstrating how governing through uncertainty exemplifies the productive nature of power, in the Foucauldian sense. Affective governance is a local expression of the antipoor epistemology, which undervalues urban livelihood and devalues poor people. If vendors' pursuits of subordination do not point to the feminist subjects we might desire, they nonetheless make claims of urban belonging and imagine a state with obligations to the poor.

Conclusion

Today, self-entrepreneurship is the norm for many people in most of the world. Indeed, today's modal worker is a woman working informally rather than a male head of household working for a wage. While entrepreneurship is often celebrated, it is a condition forced onto many by neoliberal abandonment via austerity, chronic job scarcity, or state investment in punishment rather than protection. Informalized worlds of work, once imagined to be merely stepping stones along a pregiven path to development, today shape urban life and the far horizon of the politically possible.

Vendors creatively defend the popular economy. The most insurgent vendor politics offer a vital urban imagination that emphasizes the use value of urban space for ordinary Paraguayans. Through their daily labor, vendors turn streets and sidewalks into sites of work. By claiming city space from which to sell, vendors built an urban commons, a crucial livelihood resource in landscapes of disinvestment and poverty. They also challenged dominant notions of global urbanism, which conceive of streets and sidewalks as sites of circulation rather than livelihood.

Vendors' claims are also arguments for a different distribution of social resources, in which meeting the basic needs of the poor is a primary concern. With acquired rights, vendors demand market inclusion and rights to occupy city space in order to link up to the transborder trade. Vendors assert that their work is dignified and insist that they too belong to the economic life of the city. Of course, different rights inevitably conflict. Global urbanism elevates property rights and the right to profit as fundamental rights, priorities that get written into the space of the city. Other rights fall to secondary status, like the right to dignified work and the right to freedom from poverty and its consequences, including early death. Thus, the power of vendors' claims for a more humane urbanism is their insistence that livelihood is a primary rather than secondary right.

Vendors also emphasize the context of rule-breaking, differentiating between the necessary legal transgressions enabling livelihood and the hoarding of the rich. This vision prioritizes livelihood as an ethic that supersedes legal compliance, bringing us away from the deontological terrain of law as the arbiter of social legitimacy. This is another useful injunction for humane urbanism. It is also an ethic that expands dominant visions of who belongs in the city, even if it falls short of a radical democratic redistribution of the right to shape urban space. Finally, women's embodied politics imagine a state that has caretaking obligations to the poor, even if they respond to a subject of needs rather than empower a subject of rights. As predatory forms of neoliberalism move toward evacuating social relations of their noneconomic and caretaking content, imagining an obligated state is a political act.

Liberal philosophy rests on pathological individualism and the segregation of the economic from the political. Both are epistemological maneuvers asserting "freedom from the needs of others," as Jodi Melamed and Chandan Reddy (2019) argue. Testifying disrupts this, insisting, "You should care about my vulnerability." Women perform their need to call into being an ethic of interconnection. Vendors mobilize bodily vulnerability as a shared human condition as they also name its uneven distribution. In doing so, they can also push our political imaginations toward more expansive ethics of care. They certainly pushed me to confront the ways I am enrolled in the antipoor epistemology, even as I reject its premises. The material conditions of my life as a globe-trotting researcher with a U.S. passport—the very conditions of possibility for this book—are not separate from the forces producing poverty for Magdalena, Celia, Ña Luica, and others. Like a *fiscal* crossing his arms over his chest and looking away from a woman's appeals, appeals made for her children, I sometimes keep my car window closed to panhandlers holding placards with their own appeals in the city where I live. I too claim freedom from the needs of others.

While the antipoor epistemology is experienced individually, it is organized systemically. And so street vendor politics can also teach us about urban planning practice as it actually exists. Local political techniques intensify the lived economic insecurities of street vendors. Frontline municipal enforcers manage precarity by keeping vendors' claims to space forever tenuous through legal confusion, arbitrary enforcement, and affective governance. As a consequence, uncertainty infuses the emotional lifeworlds of the street and becomes, I argue, a mode of governance. Indeed, the power of the census lay in its capacity to mystify, while Torres's claims to photographic vision instantiate authoritarian practices of power. The effort vendors invest in negotiating uncertainty, like La Colectiva's self-census, demonstrates its sway as a mode of governing.

Street vendor politics can also reinforce social hierarchies. Some vendors excluded hawkers from the imagined subjects of acquired rights. When vendors claim legitimacy through their economic productivity, they sometimes construct themselves as valuable against an unproductive and therefore less valuable social class. These politics can reinforce what Kathi Weeks (2011) describes as the work society, a hegemonic linking of productive labor with socially constructed understandings of the valuable person. Moreover, street vendor politics cannot solve the limits and contractions of a trade economy based in zero-sum arbitrage. Nor can they overcome the dislocation unleashed as supralocal forces rework the trade route. Vendors' insurgent urban epistemologies alone cannot remake urban economies, but they are nonetheless embers of worlds otherwise.

CHAPTER 5

Enclosure Devices

Over the decades, merchants, traders, and vendors built a city to facilitate global commercial flows. The trade route and the city co-constituted each other. However, by the late 2000s, worrisome political and economic changes threatened the city's economic base. Brazil had tightened border controls, upping enforcement and reducing the quotas of goods *sacoleiros* could export without paying taxes. Brazilian president Dilma Rousseff attacked contraband by lowering taxes and tariffs on items like electronics and cell phones, thereby squeezing profit margins on the reexportation of these products. Brazilian lawmakers proposed establishing duty-free zones in border towns, a strategy to draw commerce into Brazil and bypass Paraguay entirely. The Paraguayan Ministry of Industry and Commerce promoted export processing factories in the frontier region as the road to prosperity and formalization, an economic model with no place for street vendors. Who would survive these changes?

Vendors' association president Emilio Sosa convened a meeting of community leaders to strategize about defending street vending.[1] Vending leaders arrived in a slow trickle to the second story of a half-constructed building on the Nine Hectares. I chatted with a journalist from Asunción who was leaning through the opening of a future window, peering over a gravel parking lot that gave way to forested green hills, the winding Paraná River, and a tin-roofed warehouse where about two hundred vendors sold colorful blankets hemmed in the Qin Yi América factory. "Things are bad, really bad," the journalist commented. "This city must change. The million-dollar question is whether there will be a serious effort to transform the city's model, or if it will just wither and die."[2] He went on, describing the interlinkages with other cities, like the Iquique free-trade zone in Chile, a major point of entry for goods arriving to South America from East Asia: "It's all one big scheme. Iquique depends on Ciudad del Este, China depends on Iquique, Colombians are flying the planes.

In Iquique, underinvoicing is common practice. If something costs ten dollars, they write the invoice for five! If you ask them to invoice it for three, they say, 'Sure, no problem.' And this is Chile's plan—their *esquema* [scheme]—put in place by a supposedly serious and respectable state." The journalist critiqued the *esquema* for capturing rather than creating value largely through breaking laws and codes, that is, through accumulation by transgression.

When Sosa called the group to order, the journalist spoke first, sharing his dire predictions of urban decline and lamenting a corrupt political culture. When Sosa spoke, he argued for formalization by describing Ciudad del Este as "the lungs of Paraguay." He suggested a different understanding of progress:

> The authorities need to understand that progress here comes from Paraguayans. We are the ones who bring money to the barrios. Paraguayans are the ones who make purchases here. We have analyzed the lungs of Ciudad del Este, and it is us. Ciudad del Este is a purely commercial city. Our problem is not that serious. It can be solved. What we are missing is capital and a space. Right now, the system does not work because we end up in debt to the Chinese [factory and shop owners]. We have to finance on a day-to-day basis. When we sell, we are just eating up our own costs. What we need is formalization, like the project we presented to [ex-president] Lugo for a shopping mall for Paraguayan vendors.[3]

Unlike the journalist, Sosa described Ciudad del Este as central to Paraguayan development, as vital to the national whole as lungs are to a living human body. His metaphor imagines the city as the organ that draws in life force—money—from the outside and then circulates it throughout the country. Casting the city as vital to the national body contests stereotypes of the city as marginal or as a problem. Sosa also stressed the economic importance of street vendors. While most shop and gallery owners live across the bridge in Foz do Iguaçu, Brazil, street vendors nationalize global capital flows. With their earnings from the border trade, they buy goods from neighborhood shops and send money to family in the countryside. By circulating money through national space, they keep many poor families afloat. Vendors like Sosa and his members also helped build the city as a useful urban platform, enabling a vast trade network. Unlike the high-tech logistics cities lauded by global urbanists (think Oakland, California, or Vancouver, British Columbia), in Ciudad del Este the urban poor could cast their net, seeking to land some of the profits of the border trade.

A coalition of electronics importer-exporters organized by Dionel Pérez, used the same metaphor but suggested that a different brand of formalization in the form of tax breaks would breathe life into the region. The coalition argued that when taxes are less costly than the various transaction costs of smuggling, importer-exporters will choose to pay taxes. Importer-exporters are, in this view, rational economic actors seeking the most efficient way of facilitating global commodity chains. The organization emphasizes that low taxes and tariffs are the solution to informality, and one of its promotional flyers boasts that Ciudad del Este is responsible for 29 percent of the country's import tax revenue.[4] Perez's coalition was unconcerned by the contributions of street vendors, *sacoleiros*, and small-scale transport workers. Development experts likewise usually analyze popular economies like Ciudad del Este's street market as mere survivalism, structurally irrelevant to the reproduction of global capitalism. But we can learn from Sosa's analysis of street vendors as the lungs of Paraguay by paying attention to the many ways their work matters.

Learning to see how popular economies produce value is important, for when this value is rendered invisible it is easier to enclose, that is, recapture and redirect away from the popular economy. The framework of enclosure is crucial. As trade liberalization, antipiracy campaigns, and post-9/11 security initiatives rework the trade circuit, these transformations have fomented pitched battles over who will benefit and who will be cast out. Different groups—from Brazilian trade associations to Ciudad del Este's merchant bloc—seek to protect their profits, often by proposing formalization. But are these efforts for formalization or for enclosure?

I follow here four different reform efforts that impacted Ciudad del Este: a Paraguayan project to regularize the reexportation of electronics, the Brazilian government's criminalization of *sacoleiros*, a binational project to formalize *sacoleiros*, and a Paraguayan project to invest in factories. Reformers treated street and elite illegalities very differently, and the class-based results of these struggles disarticulated or criminalized the popular elements of the border trade while legalizing or protecting elite illegalities. Across the board, these reforms did not address the economic needs to which the popular economy responds.

I begin by outlining a theoretical framework for analyzing popular economies and enclosures. The next section demonstrates that street vendors create value, even as this value is often overlooked or downplayed. Then I turn to a series of reforms that played out in the early 2000s and 2010s, including two elite-led projects (legalizing the electronics trade and celebrating factories) and two reforms aimed at the popular economy (criminalizing *sacoleiros* and formalizing *sacoleiros*). While these reforms undermined the very practices constructing the city's actual comparative advantage, the flexibilities underwriting the popular economy were more harshly addressed than elite illegalities.

Formalization and Enclosure

Vendors helped produce Ciudad del Este as a commercial hub, an important node in a global trade network. Indeed, vendors' labor and knowledge provide "invisible subsidies," as Sharad Chari and Vinay Gidwani (2005, 273) might say, for the social reproduction of capitalism. Yet government officials and development experts have a hard time seeing the value these workers produce. The framing of the popular economy rather than informal work emphasizes the productivity and import of these work worlds of the urban majority, an argument made with particular force by critical researchers in Latin America.[5] Popular economies are many things at once. They provide sustenance and social protection in contexts of disinvestment, dispossession, and the chronic shortage of waged work under late capitalism. Indeed, capitalism's systemic production of poverty and a population surplus to capital's need for labor makes the persistence of popular economies both predictable and necessary. Decades of research on informalized worlds of work teach us that they are deeply intertwined with so-called formal economies as key links in chains of value making.[6] Popular economies also subsidize social reproduction.[7]

Popular economies are also never merely functional to capitalism and are never only strategies of survival. There is always an excess that escapes capital's logics and discipline. Moreover, these lifeworlds of work are always intensely social and cultural.[8] They are "forms of living," as Kathleen Millar (2018, 9) calls them, ways of making meaningful lives, constructing relationships, and building community. They can also be ways of acting politically, even if these political styles at times fall outside academic expectations or fall short of activist desires for collective resistance. Popular economies also mix logics of profit and competition with those of cooperation and community.[9]

Popular economies produce value and occupy spaces that capital targets for privatization and enclosure.[10] To analyze enclosures, many turn to David Harvey's (2003) concept of accumulation by dispossession, which popularized and expanded Marx's concept of primitive accumulation. For Marx (1894, 875), the historical process of producing waged labor required a violent separation of people from the means of reproducing life. The tumult of the Industrial Revolution unmade social worlds, as elites cut off peasants from old ways of social provisioning by enclosing their common pasture lands and banishing the poor to workhouses. Marx calls this divorce "primitive accumulation" and argues that it is constitutive of capitalism because it creates the working class out of the peasantry and renders workers dependent on the wage to reproduce themselves, their families, and society.[11]

Like the old forms, today's new enclosures—land grabs, privatizations, debt crises—cut off "communal control of the means of subsistence," as the Midnight Notes Collective (1990, 3) writes. Today, however, accumulation by dispossession expands surplus population rather than the working class.[12] Enclosure also targets resources and spaces produced through informalized work, a process that researchers have documented especially well in the case of waste pickers.[13] As cities seek to formalize and "green" these commodity chains, too often they exclude waste pickers and devalue their experiential knowledge, the very knowledge that created functioning commodity chains of recyclables in much of the world. As Melanie Samson (2015, 815) notes, "Capital values the resources to be enclosed, but not the people who must be dispossessed of them."

Harvey argues that accumulation by dispossession is a structural response to the tendency of capital to overaccumulate, a dynamic that requires strong state action to create new arenas of profit-making when old ones falter. Accumulation by dispossession highlights the key temporal and geographical dynamics of these processes. But Harvey's framing centers the logic of capital as the driver of transformation and overlooks the value produced in popular economies, seeing them as merely survivalist and subsidiary.

Rather than the structural machinations of capital, the autonomist tradition insists that the motor of historical change is class struggle (with race, gender, and other forms of difference as constitutive of class).[14] Workers and communities create social systems of provisioning, often in the form of urban commons. These commons are especially important in cities of the Global South where the long histories of colonial racial capitalism concentrate disinvestment and poverty. When these commons impede capitalist urban development or become sites of value, they are often targeted for enclosure. Thus, Tom Gillespie (2016, 73) argues, enclosure is better understood as "a reactive response to the limits to accumulation posed by a rival social force—the urban commons."

Furthermore, enclosures are at once material and discursive. Removing the work worlds of the poor is a step toward revaluing urban spaces for capital. Yet these worlds must first be understood as problematic, as outside the realm of legitimate economic practice. Feminist geographers J. K. Gibson-Graham (2006), two geographers writing under one name, show the importance of economic imaginaries, widespread assumptions of valuable work, productive activities, and corresponding ideas of valuable people.[15] The dominant economic imaginary centers waged work as the norm and universal horizon. This is a remarkably tenacious myth, given the long-standing import of popular economies in most of the world, as well as the precipitous decline and degradation of waged work in overdeveloped countries.[16] Assuming waged work as the norm is also Eurocentric, as it asserts Western countries as the blueprint for universal development.[17]

Normalizing the wage also made wageless life "invisible to science," according to Michael Denning (2010, 79). This echoes dynamics that render invisible value-producing domains like social reproduction, women's unpaid household labor, the essential inputs of nature, and noncommodified economies of reciprocity.[18] Through these processes, the so-called informal sector became a catchall for work that departed from expectations of Euro-American social scientists and policymakers and that they often defined through frameworks of deficit.[19] This deficit-based definition holds across ideological divides: neoliberal economists see low productivity and human capital; labor scholars emphasize the lack of state protections like social security and workplace protections; while orthodox Marxists see a lack of class consciousness and historical agency due to structural location in economies of informal survivalism, to use the words of Mike Davis (2006).[20]

Drawing from deficit framings of informal work, reformers often imagine popular economies as problematic or even criminal while overlooking their contributions. Conceptualizing the work worlds of the poor as problematic justifies reform or eviction. With our dominant economic imaginary biased toward formalized, waged work, policymakers usually expect that formalization will resolve the problems and precarities of popular economies. Formalization policies strive to align economic activities with legal codes by either changing the law or correcting behaviors.[21] These reforms always work through economic imaginaries, often those with antipoor biases. Indeed, the antipoor epistemology has long shaped both policy and scholarship. Its framing is rooted in liberalism's foundational but false separation of economy and politics, which casts poverty and the popular economies of poor people as social or moral questions rather than political and economic ones, thereby disavowing how uneven development and racial capitalism *produce* poverty, albeit differently in different places.[22] The antipoor epistemology also enables *blanqueamiento* to gloss over elite illegalities. It has structured policies, from the English workhouses for the so-called dangerous classes during the rise of industrial capitalism, to today's campaigns evicting street vendors, to "sit-lie"

ordinances criminalizing sleeping and sitting in public places, to various reforms targeting the border economy.[23] I analyze these reforms after demonstrating the productivity and import of street vendors in Ciudad del Este.

Work Worlds of the Street

When I arrived in Ciudad del Este in 2011, Lina and Ingrid introduced me
to the work worlds of the street. Both were sisters of a family I lived with as a
Peace Corps volunteer in a rural town four hours from Ciudad del Este by car
but a world apart. The sleepy rhythms of this farming community in decline
sharply contrasted with the commercial bustle of the frontier town. The rural
town's biggest export was "young people," as a resident wryly noted while listing friends working far away in Madrid, New Jersey, or Buenos Aires. Sending
two brothers and three sisters to Ciudad del Este, as my host Ña Constanza
did, offered the benefits of remittances without years or decades between the
good-bye and the return. Lina and Ingrid generously welcomed me into their
worlds, helping me along my slow journey to understand something of the
practices and logics of street vending.

For many years, Lina and Ingrid sold blankets, tablecloths, and other lin-
ens from self-built stalls on the sidewalk before they were allocated *casillas*—
permanent vending stalls with roofs—in the first stage of the Pilot Plan. As
part of an upwardly mobile, albeit precarious, middle class, Lina and Ingrid both bought land, built homes, and financed private school educations
for their children through their earnings as street vendors. Their twelve-by-
twelve-foot stalls were larger than most, with room to display blankets and
tablecloths on tall shelves, make calls from a combined landline and fax machine, and eat lunch perched on a stool. They paid a small monthly tax for
use rights to their *casilla*, rented warehouse space to store goods, and financed
merchandise purchases with profits or loans. For many years, Lina financed
her own trips to Iquique to purchase merchandise until it became cheaper to
buy from middlemen and the blankets produced in the nearby Qin Yi factory.
The low overhead costs associated with informality help street vendors sell
goods cheaply.

Over years and even decades, vendors built long-term relationships with
their clients, as vendors call their regular customers. One afternoon, Lina chatted with one client as her employee deftly zipped five blankets into a clear
plastic bag so they looked like one. Then she asked, "Do you need a taxi?
Jonny can take you across. He's trustworthy." After the *sacoleiro* left, Lina explained to me, "Now there are these lists about how many of each item some-

one can bring across. This is in addition to the quota. They often ask us questions about this, about enforcement."[24] Street vendors' local knowledge helped Brazilian buyers navigate the complexities of border crossing, changing enforcement trends, and shifting regulatory regimes. Street vendors thus help to lower distribution costs.

Of course, some of the merchandise itself is cheap, sourced by Chinese merchants directly from ports in the Pearl River Delta and Xiamen through kinship networks. This connects Ciudad del Este with China's SEZs, which are expressions of "graduated sovereignty" whereby the state cedes authority in exceptional spaces encoded for economic freedom and governed by disciplinary logics of productivity and optimization, as Aihwa Ong (2006, 7) notes.[25] In the 1980s China's leader, Deng Xiaoping, initiated a strategy of economic reform, including export-led development expressly organized around SEZs. These zones now symbolize a development industry common sense that pursues economic growth via export-oriented economies. As the trade circuit incorporated merchandise produced in China's SEZs, it implicitly authorized this production model and the labor exploitation behind cheap prices. Indeed, it subsidized them, cheaply distributing the merchandise produced in SEZs.

Legal flexibilities also generated streams of revenue available for capture. As in undervaluation, street vendors reduced the cost of their merchandise by not charging sales tax. The 2001 campaign of the Coordinadora Paranaense de Ciudadanos en Acción (CPCA), discussed in chapter 3, sought to shape the terms of these flexibilities, seeking both legal enforcement and nonenforcement. In seeking this selective forbearance, the CPCA proposed decreased border controls and the nonenforcement of the quota for *sacoleiros*. Yet its proposal to recover sales jobs for Paraguayans from Brazilians without work authorization required enforcement. The mayor of Foz do Iguaçu—contradicting the official Brazilian line, which was critical of Paraguayan legal laxity—requested the flexibilization of labor law and the deferment of inspections.[26] Yet even as the date of inspections neared, Paraguayan migration officials reported that few Brazilian workers applied to regularize their status. Fearing the Paraguayan government would cave under pressure from Brazil, the CPCA threatened to blockade the bridge if enforcement stalled. But after Brazilian workers organized two weeks of intermittent bridge blockades, the CPCA and Paraguayan officials agreed to halt inspections.[27]

This border economy also circulates money throughout Paraguay. Internal migrants from across the country like Lina and Ingrid arrived in Ciudad del Este hoping to find a place for themselves in the street market, especially as industrial agriculture undermined the smallholder farm economy. Street vendors send earnings to family and businesses, to barrios surrounding Ciudad del Este, and beyond. My host family in the Peace Corps was relatively well-off, with a brisk hardware business. Only later did I understand that they owed their success to remittances from family working as vendors in Ciudad del Este who also provisioned the hardware store.

Although vending is profit driven, noneconomic logics of care and obligation also shape the work. Through 2013 Lina employed two relatives to stock and sell merchandise: "I really only need one employee now, but I can't fire them. Carlos has a family to feed, and my nephew needs money for his university fees. I'm going to hold on as long as I can."[28] When I returned in 2015, Lina only employed Carlos. These noneconomic logics of care and obligation—alongside her business-savvy strategies—informed Lina's decision to employ relatives during hard times. Examples of this solidarity ethic abound. Vendors watched each other's stalls, selling another's merchandise rather than their own. A taxi driver helped Celia, a hawker described in the last chapter, hide extra sweatshirts in his truck, skirting the oversight of *fiscales*. Vendors lend to each other and to family and friends, maintaining a constant web of debts, payments, and obligations. This web is also a safety net that can catch someone who falls on hard times, although the decline of the border trade, amid other pressures, has stretched open wide holes. This is a mix, then, of entrepreneurial rationalities with a "repertoire of communitarian practices," as Verónica Gago (2017, 20) also found in La Salada, a huge informal market outside of Buenos Aires.

From Lina I learned that vending is both toil and autonomy. Reflecting on her two decades of work in the street market, waking before four o'clock in the morning six days a week, Lina commented, "We live a very agitated life, we wake up very early, it is very self-sacrificing. . . . It is not easy; we earn money, but it is not easy."[29] At the same time, Lina valued the autonomy and flexibility of street vending. She decided when to close up for the day, usually early enough to pick up her son from school or tend to family. A college graduate, she also imported medicine for a local pharmacy to supplement her income.

The autonomy of street vending contrasts with the hierarchies and rigid work times of waged labor. In Ciudad del Este, even after steep declines in the border trade, vendors with prime spots like Lina's could earn considerably more than many waged workers.[30] A motorcycle taxi driver ran the numbers for me, comparing his potential salary as a licensed public schoolteacher with his earning potential from the street: "On a good day, I can earn 100,000 guaranies in one hour with my taxi. Teaching paid 16,300 guaranies an hour. It's an easy decision."[31] Of course, income from vending varies wildly across and within cities, marked by significant fluctuations over time. Yet the rhythm of daily pay is sometimes preferable to a monthly paycheck, a timescale that can misalign with the immediacy of economic needs: a health crisis, a friend in need, a debt payment, a school bill, or simply the need to put dinner on the table. Vendors value the freedom to determine work rhythms, maintain side hustles, and escape the disciplines of the boss.

Research on informality often focuses on its challenges, what the International Labour Organization (ILO) calls its "decent work deficits": low and unstable income, dangerous working conditions, and a lack of state benefits.[32] A middle-class acquaintance of mine went further: "[Vendors] are naturally selfish. They chose this life precisely because they don't want to work hard. They don't have to keep a schedule; they don't have a boss; they can just sit around and drink *tereré* and stay home when it rains."[33] Antipoor epistemologies like this denigrate desires to escape the strictures of waged work as an individual or cultural failing. In many respects, the ILO perspective and these middle-class values differ, but they both construct informal work as a problem and promote formalization as the solution. This perspective can overlook the politics behind vendors' practiced determination to wrest time and autonomy from the discipline of the wage.

Legalizing the Electronics Trade

The merchant bloc promoted tax breaks as a solution to contraband, tax evasion, and money laundering in the border economy. They argued that low taxes would make legalized reexportation competitive with smuggling. Pérez's chamber of commerce rallied other trade groups in its campaign to slash taxes on the reexportation of electronics, including video game consoles, smartphones, and computer parts. The USAID-funded nongovernmental organization Paraguay Vende (Paraguay Sells) joined the effort, publishing two key reports backing tax cuts as a means to regularize the border economy.[34] The reports proposed investing in export processing and a large duty-free zone, which had long been the dream of the merchant bloc.[35] The Finance Ministry opposed the plan because of worries about lost tax revenue. Adrien Ojeda, an economist who had worked at the Finance Ministry, commented, "In reality, the plan was the continuation of reexportation, with a few additional components."[36]

The reports conveyed urgency. The second opened with a long epigraph quoting Edgar Allan Poe's short story "The Pit and the Pendulum." In Poe's story, a prisoner awaits execution in a dark cell, watching a swinging blade descend from above. As it falls, the rate of downward movement increases, "a natural consequence" of the blade's widening arc.[37] This use of Poe's work imagined Ciudad del Este as the prisoner and competition from Brazil—represented as a natural force—as the pendulum. The lesson is straightforward: in a world ecology of cities, Ciudad del Este must compete or die.

I interviewed the report's author and director of Paraguay Vende, Reinaldo Penner, wanting to understand more about the social life of his reports and the intellectual backing they provided for tax breaks as a strategy of formalization. Penner arrived right on time, his drawn face and confident demeanor conveying something of his lineage: a family of German immigrants with large land-holdings in northern Paraguay. I could easily envision him navigating meetings with U.S. Embassy officials and staff from Chemonics, the development firm in charge of Paraguay Vende's USAID contract. He spoke enthusiastically about his organization's successes in adding value to agricultural commodity chains but was more reserved about his role on the border. "We didn't do anything, just those reports. We don't work on reexportation anymore," he said, seeming to distance himself from Ciudad del Este and its troubled reputation as we continued chatting about government backing for contraband as if we were talking about the weather.[38]

I also was curious about the report's optimistic vision that formalization could spur investment in export processing factories and transform *contrabandistas* into businessmen of a particular type, the kind recognized within USAID logics as entrepreneurs adding value in commodity chains. From his chamber of commerce, Pérez went a step further, conjuring visions of a city transformed—a high-tech manufacturing hub creating waged factory jobs and attracting foreign investment. Ojeda remarked that these promises of factory jobs were largely "good rhetoric," more marketing ploy than reality.[39]

Penner's reports strove valiantly to capture the dynamics of the border trade. He interviewed frontier merchants and grappled with the everyday practices that built the trade route and secured its continuity in spite of endemic rule-breaking. The report described undervaluation with something like admiration, calling it "a system of great simplicity and high commercial precision."[40] Penner resorted to scare quotes when describing illegalities in the border trade, suggesting a misalignment between the word and the signified, bracketing actors and their actions: customs authorities "tolerated" undervaluation, and frontier agents "established linkages," while other "agents" were "responsible" for the shipments.[41] The quotations signaled legal transgression or its enabling relationships, moments where the language of economics fails to capture the dynamics at stake, as the discipline still assumes a functional divide between legal and illegal. Indeed, the vocabulary of development economics was a straitjacket, restricting Penner's ability to grasp the practices of outlaw capital.

Penner also sought to differentiate real businessmen—those desiring formalization—from outlaw capitalists: "Those who really favor corruption are not the established businessmen [*empresarios*] but the anonymous importers, stealthy traffickers [*furtivos negociantes*] outside the industry or foreign businessmen and customs officials, obligated 'partners' of the merchants, and a whole host of public officials assigned to control tasks."[42] Bifurcating *empresarios* from *negociantes*, he sought to separate the legal from the illegal, the good apples from the bad, and then limit the true logics of capital with legalized practices.

Even as Penner expressed concern about stealthy traffickers, the report largely blamed the state as the source of corruption, condemning the "weak rule of law."[43] In this, it echoed skeptical Finance Ministry economists who also saw a weak state. Ojeda described tax breaks for reexportation as "institutional capture," while the important historian Milda Rivarola described the region as "transnationalized territory where the state cannot impose its power or sovereignty."[44] To be sure, customs officials sometimes pressured businesses to undervalue imports. In a planning meeting I attended, one businessman described a phone call from a customs official, who directed him to declare his perfume imports under a less valuable customs category, thereby reducing his tax bill and creating a revenue stream that could be redirected. The businessman reflected, "The state made us *contrabandistas*."[45] Yet both perspectives missed the co-constitution of state and economic power.

The reports also ignored the border trade as a key site of livelihood, tapping into the antipoor epistemology. Leaked embassy cables and the Paraguay Vende reports hardly acknowledge the presence of street vendors or *sacoleiros*. In a rare mention, U.S. Embassy staff in São Paulo worried that the uptick in Brazil's border controls could result in a "potentially explosive social reaction" as displaced vendors, *sacoleiros*, and others faced the decimation of their livelihoods.[46] In Paraguay, U.S. Embassy officials dismissed former president Fernando Lugo's concerns with redistribution, putting scare quotes around his "economic justice" platform, modest as it was. Workers in the popular economy figured only as problems to be mitigated, not as value-creating economic actors, not as political subjects with rights to the city, not even as stakeholders to be consulted.

Despite opposition from the Finance Ministry and economic think tanks like CADEP, the organization that hosted some of my research, the proposal to cut taxes on the reexportation of electronics passed in 2005. The new policy reduced the overall tax burden for reexported electronics to just over 4 percent. Under the new trade rules, Congress brought inside the law activities that were once called contraband. Ojeda commented that it responded to traders' "intentionality to avoid taxes on their activities."[47] Indeed, the plan allowed electronics traders to enclose the revenue that would have otherwise gone into state coffers. The Paraguay Vende reports played a key role in the formation of this plan, convincing midlevel state officials that tax breaks would lead to formalization and jobs.

Except for the tax breaks for the electronics trade, the vision outlined in the report did not materialize. At the time of our interview, twenty-three *maquilas* employed a few hundred workers, and there were no plans for the proposed duty-free zone. To explain the continuation of contraband and the failure of his vision, Penner described tough competition from Brazilian factories. Then, sounding resigned, he said, "The state either couldn't or didn't want to do what was necessary. The state needs to change the *old system* [*el sistema viejo*] of bringing in merchandise through the Guaraní Airport, they need to change the people working in customs, and they need the navy to actually do its job to combat contraband" (emphasis added).[48]

The Paraguay Vende reports reveal the resiliency of the pro-free-trade logic even in zones of doubling, where legal and illegal, entrepreneur and criminal, fold into each other. Paraguay Vende's policy proposals—and development common sense more generally—seek to separate *empresarios* from *negociantes*, or good, rule-following capitalists from corrupt profiteers. The report spins the group's proposals, equating formalization with tax breaks as objective, technical responses to market forces, which are represented as inevitable, as natural as the law of gravity pulling on Poe's pendulum. Identifying contraband and undervaluation as "the old system" locates it as a remnant of the past even as it persists in the present. At the same time, blaming the state for contraband exculpates the private sector and avoids the conclusion that outlaw capital is central to the logics and practices of capitalism. These are all core tendencies of the liberal epistemology of corruption that miss the constitutive power of outlaw capital.

Criminalizing *Sacoleiros*

"Paraguay is dead," Chinese shop owners in Ciudad del Este announced anxiously in 2015 to anthropologist Rosana Pinheiro-Machado (2017, 97). In her elegant ethnography of the China–Paraguay–Brazil trade route, Pinheiro-

Machado argues that the rise of a neoliberal intellectual property rights discourse criminalized *sacoleiros* and shuttered Chinese-owned stores in Ciudad del Este, causing the circuit's "collapse."[49] Her work (2017; see also 2008, 2010) and the research of Eric Cardin (2006, 2012, 2014) describe the work lives of *sacoleiros*, the criminalization of the *sacoleiro* circuit, and the dislocations that resulted. In 2002 the USTR designated Brazil as a priority country for facilitating intellectual property rights violations, expelling it from the General Agreement on Tariffs and Trade. Under this pressure, and with U.S. technical and financial support, Brazil unleashed an array of policies aimed at "criminalizing and dismantling a trade system."[50] It also invested in infrastructure. In 2006 a new customhouse on the Brazilian side of the bridge symbolized the renewed commitment to border enforcement.

With creative tactics, *sacoleiros* skirted the quota restrictions that limited the amount of tax-free merchandise they could bring into Brazil (see the appendix for details of the border trade's complex labor niches). Shops and vendors did not charge sales tax, reducing prices. *Sacoleiros* hired help to carry overquota purchases across the bridge. In addition, enforcement was lax, and Brazil customs agents deferred to unwritten codes and flexible enforcement. They often allowed *sacoleiros* to travel with three large bags of goods, regardless of whether their content was compliant with quota restrictions. During enforcement actions, agents confiscated some rather than all of a trader's merchandise. These forms of flexibility shrank in the post-9/11 security era.

As the Brazilian state cracked down on piracy and smuggling, *sacoleiros* and street vendors defended their ways of work in an increasingly hostile environment. *Sacoleiros* turned to backcountry roads to evade police raids. When the Brazilian government started ticketing bus companies for transporting *sacoleiros*, traders briefly caravanned in individual vehicles, collectively protesting confiscations and detentions on the International Friendship Bridge by stopping traffic and honking. They pressured authorities to respect old practices of "leeway in the form of tacit agreements," like pooled payments to Paraguayan police officers to overlook transgressions.[51]

Brazilian trade groups sought to enclose the value circulating through the *sacoleiro* circuit by constructing the popular trade route as a criminal problem. The move to criminalize *sacoleiros* was epistemological as well as material. Powerful actors sought to cast some people and practices as outside of what they saw as the real Brazilian economy. Brazilian policymakers grouped informal trade, counterfeiting, smuggling, and drug trafficking together and "ceased drawing moral or legal distinctions between the categories."[52] Imaginatively constructing an outside—a world of bad economic actors and activities—helps stabilize an understanding of what counts as inside, that is, what is considered to be the real, formal economy. Indeed, labeling an economic world as problematic is a necessary step toward instituting policies to transform or eradicate it. As frontline enforcers, border agents wielded considerable power to sort the licit from the illicit. As part of the reforms, the Brazilian government hired a new crop of border agents to replace those with connections to the *sacoleiro* circuit. In interviews with Pinheiro-Machado, the new agents called *sacoleiros* a "band of criminals" and "a gang of shifty, corrupt outcasts," imagining them as criminals engaged in an illegitimate economy rather than petty traders or fellow Brazilians.[53] This criminalization pushed many *sacoleiros* to abandon their work.

Brazilian trade groups joined in constructing contraband as a national problem and collapsing the *sacoleiro* circuit into the same category as smuggling. In the 2010s smuggling became a high-priority concern in Brazil. As Fernando Rabossi (2018) demonstrates, trade groups generated implausible estimates of contraband's precise negative impact on Brazil's economy—purported annual losses of 100 billion reais—despite untenable assumptions and glaring gaps in official knowledge of how these trade routes actually work. This self-serving research was largely uninterested in analyzing a social field and instead aimed at "[transforming] smuggling into a worrying problem that must worry everybody," a goal trade groups also promoted with publicity campaigns and stunt protests.[54]

Criminalizing *sacoleiros* reorganized the trade route. Risks increased, pushing more trade through clandestine contraband routes. Daily bridge crossings dropped sharply, down from forty thousand per day in the early 2000s to one-tenth of that fifteen years later.[55] As the flow of *sacoleiros* slowed, many of the city's six thousand shops folded.[56] *Sacoleiros* shouldered increased costs and risks. They could pay *laranjas* to carry some of their purchases across the bridge so that each complied with the Brazilian quota. They could turn to the network of clandestine ports and the labor of traffickers. Or they could take purchases across themselves and risk losing their merchandise at a checkpoint. Indeed, the Brazilian crackdown on the *sacoleiro* circuit increased uncertainty, insecurity, distrust, and danger. One Brazilian trafficker, known as a *batedora* (see the appendix), reflected on the consequences of working in a world now designated as criminal rather than informal: "In Paraguay, there aren't real friends. Because when you deal with illicit things, it's like you are drawn into the other side. To have a real friend requires having compassion; it's a feeling that *muamba* [contraband] doesn't have, that trafficking don't have either. Because you are illegal, it gets into you, there is a lot of falsehood. Scary stuff. There is no true friendship, there is only friendship of interest" (quoted in Cardin 2012, 217). Thus, the crackdown on the *sacoleiro* circuit intensified the underworld it was supposedly designed to address.

Street vendors in Porto Alegre, Brazil, responded to the crackdown through new discourses of authenticity, even as many still sold counterfeit goods. In the earlier days of the *sacoleiro* circuit, goods from Paraguay were associated with shoddy merchandise. Later, however, Paraguay became even more strongly associated with transgression, smuggling, or piracy, connotations that overlaid the association with cheap merchandise. A manager of a mall (*camelodromo*) built to formalize vendors said to Pinheiro-Machado, "We do not accept smuggling here: that low-quality merchandise from Paraguay."[57] However, shopkeepers did sell counterfeits, just routed through a warehouse at 25 de Marzo in São Paulo rather than through Paraguay. Even the production process cannot easily divide brand-name goods from knockoffs, as some Chinese factories produce generic, counterfeit, and brand-name goods in the same facilities.[58] Authentic merchandise, then, in the eyes of these Brazilian street vendors meant goods purchased from a formal establishment with a receipt rather than on the streets of Ciudad del Este. This perspective mixed components of the neoliberal antipiracy discourse, even as it conflicted with official copyright logics.[59] While dealmaking and rule-breaking were common throughout the trade circuit, this particular spatial imaginary located contraband as a Paraguayan problem. The solution, then, was to cut Paraguay out of the trade circuit, criminalizing some—but not all—traders and entrepreneurs who dealt with counterfeits.

Even Rosana Pinheiro-Machado reiterates this problematic spatial imaginary. Her ethnography, which I draw from here, richly details the experiences of Brazilian *sacoleiros*, street vendors in Porto Alegre, Chinese merchants working in Ciudad del Este, and factory owners in the Pearl River Delta as key actors in materializing the trade route. This expands our understanding of the agents of globalization. She also demonstrates that antipiracy efforts succeeded in reworking the trade circuit, even as these policies failed to address the fallout for those whose livelihood depended on that circuit. However, she overlooks Paraguayan state power, the agency of the merchant bloc, and the participation of Paraguayan street vendors in constructing this trade route. Ciudad del Este shows up only as a stage for a play directed and acted by non-Paraguayans. In part, these omissions are the necessary limitations of any ethnography, which must choose the direction of its limited attention, making what are always political choices to look in some places rather than others. Nonetheless, this telling reinscribes the spatial imaginary that excises Paraguayan agency from geographies of contemporary capitalism.

What dies, then, in the metaphor of Paraguay's death? Like Sosa's image of lungs, the metaphor of death invokes the centrality of both the trade route and the city in the life projects of *sacoleiros* and street vendors. Paraguay contributed particular forms of forbearance, flexible enforcement, and dealmaking that enabled street vendors and *sacoleiros* to participate in and construct the trade circuit. This was a resource that could be used by the many, not just the few. Thus, Paraguay represents not just transgression but also popular access to global commercial circuits. While they flourished, the popular economies embedded in these trade routes confronted hegemonic forms of exclusionary global urbanism, which have little place for the make-do economies of the urban majority. The death of Paraguay is the foreclosure of popular access to socially accepted forms of provisionality and dealmaking as antipiracy advocates push for policies that enclose the value circulated through the popular economy.

From the vantage of Chinese merchants in Ciudad del Este and Brazilian *sacoleiros* from Porto Alegre, these trade circuits collapsed. Yet until the devastations of the coronavirus pandemic, Paraguayan street vendors continued to ply their wares. Some segments of the merchant bloc, like electronics importer-exporters, adapted by successfully changing legal codes to protect their profits. Counterfeits are still sold in street markets across Latin America. Some Chinese distributors, once connected through Ciudad del Este, now ship directly to warehouses in São Paulo. And contraband trails have fractured. Trade across the northern, less patrolled Paraguayan border town of Pedro Juan Caballero picked up, while large-scale *contrabandistas* turned to the vast network of clandestine ports to smuggle goods across the river. Thus, rather than collapse, more diffuse and riskier trade networks today connect Latin American consumers with cheap goods from China: name brand, generic, and counterfeit.

Formalizing *Sacoleiros*

As Brazil tightened border controls, policymakers also pursued other strategies to stem the flow of contraband across the Paraguay-Brazil border. One project called Régimen de Tributo Unificado (RTU, Unified Tax Regime) sought to formalize the *sacoleiro* circuit.[60] Brazilian policymakers also strategized to absorb the *sacoleiro* circuit into Brazil, a national enclosure project.

In 2013 the legislature initiated plans to set up duty-free shops in any of Brazil's thirty-two border towns.[61] The free zone legislation promised to bring investments, jobs, and commercial flows to Brazilian border cities. The legislation extended the duty-free import quota of U.S.$300 to the duty-free shops inside Brazil while reducing the amount to U.S.$150 that *sacoleiros* and shopping tourists could bring into the country tax free. Thus, the plan expressly disincentivized Brazilians from crossing borders to make purchases as part of a move to nationalize commodity circuits.

The RTU formalization plan offered registered *sacoleiros* lower taxes on a restricted list of consumer goods purchased from registered shops and tracked through an electronic system. The plan allowed individual petty traders to import up to U.S.$5,000 per year. The RTU would "convert *sacoleiros* into legal buyers," as one journalist commented, or into "minientrepreneurs," in the language of one of the plan's architects.[62] Eventually, Brazil and Paraguay agreed on a unified tax rate of 25 percent, well below Brazil's combined rate across several taxes of about 60–70 percent for goods not on special lists.[63] RTU proponents argued that lowering taxes would make legalized trade competitive with smuggling and therefore increase tax revenue. This is the same logic behind the tax breaks for the reexportation of electronics. However, when formalizing the popular economy, policymakers offered much smaller tax cuts.

The program's director described RTU as a success, proudly asking if I would like a picture of the first receipt of RTU purchases framed on his wall.[64] He described RTU as an innovative model of frontier commerce that would differentiate between two flows of goods crossing the border: merchandise purchased by tourists for personal consumption (subject to the fluctuating Brazilian quota of U.S.$150–$300) and the commercial *sacoleiro* circuit. Brazilians, he explained, "dress up like tourists" but then resell the goods they purchase, pretending to belong to one circuit when in fact they belong to the other. "The goal is to make honest [*sincerar*] their activities and formalize the city," the director continued. The program's innovation was therefore to officially acknowledge and attempt to regulate *sacoleiros* as petty traders.

The director described the plan as a win-win for Paraguayan businesses and Brazilian *sacoleiros*. Generating buy-in required many meetings with different stakeholders. However, Paraguayan street vendors were not invited to participate. Indeed, the plan excluded vendors from the formalized *sacoleiro* circuit, as only purchases with registered businesses could qualify for the special tax exemptions. For the director, this exclusion did not even merit comment, a form of blindness that does not recognize the economic value and lifeworlds of street vendors. However, the plan included Paraguayan taxi drivers as necessary for the distribution circuit. When I asked about the plan's implementation challenges, the director said quickly, "The taxi drivers." He went on, "They are people who do not have a high level of culture; I mean with this low, this low, hmm.... They are not taken to formalization, and they must formalize themselves. They must issue receipts, pay their taxes, and train themselves, because they need to use the computer system. They must give conformity to transport. This is just pressing a button, but there was a certain resistance among drivers to register in the computer system." He emphasized that the RTU operators' manual required two forms of translation for drivers: from Portuguese into Spanish and then into the vernacular forms of taxi drivers. The director explained that training would correct these deficiencies. However, formalization also directly raised costs. In 2013 the price of RTU-registered taxi rides was fixed at a much higher price than the negotiated rates offered by ordinary taxi drivers, potentially disincentivizing ridership.[65] Likely because of these high fixed prices, few taxi drivers registered, just as they also resisted bureaucratic hassles and state surveillance. Through a deficit framing, the RTU treated taxi drivers as objects of reform, aiming to shape them into compliant transportation entrepreneurs who voluntarily make themselves visible and legible to government officials. The director interpreted their resistance to border surveillance as a cultural flaw. Yet there was a host of reasons why taxi drivers rejected the RTU, including a rather entrepreneurial cost calculus.

The RTU also generated considerable resistance from Brazilian businesses and U.S. foreign policymakers. A leaked cable from the U.S. Embassy in Brasília, titled "Calling All Smugglers," wrote derisively of the plan, describing the "threat from across the border" as "costly to U.S. industry" while laying out a strategy to quash the bill. In the hearing, the representative of the Brazilian Institute for Defense of Competitiveness (Instituto Brasileiro de Defesa da Competitividade, IBDC) mobilized the global antipiracy discourse. This was reported by U.S. Embassy officials: "It may have been Edson Vismona of IBDC who made the point that resonated most with the Senators. He called the tariff reduction a subsidy to Chinese and Taiwanese manufacturers of pirated goods and showed a Brazilian newspaper ad for submarket priced products with the website address www.chinadirect.com."[66] Thus, even as the plan responded to new security logics—electronically monitoring the movement of goods and people across the border—the United States sought to sink the proposal. In contrast, USAID-funded studies backed the legalization of the electronics import-export business as a pragmatic strategy to outcompete the *contrabandistas*. Yet the IBDC, with US Embassy backing, called for a more punitive approach to street vendors and *sacoleiros*.

While the tax official described RTU as a successful example of formalization, many in Ciudad del Este expressed deep disappointment. While Paraguayan negotiators had pressured Brazil to drop the unified tax rate from 50
to 25 percent, it was still higher than the estimated 18–22 percent that would
make the transaction costs of smuggling comparable to regularized sales.[67] By
2013 only thirty-three businesses had registered, and by 2019 only thirty-seven.
The volume of commerce registered with RTU was also low; by 2018 some
commentators proclaimed the "end of the *sacoleiro* era" (Alvino da Silva 2018,
175).

The RTU sought to maintain Ciudad del Este's role in the trade route while
incentivizing commodity flows through formalized businesses, *sacoleiros*, and
drivers. The plan excluded vendors, attempting to redirect trade from the
street economy into registered shops. Yet the profit potentials available in Ciudad del Este rely on how it has been strategically produced as a gray space
of legal flexibilities. Paradoxically, the plan struggled because the logics of formalization undermine the very economic capacities that made this trade network possible: provisionality, negotiability, flexibility, and low costs. Formalization sought to eliminate the very practices that made the city work.

Celebrating Factories

The Maquila Regime (Régimen de Maquila) is a program of tax breaks and
special import-export exceptions designed to attract foreign investment and
spur export-oriented development. Like SEZs, *maquilas* are regimes of neoliberal exception oriented around market logics. Unlike the tax exemptions for
the reexportation of electronics, in theory *maquilas* add value and spur production. The Qin Yi factory is the poster child of the Maquila Regime. Established in 2008 with an investment of U.S.$7.7 million, the factory won a na-
tional award and garnered favorable press coverage.[68] The owners were once
involved in the reexportation business. Thus, for some, the Qin Yi factory represented the much-sought-after transition from economies of commerce to
production. Qin Yi's popular Kamamia brand blankets sold well to Brazilian
buyers and could be purchased from street vendors throughout the market.
Their printed fabric was made in family factories in mainland China and then
shipped to Ciudad del Este, where 246 Paraguayan workers hemmed the edges
in the Qin Yi factory. By using Paraguayan workers for this final production
phase, Qin Yi could add a "Made in Paraguay" tag, earning significant tax
breaks and advantages.

The "Made in Paraguay" tag represented a key development common sense.

Waged factory jobs symbolized the formal sector, a desirable rung on an imagined ladder of economic development. Factory jobs were therefore understood as the solution to the problem of informal work. This is why USAID, via its Threshold Project, backed the Maquila Regime. The U.S. Embassy praised Qin Yi, calling it an exemplar of "economic formalization" that "increased the ease of doing business."[69] Embassy officials wagered that the Maquila Regime would generate four thousand factory jobs in the frontier region and lauded Qin Yi's modest contribution of over two hundred jobs as a success.

What does the "Made in Paraguay" tag emulate here? Formalization means importing the Chinese factory production model, often with direct supply-chain links to Chinese factories in SEZs producing the nearly finished products, like Qin Yi's printed bolts of fabric. In China, hundreds of millions of peasants migrated for factory jobs, while rapid industrialization via low-wage labor catapulted China into position as a major economic player. In China, as in Paraguay, an alliance of business elites and state officials backs this production model as the pathway toward national economic growth. Chinese state officials justify harsh factory conditions as a necessary stage of sacrifice along the road toward national development, dismissing workers' rights with a discourse of nationalism and exceptionalism. In addition, the myth of what Melissa Wright (2006) calls the "disposable third world woman" and paternalist shop-floor management techniques discursively decouple workers from the value they produce. The scale of transformation pushed by Paraguay's Maquila Regime is orders of magnitude smaller. Yet the discourse of formalization by factory is powerful in both places. The Paraguayan Maquila Regime aims to replicate the production model and successfully invoke the developmentalist dream of formalization, even as a few hundred waged jobs and thirty-seven factories cannot transform the political economy of production.

Paradoxically, the Qin Yi model invokes formalization even as the factory utilized the city's cheap distribution network to move its merchandise to consumers across the Southern Cone. Initially, vendors profited from selling Qin Yi products, earning one to three dollars per blanket.[70] This profit potential attracted many vendors, and soon Kamamia blankets were everywhere in the street market. But the relationships between street vendors and Qin Yi quickly soured. Qin Yi raised prices, and profit margins dropped to thirty cents per blanket. Even worse for street vendors, Qin Yi began selling directly to *sacoleiros*, cutting out vendors from the trade circuit. This echoed the RTU formalization project, as empowered actors ignored how transformations impacted the livelihoods of street vendors.

In 2013 street vendors began organizing against Qin Yi. After the meeting that opened this chapter, vendors filed an official complaint, a *denuncia*, arguing that Qin Yi had broken *maquila* regulations by selling more than 10 percent of its blankets locally. The *maquila* tax breaks, after all, were designed to promote export-oriented production. How could so many blankets be for sale locally? A local politician and lawyer backed the vendors' cause, asserting that Qin Yi is "up to something fishy [*ojapo hikaui imacanada*]" and proposing a twin plan of protest and legal action.[71] The regional Ministry of Industry and Commerce representative, who received the *denuncia* in person, assured the vendors: "It's unacceptable that outsiders come to our country and hurt those that are working for their daily bread. I am going to personally deliver this letter to headquarters."[72]

National Ministry of Industry and Commerce regulators were less sympathetic to the street vendors' cause, insisting that Qin Yi only received tax benefits for the portion of its product designated for export and used an idle capacity designation to produce for the national market. Curious about this exception, I joined ministry regulators on their oversight visit to Qin Yi. The visit was cordial, a sharp contrast from the adversarial and disrespectful tone of *fiscales* overseeing street vendors. The regulators joked and chatted as they helped a young secretary fill out a series of forms with the correct responses. "We are here to collaborate with these businesses," a state official is quoted as saying in a 2011 publication of the Ministry of Industry and Commerce.[73] I saw no evidence of the detailed accounting required to differentiate the use of machines and materials for export from their use for sale within Paraguay via the idle capacity designation. Yet the regulators insisted that Qin Yi was in compliance. To me, the visit seemed like a rubber stamp, a clear example of how the regulatory gaze turned toward elite illegalities is fundamentally different from the gaze turned toward street informalities.

Qin Yi also transformed distribution systems within the street market to get its blankets to market. Each morning before daybreak, a small army of Qin Yi employees distributed blankets to vendors on credit. In the midafternoon, as the bustle of commerce settled, these employees made their rounds again to collect payment. Sosa's wife commented, "It's tough, with so many people selling Kamamia. By the end of the day many vendors have to give away their merchandise just to be able to pay off their debt to Qin Yi."[74] Like Sosa's comment at the meeting that opened this chapter ("Right now, the system does not work because we end up in debt to the Chinese. We have to finance on a day-to-day basis"), she lamented street vendors' indebtedness to Qin Yi and the cycles of loan repayment, now compressed into a single day. While vendors had traditionally financed their merchandise on credit, the old arrangement had more room for delays and favors than the unforgiving time-credit rhythms of Qin Yi.[75]

Although factories look legal and invoke the formalized city, the Qin Yi factory relied on the *sacoleiro* circuit to move merchandise to end consumers. The symbolic power of the factory and the desire for all it represents help Qin Yi to stand in for the formalized city. Regardless of Qin Yi's level of compliance with Maquila Regime rules, vendors' visceral sense that Qin Yi benefited while they suffered is important. It underscores how the antipoor epistemology influences how legal codes are written, as well as how they are enforced. It also reveals how this system benefits factory work over street livelihood without much regard for the system's casualties.

Conclusion

Ciudad del Este was produced as a zone of useful transgression. Forms of provisionality, forbearance, and flexibility produced profit potentials in both elite and street economies. Vendors and *sacoleiros* built Ciudad del Este's city center as an urban commons that cheaply moves commodities through globalized space, connecting producers to consumers. Vendors siphon money from the border trade to poor barrios as they buy dish soap from a corner store or send cash back to family members in the countryside.

The impacts of reform efforts were uneven. As conditions changed, everyone sought to defend their ways of work and profit-making. The popular elements of the China–Paraguay–Brazil trade route were most vulnerable to disarticulation, criminalization, and enclosure. Indeed, the reforms targeting the *sacoleiro* circuit sought to regulate away the flexibilities and forms of dealmaking that made the trade route work. Disarticulating the popular elements of this trade network does not eliminate piracy or rule-breaking. Indeed, criminalizing the *sacoleiro* circuit across the bridge increases smuggling across the river, intensifying risk rather than reducing illegality.

While workers in the *sacoleiro* circuit faced criminalization or ill-conceived formalization, some elements of the elite trade network managed to protect their extralegal economies. Electronics traders managed to rewrite trade rules to reduce their tax bills, while networks of *blindaje* protected the president's contraband cigarettes, as discussed in chapter 2. Meanwhile, the export processing factory, with its promise of waged work, epitomizes the image of the formal city. Export processing will likely remain a token industry, a means to claim movement toward formalization and job creation without addressing the dislocations wrought through the slow reworking of the trade circuit. Yet these factories can stand in for progress without significant transformations in urban political economy while obscuring questions about whose livelihoods are lost in the transition.

The work of reform is both material and symbolic. While officials in Paraguay and Brazil largely tolerated the *sacoleiro* circuit for decades, in the 2000s the discursive environment shifted. The global discourse on piracy, followed by antismuggling campaigns sponsored by Brazilian trade groups, engaged in this epistemic work, attempting to stabilize boundaries between economies understood as legitimate versus illegitimate. Imaginatively claiming the boundaries of legitimate economic practice constructs some worlds of work as *outside*, a step toward formalization, criminalization, or enclosure. Antipiracy and antismuggling advocates laud these transformations as successful, but these interpretations require ignoring the lived impacts of these transformations while also devaluing the lives and livelihoods of displaced *sacoleiros* and street vendors. Normalizing callousness toward these inequalities is a core function of the antipoor epistemology at the center of global capitalism.

CONCLUSION

The politics of outlaw capital have taken a troubling new turn as rising authoritarian populisms enfold anticorruption activism as their own. Take, for instance, the historic defeat of the Colorado Party by the young outsider Miguel Prieto in Ciudad del Este's 2019 mayoral elections.[1] While the power of the Zacarías coalition had felt unassailable for so long, Prieto's win revealed its fallibility: for the first time in sixty-two years, residents in Ciudad del Este would not be governed by a mayor from the Colorado Party. This repudiation of strongman politics reverberated across the region, with the Colorado Party losing mayoralties in the state's four biggest cities.[2] Prieto's election by unprecedented margins signaled a deep exhaustion with the political class and widespread support for a new kind of urban politics, dynamics occurring across the Americas.[3] But the currents that sustained Clan Zacarías did not disappear with its electoral defeat. Furthermore, the city's core contradiction—its simultaneous reliance on the extralegal border economy and its antipoor disavowal of the same—remains.

Indeed, this moment distills the challenges of anticorruption politics, which risk rearranging rather than transforming social orders predicated on deep inequalities. Prieto ran as an anticorruption outsider promising change, yet he may only offer a change in political style that does not challenge the global urbanist project of reform without redistribution. This bind is evident in the municipal priority of formalization. Early on, the municipality rolled out a new vendors' census, offering vendors ten-year, renewable contracts. Ten-year contracts protect vendors from the rhythms of election-driven vote-bank politics and represent a significant departure from the McLeod municipality's push for one-year contracts. Yet while Prieto's municipality is more rule oriented, evictions persist. For instance, in aiming to "order" a central market, a new batch of more respectful *fiscales* followed official rules, notified vendors before eviction, and proposed relocating displaced vendors, thereby departing from prior practices of governing through uncertainty. Yet officials called the eviction an operation to clear (*despejar*) the plaza, using revanchist military language that resonates with the antipoor epistemology.[4] Likewise, in a dispute with an unauthorized motorcycle taxi driver, Prieto used an antipoor slur commonly used to disparage the occupations of landless peasants: "Here we have a lot of *these kinds of people*, who justify [their occupations] with their economic situation, just like with the invaders [*invasores*]."[5] Dismissing the long histories that produce both rural and urban poverty with his comment "these kinds of people," Prieto instead blamed an "underclass," a theory that suggests that the poor are responsible for their own destitution.[6] Likewise, Prieto hopes to transform Ciudad del Este into a tourist destination, the kind of place imagined as the antidote to the informal trade city. Yet the gray spaces and economic practices that planners aim to banish with the tourism plan are precisely what make the city work. At the same time, attracting casinos, shopping malls, and themed restaurants entails tax breaks and concessions, deals not usually called corruption, even though they are often secured through exceptions, rule bending, and revenue streams that circumvent the public benefit.

Furthermore, elite illegalities stubbornly resist attempts at reform or accountability. Javier Zacarías and Sandra McLeod, for example, embody this trend, as their lawyers have stymied all legal challenges against them with such success that Zacarías remains a senator and McLeod plans to run for reelection in 2023. Indeed, across the continent, the politics of anticorruption muddies vociferous statements about the sanctity of the rule of law with actions oriented toward gaining the political power to *apply* the standards and, as importantly, to activate exceptions to them. In Ciudad del Este, Prieto's opposition has filed more than twenty *denuncias* (legal complaints) against him, complaints that mix legitimate grievance with political theater and reveal the extent to which corruption accusations can be weaponized against political opponents.[7] Furthermore, the politics of anticorruption reasserts the law as the source of redress even as it sidelines debates about the social distribution of wealth. In its most problematic form, anticorruption detaches completely from meaningful projects aimed at solving social problems.

In this conclusion, I explore contemporary configurations of outlaw capital. After summarizing the book's main arguments in the next section, I engage a "comparative gesture" to outline how the ideas laid out in this book can be useful in other contexts.[8] The following section looks at the submerged racism of anticorruption campaigns, exploring how it has fueled rising authoritarian populism in Brazil, dynamics also relevant in places like India and the United States.[9] In order to contest the resolution of outlaw capital's contradictions through racism, I draw inspiration from Brazilian Black feminists Marielle Franco, Joice Berth, and Djamila Ribeiro to offer alternative frameworks through which to think and act. The final section asks how we can move toward more just and humane cities, given the duplicitous impact of many reform efforts that risk reproducing the very violences they aim to overcome.

The Economy of Illegalities

This book has argued that illegalities are a terrain of race-class conflict constitutive of urban development. In his writing on the birth of prisons, Foucault (1995, 87) described how an "economy of illegalities" emerged alongside the transition to capitalism as states developed new techniques to differentially administer, punish, or allow illegalities.[10] The careful management of illegalities hinged on separating the *illegality of property* (crimes like theft, trespass, and poaching or wood gathering on landed estates) from the *illegalities of rights* (the power to transgress the law without punishment).[11] These two domains of illegality are related via a "class opposition" in which the illegality of property is largely the domain of the poor, while "the bourgeoisie . . . reserve[s] to itself the illegality of rights: the possibility of getting round its own regulations and its own laws, of ensuring for itself an immense sector of economic circulation by a skillful manipulation of gaps in the law."[12] Indeed, the state apparatus of law, punishment, discipline, and surveillance emerged as attempts to contain the illegalities of property of the working class. Affiliated regimes of knowledge constructed delinquency as a stand-in for all crime, thereby hiding away the vast field of profitable illegalities claimed by elites.

This class opposition holds today, even in the face of vast transformations in forms of social life in the intervening centuries. What is at stake is new articulations of these old dynamics, including their space-making powers. Indeed, outlaw capital arises out of a contemporary economy of illegalities that administers street and elite illegalities quite differently. Outlaw capital is thus a mode of accumulation that negotiates profits and distributes rents from legal transgression. Throughout this book, I have argued that it is constitutive of contemporary landscapes of capitalism, indeed, that it is a form of capital. This is not to suggest a new binary differentiating transgressive from clean capital but rather to emphasize the transformations of capital through different forms as it circulates through different moments in economic circuits. The outlaw moment along circuits of capital is like a swirling eddy in a swift river where water briefly escapes the inexorable currents. While the water in this eddy is momentarily freed from the pull to the sea, it will eventually return to the flow. Likewise, outlaw capital is temporarily unbound from the core expansionary logic, the pull to self-expand, but this pause along global capital circuits does not mean it is outside the system. Indeed, the practices of outlaw capital may be on the rise as profit-making opportunities in the real economy contract amid a global manufacturing glut, thus increasing the temptation to invest in transgression, speculation, and fantasy markets like bitcoin. Of course, the transgressive is capital's old friend, foundational to and constitutive of capitalism through enclosures and dispossessions that first transgress and only afterward generate the legal justifications for the thefts.[13] Outlaw capital's profitable transgressions echo this foundational logic, showing us, if we care to look, that nothing is sacred within the actually existing social complex of capitalism, not even its own laws and codes, beyond its inexorable, acquisitive drive for self-expansion.

The transgressive nature of outlaw capital's profitability means that its advocates must seek ways to hide and obscure it, what I have called "obscuration," to emphasize that the social relations that constitute this hiding are themselves processes. This furtive quality of outlaw capital makes it hard to study and amenable to all sorts of wild tales as to its origin, nature, and consequences. One of these misapprehensions, I have argued, is the tendency to label outlaw capital as corruption, as an aberrant practice of a few bad apples that can be legislated away with the right kinds of policies and oversight practices. This view sees corruption as outside or as a distortion of the ordinary workings of capitalism, whereas I have argued instead that it is decisively inside, part and parcel of our capitalist conjuncture. Even anticapitalist thinkers like Marxist geographers, progressive urbanists, and radical planners tend to elide outlaw economies, reserving their essential critiques of the core tenets of mainstream economic thinking for the legalized economy. This leaves the vast powers of outlaw capital largely unexamined, including its affiliation with the rise of authoritarian populisms across the Americas.

Another misapprehension obscures the spatial dynamics that interlink celebrated spaces of commerce with places zoned for transgression. Just as uneven development produced places like Shenzhen, China, as a regime of low-wage labor and state policies built Silicon Valley as a technology hub, Ciudad del Este was produced, through considerable struggle, as a gray zone of profitable legal trespass. Indeed, far from being a space of state absence, Ciudad del Este became a site where Paraguayan state practice promoted contraband as a path to development with state policies to create arbitrage opportunities, promote reexportation, and build the urban infrastructures of a nodal city and zone of transgression useful to global capital. Global urbanists celebrate East Asian SEZs as model sites of economic innovation and productivity but overlook how the products produced there circulate along the China–Paraguay–Brazil trade route. Indeed, the gray spaces and practices enabled by Ciudad del Este's entrepreneurs—from street vendors to authorized Sony dealers to *contrabandistas*—subsidize the profitability of the export-oriented model by providing cheap transit for producers to reach the booming markets of Brazilian and South American consumers.

Thus, at every scale, extralegal networks are integral, not anathema, to so-called formal systems of power and profit. This book demonstrates how the emergence, boom, consolidation, and transformation of Ciudad del Este—an entire city—shaped and, in turn, was shaped by these global networks. But outlaw capital is not restricted to the "unruly" Global South. Entrepôt cities and transborder regions are historically recurrent forms produced by and productive of gray spatioeconomic practices, concentrating flows of goods and sibling streams of capital. The stigmatized entrepôt city or "lawless" border region is materially connected to cities and spaces widely interpreted as clean, from banks in Bern, Switzerland, hiding ill-gotten wealth to Russian oligarchs investing in property in Londongrad to any U.S. city benefiting from migrant labor passing through the U.S. southern border. These gray spaces also concentrate the anxieties of the administrators of global capitalism who promote the free movement of goods as necessary for globalization while criminalizing the free movement of people.[14]

Within Ciudad del Este, the global urbanist tendency to read legal compliance off spatial form expresses the antipoor epistemology, celebrating elite spaces while condemning those of the poor. The spatial and economic reforms targeting the border economy in the 2000s and 2010s—shaped by a neoliberal antipiracy milieu and U.S.-backed Islamophobia—had deep, class-based impacts. The rule-breaking practices of street vendors were criminalized while some practices of politically connected elites were protected. But more than a simple and familiar tale of the race-class biases of law, the reforms aimed at banishing corruption and informality have undermined the conditions of possibility for the gray in the border trade, especially in targeting the illegalities of rights in the *sacoleiro* circuit by pushing them more and more into the black. Paradoxically, this punitive response to popular economies intensifies illegalities and therefore risks rather than banishing them. White here is both the invisible referent and a racialized code, white as authorized, legalized, and desirable.

Indeed, racism helps hide outlaw capital. The Paraguayan vernacular term *blanqueamiento* describes the relational networks that launder licit the widespread profitable rule-breaking of the politically connected. This local grammar of critique names elite illegalities as common practices and as forms that are constitutive of state power. But even further, criminality and innocence are deeply racialized registers deployed to assess the perceived legitimacy of economic practices, spaces, and people. I argue that whiteness—more than merely an identity or form of privilege—is a mode of obscuration that hides outlaw capital. On one level, whiteness is a resource in the dramas of performing legitimacy available to empowered actors as they mobilize cultural and social capital and embody ways of being that signal their race-class status. More than simple compliance with law, assessments of legitimate spatioeconomic practice hinge on proximity to ontologies of whiteness. On another level, whiteness is a form of property and a possessive investment, following here Cheryl Harris and George Lipsitz, in that it enables access to wealth that is imagined to be self-generated and therefore deserved rather than the result of social position in relational white supremacist landscapes that expose some to toil and death so that others may live and thrive. Furthermore, this entitled sense of righteous possession is undeterred by transgression, as elites have long felt justified in their illegalities of rights. This framing challenges the durable capitalist mythos of innovative job creators generating wealth by demonstrating the power of this class of capitalists who simply loot. Their social sanction to do so cannot be pulled apart from racialized imaginaries of criminality and innocence alongside related mappings of the spaces of progress and places of problems or dangers.

In Latin American cities, elite and street illegalities are managed quite differently. Globally, uneven development concentrates survival economies in the informal cities of the Global South, where vast worlds of livelihood-based, rule-breaking work remain managed through complex mixtures of forbearance, toleration, reforms, and evictions. Notably, across Latin America, workers in popular economies have retained a considerable measure of their illegalities of rights, successfully defending their work worlds from inscription as delinquency, the tendency in the Global North.[15] The criminalization of the *sacoleiro* circuit is but one front in an ongoing battle between revanchist growth coalitions seeking to inscribe popular economies as delinquency and workers fighting back with diverse claims and strategies. Within Latin American cities, the dynamics of capitalist urban development spatially contain street illegalities in popular markets and in disinvested, peripheral neighborhoods. Here, planners join with the police, the former constructing a field of poverty knowledge that tends to disempower informal workers by constructing them as victims of circumstance or objects of reform while the latter fabricates and protects a callous social order of racialized inequality. Euro-American cities, for their part, have more successfully inscribed popular economies within the framework of the illegalities of property, even as the dynamics of informalization are intensifying throughout the Global North. Let us not forget that New York City police officers murdered Eric Garner as they harassed him for selling loosie cigarettes, a livelihood strategy of the racialized poor. These class struggles over the economy of illegalities will likely intensify as global capitalist urbanization pushes more people into rule-breaking popular economies.

Alongside these processes, the Panama and Pandora Papers—massive leaks of the financial and legal records of the superrich—detail their illegalities of rights as they hoard some $11 trillion in tax-avoiding wealth, all while creating a giant slush fund available for lobbying and public relations campaigns aimed at shaping the terrain of law, policy, and public discourse about the contours of legitimate economic activity.[16] Their efforts have remade policy landscapes and physical spaces, for instance, turning South Dakota into the new Cayman Islands, where trusts shelter U.S.$360 billion not just from taxes but also from the claims of creditors or lawsuits seeking redress for potential wrongdoing.[17] With thirty-five current and former heads of state and more than four hundred elected officials listed in the Pandora Papers, journalists are quick to note that the people with the power to regulate these forms of outlaw capital are the very people benefiting from them. Further complicating matters, the mobility of money and competition between individual jurisdictions for ever more laxity and secrecy create a perverse specialization that materializes into a seemingly intractable geography of the illicit. When governments push through even modest reforms, like a new registry in the Bahamas requiring that some trusts list ownership, the superrich simply move their wealth elsewhere. Most reporting remains people centered and legalistic, framing the problem as weak regulations and a lack of alignment between individual actions and extant legal codes. This perspective assumes that policy change is a sufficient solution, even as it acknowledges that this as a Sisyphean task. Against this tenacious common sense, so many of these practices dismissed as aberrations are actually at the very core of globalization. Seeing from Ciudad del Este helps us analyze the various powers of transgressive forms of profit-making as part of the multiple historical agencies of capitalism.

The Unbearable Whiteness of Anticorruption

As pink tide projects faltered over the past decade, the politics of anticorruption have become central to the rise of the Right. The 2008 global economic crisis and falling commodity prices undermined the pink tide neodevelopmentalist-growth-with-redistribution model. Across the region, governments faced pressure from international capital markets to enact austerity, exposing their constituencies to intensifying hardship. As people experienced downward social mobility after a period of uplift and hope, antiestablishment sentiments turned against incumbent pink tide governments. While the pink tide could claim twelve Left or center-Left governments in 2011, including Paraguay, that number had fallen to six by 2019, including major losses in Brazil, Chile, and Ecuador.[18] At the same time, the urban middle classes across the continent organized mass protests condemning corruption, in Guatemala wearing white and gathering as "the indignant ones" and in Brazil wearing the yellow and green of the flag of South America's largest country. The protests channeled pent-up frustration at the flagrant self-enrichments of political elites. In Brazil they also expressed revanchist resentments among middle classes and elites angry at prosocial policies that threatened entrenched social hierarchies through projects benefiting poor, working-class, Black and brown Brazilians. Scandal after scandal broke, from a Federation Internationale de Football Association (FIFA) bribery ring to La Linea, a secret phone line in Guatemala used to negotiate reduced customs taxes that resulted in lost tax revenue equal to an astonishing 1.8 percent of the country's GDP.[19] In places like Brazil, authoritarian populism articulated with these anticorruption social movements, mobilizing a forceful reaction against Left projects of redistribution and social uplift.

Thinking with outlaw capital, *blanqueamiento* and the antipoor epistemology can help us analyze the dangers of anticorruption, including its slippery doubleness, which launders licit elite illegalities of rights and unleashes punitivism toward the racialized poor. These dynamics were on display in the hemisphere's largest corruption scandal, Brazil's Operação Lava Jato (Operation Car Wash). This anticorruption crusade toppled the Partido dos Trabalhadores (PT, the Workers' Party)—an exemplar pink tide government—and helped pave the way for the terrifying rise of the "Trump of the Tropics,"

Jair Bolsonaro. Lava Jato reveals how anticorruption articulates racialized notions of economic legitimacy, sister dynamics to the antipoor epistemology and *blanqueamiento* that shaped Ciudad del Este. By locating corruption as the central social problem, Lava Jato decentered racialized inequality. Furthermore, anticorruption depoliticizes. By imagining the law as above politics and positing it as the source of redress, Lava Jato undermined democratic mass politics and depoliticized collective struggles over redistributing the social surplus.

Lava Jato also reveals the extent to which deals, bribes, and schemes are ordinary practices of state power, decisively inside the political economy of late capitalism, a key lesson from Ciudad del Este. The scandal started when agents uncovered a massive overinvoicing scheme on contracts with the state-owned oil company, Petrobras, a mirror image of the underinvoicing so profitable in Ciudad del Este's border trade. The scheme involved more than U.S.$5 billion in bribes.[20] By July 2019 prosecutors had logged nine hundred indictments and two hundred convictions, including within Brazil's hitherto untouchable political elite.[21] The scandal went continental, and the Brazilian construction company Odebrecht eventually admitted to offering another U.S.$788 million in bribes and campaign contributions in eleven countries. Just as anticorruption reforms transformed the China–Paraguay–Brazil trade route, anticorruption also remade Brazil's political landscape. The fallout of Operação Lava Jato led to Dilma Rousseff's impeachment in a 2016 parliamentary coup, ending thirteen years of Workers' Party governments and their bold, redistributive social programs. Two years later, alleging corruption, Judge Sérgio Moro's court jailed the popular presidential candidate, ex-president Lula da Silva of the Workers' Party, then leading by a wide margin in the polls. Judge Moro barred Lula from running and even forbade press interviews, setting the stage for Bolsonaro's win.

Initially, Lava Jato was the poster child for a global anticorruption industry on the move, promoting the liberal epistemology of corruption I described in chapter 1.[22] Lava Jato judges and the prosecutorial team were lauded as national heroes, and *Time* magazine even named Judge Moro as one of the world's one hundred most influential people. Yet, years on, it is increasingly clear that Lava Jato was a project of anti-Left "lawfare," that is, the selective use of law to attack political enemies.[23] Revelations by investigative journalists at *The Intercept* and subsequent scandals detailed collusion between Judge Moro and prosecutors that was expressly designed to undermine the Workers' Party.[24] Indeed, once Lava Jato had removed the Workers' Party from power, prosecutions slowed considerably.[25] One journalist summed up these dynamics, writing that Lava Jato was "not designed to punish corruption, but to protect it."[26] Indeed, shortly after Bolsonaro assumed the presidency, he absurdly declared that "there is no more corruption in government" and shut down the investigation.[27]

Public narratives about corruption communicate deeply held sentiments about the abuse of entrusted power, often entangling with ideological assessments over the appropriate role for the state. Indeed, anticorruption can activate deep feelings over who deserves state support. Elite and middle-class anger over the Workers' Party projects of redistribution and social uplift coalesced into *antipetismo*, a resentful politics of hate directed at the PT that expressly supported authoritarianism.[28] *Antipetista* corruption talk sought to link the Left and welfare projects with criminality. Indeed, Workers' Party opponents vilified social welfare as "handouts," classifying these measures as "fraud" and "swindling" and equating state projects to redistribute wealth to the poor as corruption, a position aligned with neoliberalism.[29] Media monopolies amplified this message by villainizing the Workers' Party as responsible for corruption, obscuring the ubiquity of dealmaking as a mode of politics.[30] This antipathy to using state power for prosocial redistribution is also part of tough-on-crime politics, which invests in poor communities through policing and prisons, that is, via the coercive rather than caretaking powers of the state.

This politics of anticorruption helped construct consent for rising authoritarian populisms, a project exemplified by Jair Bolsonaro. Populism has long flourished in Latin America, bolstered by deep inequality, regular elections, and an entrenched oligarchic elite fiercely resistant to sharing power. These conditions are ripe for political discourses that set a so-called pure people against a corrupted elite.[31] Populism, itself lacking a consistent ideology, makes use of available narrative frames, including neoliberal ones that construct the corrupt elites as those advocating for a strong state.[32] Indeed, in the 1990s leaders in Argentina, Brazil, and Peru blamed the widespread hardships of neoliberal structural adjustment on a corrupt political class favoring a strong state.[33] Today, Lava Jato campaigners and authoritarian populists both decry attempts to use state power to redistribute social wealth, state actions they frame as corruption. Furthermore, the populist discourse of friend and enemy dovetails with the authoritarian scapegoating of those marked as other, denigrations that also justify violence.

In Brazil, racialized notions of crime and innocence alongside the success of prosocial state investments activated resentful, revanchist feelings that the wrong people (read: poor, Black, and brown) are getting state help. These messages were on display as protests rocked Brazil in the years following the Lavo Jato revelations. Most anticorruption protesters were white. Black and brown Brazilians were present largely as workers (street vendors, maids, or military police), not as disaffected citizens. Protest signs depicted members of the Workers' Party as thieving criminals, sometimes with expressly racist imagery, like a protest sign showing Rousseff as the popular Black entertainer Mussum, smiling widely with the tagline, "You're being screwed."[34] One white protester smiled as he mocked lynching another white protester in blackface. These anti-Black performances mobilized racist associations linking criminality with Blackness as a means to criticize the Workers' Party. One emblematic photograph of the protests showed a white couple walking a few paces ahead of a darker-skinned nanny pushing their child in a stroller. The nanny wears the traditional white clothing of today's servants and yesterday's slaves, symbolically marking her subordinated status and a tenacious sense of white entitlement to Black labor. The Workers' Party's modest redistribution policies threatened these sorts of social relations, fueling resentment against challenges to racialized hierarchies.

Indeed, anticorruption articulates racism. In a blog post published early in the Lava Jato scandal, feminist Joice Berth (2016) argued that anticorruption hides a racist agenda, while, more recently, sociologist Jessé Souza (2021, 498) argues that a "racist affect" within anticorruption campaigns associates honesty with elites and the largely white middle class. Indeed, in a Brazilian version of *blanqueamiento*, whiteness protects Brazilian elites facing corruption charges by acting as a taken-for-granted innocence.[35] Even further, light-skinned Brazilian elites interpret the desires for social mobility of dark-skinned, working-class Brazilians as corruption even as they interpret their own "rapacious acquisitiveness as rights."[36] These racialized assessments of corruption entangle with equally racist notions that associate criminality with marginalized and Black urban spaces and young, Black men.[37] A devastating level of anti-Black state violence effectively renders these young men as killable.[38] In 2020 police killed an average of seventeen people per day, three-quarters of whom were young men of color living in marginalized neighborhoods.[39] The tough-on-crime philosophy behind these killings is a cornerstone of authoritarian populism. Both Lava Jato and authoritarian populism tout the rule of law, but this stated commitment to the law is always haunted by the question, the rule of law for whom?

Corruption means many things in the discursive landscapes of anticorruption protesters and Lava Jato prosecutors, discourses working through what Ernesto Laclau and Chantal Mouffe (1985, 130) call a "logic of equivalence," or discursive simplifications that confuse one thing for another in order to construct political enemies. The term *corruption* slips into the term *criminal,* which itself is overloaded, meaning both the Workers' Party and the racialized poor. By slipping between discourses of corruption and crime, anticorruption campaigners conjure multiple enemies, both the criminal-bandit and the corrupt Workers' Party. Thus, they can speak to multiple publics: those exhausted by crime, those outraged at elite illegalities, and the revanchist classes desiring to take back social space after a period of multiracial inclusion and upward mobility. The politics of anticorruption and tough on crime, as discursive twins, elide racial capitalism's inequalities as criminogenic, as the condition of possibility for both economies of desperation behind crimes of poverty and the deep-seated elite sense of entitlement to loot.

While anticorruption movements importantly critique elite greed and entitlement, they also lack organization and grounding in a political theory of transformative change. Indeed, the subject position of the anticorruption campaigner is the outraged individual rather than a member of the working class or an identity-based collective. This makes these movements vulnerable to expression through revanchism, like Lava Jato's *antipetismo* or the punitive populism that seeks to address social problems with the coercive powers of the state. Furthermore, indignation at individual wrongdoing is liable to fade after the resignation of key players but before structural reform is achieved. This is precisely what happened after the *indignado* protests in Guatemala forced the resignation of President Otto Fernando Pérez Molina and voters replaced him with the comedian Jimmy Morales, who, five years later, only escaped prosecution for corruption by presidential immunity and deals to prosecute eight of his allies.

Racialized and spatialized imaginations of criminality justify punitivism toward the poor. Brazilian Black feminists like visionary city council woman Marielle Franco, urbanist Joice Berth, and philosopher Djamila Ribeiro have identified the places where racism and anticorruption meet to insist that Brazil's central challenge is the corrosiveness of inequality and anti-Blackness, not corruption.[40] In contrast to the placeless knowledge of universal metrics and standardized best practices promoted by the global anticorruption industry, these feminists ground their analysis in their own experiences of intersecting oppressions. Ribeiro translates feminist standpoint theory as *lugar de fala* (one's place of speech), which Black feminists occupy as a site of knowledge production and a source of transformative politics.[41] Marielle Franco embodied this: "One thing is to be born and live in the *favela*; a different one is to use this place of being a *favela* woman to make claims and to make politics in a different way."[42] Claiming their *lugar de fala*, these feminists challenged discourses of corruption that naturalized racialized inequality and mobilized revanchist sentiments.

I titled this section "The Unbearable Whiteness of Anticorruption" to highlight the constitutive blindness of the perspective that positions anticorruption as a social good beyond question while refusing to see its connections to racialized violence. Early in the scandal, Joice Berth (2016) warned the Left against jumping on the anticorruption bandwagon. Lacking a robust theory of anti-Black racism and perhaps taken with the national mythology of Brazil as a racial democracy, much of the Left missed how corruption talk mobilized racialized notions of criminality.[43] Ribeiro critiqued the color-blind, cross-ideological consensus on punitivism and anticorruption by writing, "Absence is also an ideology."[44] Tough-on-crime policies, after all, continued through Workers' Party governments through spectacular campaigns like deploying the military in peripheral neighborhoods to prepare for the 2014 World Cup and the 2016 Olympics. Furthermore, Ribeiro argued, penal populism acts as the deadly relay between anticorruption and tough-on-crime politics.[45] The "exaltation of punishment" central to penal populism and celebrated by Lava Jato, Berth (2016) blogged, was a cultural orientation inseparable from racialized notions of crime and innocence. Indeed, tough talk about punishment for corruption transmutes in practice and "hits the Black and the poor" through expanded investments in a deeply uneven, racialized criminal justice system.[46] Thus anticorruption upholds racialized violence.

In her dissertation, Franco demonstrates that Brazil's militarized security policy manages poverty through containment and punishment, strategies that seek to displace politics with policing.[47] Indeed, anticorruption is the new antipolitics machine. In 1994 James Ferguson argued that development as both a discourse and a field of practice depoliticizes by constructing poverty as bounded from colonial histories and (exploitative) regional political economies, while anemic forms of expertise reduced complex social relations to market ones. In a similar way, anticorruption depoliticizes social struggles over the form, content, and end of political life. Mobilizing the notion that the law is somehow above politics, anticorruption reduces political struggles over the social surplus to technical and juridical questions, what Brazilian scholars have called the "rhetoric of technique," or a "negationist" politics that strives to negate the terrain of the political via law.[48] These claims to the neutral, technical application of the law depoliticize intensely political questions about the contours of public life and the distribution of social wealth. They also obscure the life-and-death stakes of these battles. In March

2018 gunmen assassinated Marielle Franco as she campaigned against racism and police brutality, terrible proof of the threat she posed to entrenched structures of power. Across Brazil and around the world, mourners expressed their collective grief, calling out "Marielle, presente!" (Marielle is still here) and "Marielle é semente!" (Marielle is a seed), amplifying her voice beyond her precious mortality. While much remains uncertain in Brazil and beyond, contesting the racialized politics of anticorruption will be a key terrain of struggle for those seeking to enact the radical projects of justice, equality, and democracy that Marielle and other Black feminists invite us into.

Dignified Work and Urban Commoning

Urban livelihood rights will also be at the center of contests over the form, function, and future of twenty-first-century cities. In this, street vendor politics have useful lessons for troubled times. The most insurgent vendor politics center life and urban livelihood, as vendors put forth a vision of the city in which public spaces are sites of work, not just of circulation or consumption. Their vision seeks more inclusive market relations rather than anticapitalist alternatives. At the same time, by claiming space for life and livelihood, vendors helped materialize Ciudad del Este's city center as an urban commons. Commoning, as a verb, is a practice of care, conviviality, and horizontality that holds livelihood—not the law—at its center. Within the street market, all sorts of relationships of care provide noneconomic forms of value, a solidarity ethic that sutures together the social life of the street market. Stereotypes of street vending as only organized by relentless competition, survivalism, or the logics of profit miss the intertwining of life and work. Indeed, with an insurgent spatial imagination, vendors prioritize the use value of urban space, thereby challenging global urbanist framings that offer only template cities with sports stadiums, malls, shopping districts, and the like but with little room for the poor. In contrast to this view, vendors like Obdulio, whom we met in chapter 4, envisioned Ciudad del Este as a collective soup pot. This urban epistemology can orient us toward more humane urbanisms, in that vendors challenge the unquestioned dominance of exchange value in cities built by and for capital. For their part, women's affective politics of the body are also key modes of making claims to the right to extract livelihood from the city. These women invite us to feel their precarity and to care about their vulnerability, militating against liberalism's logic that we are free from the needs of others.

As the pandemic shuttered borders and devastated Ciudad del Este's popular economy, vendors insisted that they deserved dignified work, *trabajo digno*. The pandemic intensified contests over meanings, terms, and valuations of work, laying bare the life-and-death stakes of struggles for *trabajo digno*. Certainly, the pandemic illuminated the worlds of work enacting our collective lives, including our deep dependence on unpaid, low-paid, and informal workers. With a rapidity that defies the term *structure*, social distancing and quarantine forced significant shifts in the social relations of work that are wrought differently across lines of race, class, gender, and geography.[49] Ordered into quarantine, street vendors around the world faced a terrible double bind: stay at home and forgo the earnings needed to put food on the table, or work and risk exposing themselves and their loved ones to infection and death. New vocabularies emerged from these material changes, including *essential work*, a term resonant with *trabajo digno*. Essential work frames the central late-capitalist paradox that workers most necessary to the social reproduction of collective life are often unpaid, low paid, and underprotected. While this observation was a revelation for some living in fortresses of privilege, frontline communities certainly have long known this reality. Indeed, the pandemic also revealed the terrible capitalist paradox that twins the essential with the disposable. While the pandemic highlighted our collective dependence on devalued work and inspired solidarity with essential workers, a chasm still looms between the recognition of essential work and the material conditions required to dignify it.

To be sure, in dire and diverse conditions, workers organized. From U.S. street vendors launching a national agenda for street vendor justice to mass mobilizations of striking feminists across Latin America, workers' movements pushed for material changes that challenged old notions of valuable work and deserving workers.[50] Worker organizing influenced policy as governments drew boundaries around what work qualified as essential. Officials in Montevideo and some districts in Guatemala included informal food vendors in essential work legislation, while six other Latin American countries, including Paraguay, defined essential work regulations broadly such that informal food vendors could make the case for their inclusion.[51] Furthermore, across the region and often for the first time, state relief programs included vendors as workers, as "legal subjects in their own right," a seismic reframing of vending as productive and essential rather than as a problem.[52] Furthermore, the infusion of cash aid to millions reminds us of the vast, untapped caretaking capacities of states, even as recovery supports have been insufficient and allocated along old fault lines. For instance, as in the United States, an emergency aid program in Argentina excluded undocumented workers, including the 77 percent of street vendors who are migrants, many from Paraguay.[53]

To fill the gap left by insufficient pandemic aid, poor women in Asunción opened soup kitchens. These kitchens met urgent basic needs, feeding thousands of people during the pandemic as they also embodied a spirit of mutual aid and community caretaking key to stewarding the urban as a commons.[54] Furthermore, community organizers won federal funding for these soup kitchens, a successful example of claiming state resources for poor communities.[55] Yet in the long tradition of neoliberalized states outsourcing community caretaking, these kitchens were largely run by poor women already overburdened by the nearly impossible task of making life work in zones of "organized abandonment."[56] One organizer said, "The crisis is permanent in our neighborhoods," underscoring the cascading hardships of poverty and critiquing privileged communities that experienced the vulnerabilities of the pandemic as a novelty and desired a "return to normal," blind to the violences upon which this normal is built.

Vendors' struggles against the Pilot Plan can also teach us to be wary of formalization for its own sake. All formalization projects necessarily value some economic forms, social spaces, and urban subjects over others. Because the terms of formalization are a terrain of struggle, the end results often express the visions of dominant social groups and risk reproducing the antipoor epistemology. Indeed, in Ciudad del Este, the logics of formalization sought to banish the illegalities of rights claimed by ordinary street vendors and Brazilian *sacoleiros*, even as reforms protected those of elites. Formalization projects rely on—and produce—powerful spatial imaginaries that divide up places, people, and activities to then slot them into pregiven categories: formal or informal, legal or illegal, modern or underdeveloped. These projects often promote ready-made ideas from global urbanism's repertoire: frontier factories, shopping malls, and standardized vending stalls. These spatial forms of global urbanism are widely interpreted as legal and formal, regardless of their alignment with the law. While elite high-rises, gated communities, shopping malls, and sports stadiums can be as noncompliant as street vendor occupations, they convey the look of legality. In Ciudad del Este, a singular focus on formalization authorized urban forms with this look—legal, formal, modern, global—without sufficient concern for the lifeways to be replaced. Through these dynamics, formalization is implicated in criminalizing the livelihoods of the poor. It also blinds academics, policymakers, and other reformers to the illegalities of the rich and the networks of outlaw capital shaping urban environments.

Rather than formalization, we need ways forward that center the power and knowledge of informal workers, ways that target the subjectivities and actions of planners and policymakers more than workers. Inspired by the Black radical tradition and writing with coauthor Manisha Anantharaman, I recently framed this as an ethic of reparation that insists on collective redress for the living histories of racialized and spatial inequality with the unspeakable violence of slavery as the emblematic case.[57] Reparation remembers and repairs historic injustices, a radical stance in the face of the socially sanctioned amnesia that orders so much contemporary policymaking and political debate. Clear-eyed about what Cornell West terms the "catastrophe" of racial capitalism and related oppressions and centering the experiences of those on the front lines, reparation calls for transformational change much beyond the tepid imagination of reformers tinkering around the edges.[58] At the center is the redistribution of resources and social power to the grassroots. This road is long and hard, but the pandemic has also illuminated other ways of being, seeing, and knowing otherwise in the world. The virus highlighted racial capitalism's death-dealing inequalities, as well as our inescapable interdependencies and mutual vulnerabilities, potentially inspiring the inspiration, resolve, and organization necessary for projects of transformation.

Transformative social change requires new modes of thinking and acting. The urban epistemologies provided by the most insurgent vendor politics are a useful resource along this long road into ways of being otherwise in the world. If we listen, we can learn other ways of valuing work and life as we also allow ourselves to be affected by the vulnerabilities of others, vulnerabilities that are shared even as they are distributed in deeply uneven ways across lines of race, class, gender, and geography. This mode of deep solidarity also must refuse the mythologies of the antipoor epistemology and racialized criminality, deeply harmful politics that justify violence and divert public money into punitive policies that leave the root causes of crime and inequality untouched. Relatedly, and following Brazilian Black feminists, we must resist depoliticizing, technocratic, and racist versions of anticorruption and continue contesting the distribution of social wealth.

While essential, transforming the epistemological terrain is insufficient to generate worlds otherwise. Transformation requires liberatory praxis. Vendors' insurgent politics and pandemic challenges have pushed us to theorize urban work differently, but our true challenge is to act together toward transformation. Local, placed histories always shape the far horizon of the politically possible. Thus, while the ideas in this book are relevant in many contexts, they must be put to work and transformed in the process of seeking to create worlds otherwise. I hope the ideas from this book will be useful to diverse projects aimed toward enacting geographies of justice.

Worlds of Work

Traders

batedoras Support workers who drive in front of *sacoleiros* to evaluate the intensity of border checks and communicate with *sacoleiros* about the likelihood of getting stopped.

compristas "Buyers," sometimes called "tourists," who purchase goods in Ciudad del Este and bring them back to Brazil, supposedly for personal use, not resale. The Brazilian quota system allows tourists to bring back duty-free merchandise valued under a fluctuating cap of U.S.$150–$500. There is an additional list of items subject to quantity restrictions. Nearly all visitors to Ciudad del Este are *sacoleiros*, or shopping tourists, to the extent that Paraguayans double the term to identify sightseers (*tourist tourists*). A Paraguayan official commented that *sacoleiros* "dress up as tourists; they lie," underlining that the activities of *sacoleiros* and *compristas* overlap and are difficult to distinguish.[1]

laranjas Workers contracted to carry items across the bridge for *sacoleiros*, helping them skirt the quota by dividing up merchandise among multiple bridge crossers. As border checks on the bridge intensify, *laranjas* are losing ground to *barqueiros*. Also called *pasadores*, or "the ones who pass [goods]."

sacoleiros Traders traveling from Brazilian cities to Ciudad del Este to source cheap goods for resale in Brazilian markets. These petty traders often borrow to finance purchases and take on considerable risk, as Brazilian policies criminalize the *sacoleiro* circuit. *Sacoleiros* often contract additional services to support their trading trips, *laranjas, pasadores, taxistas,* or *bateadores*. Some *sacoleiros* are contracted by a *patron* (boss). The name derives from the Portuguese word for "bag," *saco*, referring to their large bags of merchandise. Street vendors call *sacoleiros* with whom they have long relationships *clientes*.

Transportation

barqueiros Boaters who ferry merchandise across the river, working closely with particular ports.

cigarreros Barqueiros specializing in transporting cigarettes across the river, a trade that stretches from the northern town of Pedro Juan Caballero to the southern town of Encarnación.

encargados or *negociadores* Operators and negotiators who make connections and organize logistics between *sacoleiros*, *barqueiros*, and port owners.

estivadores Port workers loading and unloading merchandise for the trip across the river.

propietarios de puertos Landowners on the waterfront along the Paraguayan and Brazilian sides of the Paraná River and Lake Itaipú who control access to the ports.

transportistas In Ciudad del Este, a fleet of 2,500 *taxistas*, 800 *mototaxistas* (motorcycle taxi drivers), and 1,800 *combistas* (van drivers) take *sacoleiros* across the bridge with their purchases or organize transportation of their goods to the ports and *sacoleiros* across the river.

Vendors

ambulantes Peddlers or hawkers with no fixed claims to space who are officially required to walk while selling and forbidden to spread their wares on sidewalks. In practice, many spread strips of cardboard on the sidewalk or prop DVDs or newspapers along a building front to claim a space from which to sell.

cambistas Money changers working from the street who store four currencies—U.S. dollars, Brazilian reais, Argentine pesos, and Paraguayan guaranies—in their fanny packs and tap out exchange rates on small calculators. They are nearly always men.

casilleros Street vendors with the most established vending infrastructure, called *casillas* (little booths). Their stalls have roofs, glass display cases, and on-site storage.

empleados Hired sales staff, either Brazilians or young Paraguayans. Shops and galleries often pay *empleados* under the table. Wages are low. Successful street vendors also hire *empleados*, often family or friends, to assist with stocking and sales.

guías turistas "Tourist guides" are roving salesmen, young men who wear standardized vests and offer to help shoppers find deals. They are paid with tips.

mesiteros Street vendors who sell from tables (*mesitas*). Vending infrastructure varies: some have on-site storage lockers, while others set up and break down infrastructure daily, storing merchandise off site. The Pilot Plan is slowly replacing the incrementally built, ad hoc infrastructure of *casilleros* and *mesiteros* with standardized, state-owned stalls.

quineleros Lottery ticket sellers.

vendedores de comida Food vendors, often specializing in serving Paraguayans working in the street market. *Tereré* vendors sell cold tea, *fruteros* push large wooden carts piled with fruit, women cook lunches on the street, and *pancheros* sell hot dogs. Food vendors are often unlicensed.

NOTES

INTRODUCTION

1. I follow standard ethnographic practices of anonymization, using pseudonyms and changing identifying details for all interlocutors except elected public officials. Unless otherwise noted, all translations are my own.

2. Personal communication, Dionel Pérez, October 16, 2013, Ciudad del Este.

3. R. Brown 2009.

4. Observations, October 13, 2013, Ciudad del Este.

5. Personal communication, June 16, 2011, Ciudad del Este.

6. Mathews and Ribeiro 2012.

7. Contraband reduces costs by tax evasion, a form of oblique value capture for *contrabandistas* who buy cheap—in part by avoiding taxes—and sell dear. With drugs, illegality inheres in the commodity form itself, as the risks associated with illegality increase production costs and prices. Yet illicitness is not a fixed characteristic but a "transient quality" of different intensities as commodities move through different regulatory environments (Gregson and Crang 2017, 213).

8. Observatoria de Economía Internacional 2014.

9. Anthropologist Roberto Abínzano (2005) wrote that the city's border trade moved U.S.$10 billion. Press accounts estimated upward of U.S.$15–$20 billion, usually without citing sources (Webber 2010). Reinaldo Penner (2006b), in a USAID-funded report, argued that unregistered trade (i.e., contraband) exceeded the value of registered reexportation until 2001. U.S. Embassy officials in leaked cables described such trade as "one-half the size of the formal economy" (U.S. Embassy unclassified cable, "Unclassified Scene-Setter for Codel Reid," November 20, 2007, 07ASUNCION970_a, 3, accessed through Wikileaks).

10. Pinheiro-Machado 2008, 2010, 2017; Cardin 2006, 2012, 2014, 2015; Rabossi 2008, 2010, 2011a, 2011b, 2012.

11. Pinheiro-Machado 2010, 2017; Cardin 2012.

12. Pinheiro-Machado 2017.

13. While I was not able to locate the original quote from Stroessner, it is frequently cited in the secondary literature (Nickson and Lambert 2002, 166).

14. As scholars of neoliberalism demonstrate, it is a collection of regulatory tendencies that vary across space and mutate over time (Brenner, Peck, and Theodore 2010). Promoting austerity (often by moving private debts onto public ledgers), neoliberalism hallows out the social capacities of the state as it also expands other state powers, especially the punitive, carceral, and war-making. Thus, a potent mix of de- and reregulation strips away some state capacities and enhances others as an actively produced process. William Davies (2016, 126) describes evolving forms of neoliberal reason, with its birth as a combative political project aimed to "demolish non-capitalist avenues of political hope," to a normative project to extend economizing logic throughout the social—as captured by Wendy Brown (2015)—to the current punitive and postcritical version.

15. The pink tide includes Bolivarian socialism, including Venezuela's Hugo Chávez (1999–2013) and Bolivia's Evo Morales (2006–19), as well as the center-Left governments of Brazil (Lula da Silva and Dilma Rousseff, 2002–16), Argentina (Nestor and Christina Kirchner, 2003–15), and Paraguay (Fernando Lugo, 2008–12).

16. Gudynas 2009.

17. Fernando Lugo's impeachment trial was a sham. He was ousted for "bad performance" in the wake of political violence after police stormed an occupation of landless peasants that left eleven *campesinos* and six police officers dead. Yet prosecutors presented no evidence of Lugo's involvement. In the two-day trial, Lugo was given less than twenty-four hours to prepare his two-hour defense. Similarly disingenuous legal maneuvers removed Brazil's Dilma Rousseff of the Workers' Party in 2016, although on a less breakneck timeline.

18. Colectivo Situaciones 2009.

19. Castells 2010.

20. Galemba 2017; Jaffe 2013.

21. Illicit trade also includes other outlawed or controlled commodities like drugs and weapons. Economists estimate the value of this global shadow economy at U.S.$10 trillion using quantitative methods that, while elaborate, are rooted in an untenable dual economy model in which legal economies are assumed to be separate from their illegal counterparts (Schneider and Enste 2000, 2013).

22. Van Schendel and Abraham 2005.

23. See World Bank, "GDP (current US$)," https://data.worldbank.org/indicator/NY .GDP.MKTP.CD.

24. Over 250,000 people have been killed since the 2006 inauguration of the U.S.-backed drug war in Mexico, which backs Dawn Paley's (2014, 15) assessment that the drug war is a "strategy that ensures transnational corporations access to resources through dispossession and terror."

25. "Symbiotic relationship" is from Muehlmann (2013, 12). For the description of Mexico as a narco-state, see González and Luis (2013).

26. Corning 2017; Haberly and Wójcik 2015.

27. As "too big to fail" banks teetered perilously close to collapse, U.S. and European banks lost more than U.S.$1 trillion in toxic assets. Highly leveraged banks stopped lending to each other as the paper market froze.

28. Rajeev Syal, "Drug Money Saved Banks in Global Crisis, Claims UN Advisor," *The*

Guardian, December 13, 2009, sec. World News, https://www.theguardian.com/global/2009/dec/13/drug-money-banks-saved-un-cfief-claims.

29. Gibler 2010.

30. Assistant Attorney General Larry Breuer cited in Taibbi (2012).

31. Ballvé (2020) demonstrates that particular forms of drug-fueled state presence—not absence—create zones of violence in rural Colombia.

32. Van Schendel and Abraham 2005; Luke and Toal 1998; Chabal and Daloz 1999; Callejas 2014.

33. Das and Poole 2004; Jaffe 2013; Wilson 2009.

34. Foucault (1995, 280) says, "The existence of a legal prohibition creates around it a field of illegal practices, which one manages to supervise, while extracting from it an illicit profit themselves illegal, but rendered manipulable by their organization in delinquency." See also Heyman (1999).

35. Marez 2004; Bhattacharyya 2005.

36. Anthropologists demonstrate that the political authority of the state is both processual (Joseph and Nugent 1994; Nugent 2009) and performative (Aretxaga 2003; Abrams 1988; Hansen and Stepputat 2001; Trouillot, Hann, and Krti 2001; Krupa and Nugent 2015).

37. Marx (1894) describes capital as value in motion to capture how capital moves through circuits of production, distribution, and exchange in different forms. In these circuits, surplus value is the increment of value produced by the workers that they are not compensated for in wages because it is captured by employers.

38. See Lexico dictionary, https://www.lexico.com/en/definition/obscuration.

39. Byrd et al. 2018.

40. Rosa Luxemburg's (1921) visionary work argues that capitalism requires resources, waged workers, and markets outside its domain and thus commandeers them through colonial and imperial violence. Against Marx's claim that what he calls "primitive accumulation" marks the early stages of capitalism, Luxemburg (1921, 350) wrote, "This process is still going on."

41. Many convincingly argue that primitive accumulation is ongoing, an iterative necessity for the reproduction of capitalism (Perelman 2000; De Angelis 2004; G. Hart 2006; Luxemburg 1921). Massimo De Angelis (2004, 62, emphasis in original) describes this dynamic well when he says, "Enclosures are a continuous characteristic of 'capital logic' once we understand capital not as a totalized *system*, *but* as a *force* with totalising drives that exists together with other forces that act as limit on it."

42. Marx 1894, 899.

43. Jim Glassman (2006) includes primitive accumulation as a separate, original category of extraeconomic appropriation, while Jason Moore (2018) adds the unpaid energy and work of cheap nature.

44. While Glassman and others propose a conceptual split between waged-based exploitation and extraeconomic accumulation, other scholars propose a more messy articulation in which postindustrial relations of exploitation, dispossession, commodification, financialization, and debt bleed together (Gago 2014; Melamed 2015).

45. Sometimes outlaw capital appropriates value in the form of unpaid taxes, a kind of

unactualized collective resource that differs from the collective resources at the heart of social movement struggles against enclosures.

46. This is not to say that only outlaw capitalists engage in dealmaking but that deals are an indicator of the transgressive moment generating profit possibilities.

47. Luminary Cedric Robinson (1983) traces how capitalism in industrializing England was not born through a revolutionary overthrow of the feudal system, rationalizing and modernizing the economy, but rather that capitalism used existing racial hierarchies to justify dispossession, imperialism, and other violences linked to value extraction. Groups dispossessed by enclosure—the Irish, Arabs, and the Roma—and later colonized peoples the world over were imagined to be unruly and defective racial others. These present histories are extensively analyzed by scholars in the Black radical tradition (Du Bois 1935; A. Davis 1983; C. James 2001; Gilroy 1993; Kelley 2003; McKittrick 2006; Gilmore 2007).

48. Capitalism both severs and binds, destroying dense webs of noncommodified social relations as it sutures together other geographically expansive connections useful to capitalist sociality. Ruth Wilson Gilmore explains this through the metaphor of partition, which Jodi Melamed (2015, 78) describes as a "technology of anti-relationality," a core logic of capital.

49. Roediger 2017; Ignatiev 2008; Wolpe 1972.

50. Telles 2014.

51. Fields and Fields 2014; Kendi 2016.

52. D. Harvey 1982.

53. Chiodelli, Hall, and Hudson 2017, 2.

54. Keefe 2013, 98, 100, 102.

55. The power of capital to build cities of industry, finance, or technology has been well documented by scholars in urban studies and economic geography (Abu-Lughod 2000; Sassen 2001; N. Brenner 1998). Neoliberal globalization, oriented around the logic of free trade and competitive cities, pushes the spatial division of labor (Massey 1995), stretching out the economic relationships that connect manufacturing to end consumers alongside the rise of finance capital, knowledge economies, and the creative class.

56. Henri Lefebvre (1991) argues that space is simultaneously a medium of social relations and a historically specific product of those relations. Just as Marx demystified the commodity as a set of fetishized labor relations, Lefebvre denaturalized space. Each society has particular social relationships of production and reproduction and produces its own sort of space.

57. Braudel 1992, 163; R. Brenner 2003; Cowen 2010; Mezzadra and Neilson 2013; Easterling 2014.

58. Cowen 2014, 3.

59. Negrey, Osgood, and Goetzke 2011.

60. Personal communication, street vendor, June 11, 2013, Ciudad del Este.

61. According to Global Property Guide (https://www.globalpropertyguide.com/), property in Tokyo in 2018, at the eleventh most expensive worldwide, is $10,784 per square meter, followed by Tel Aviv at $10,166 per square meter. Vendors in Cochabamba sold similar use rights to vending space (Daniel Goldstein 2016).

62. I draw from Yiftachel and Huxley's (2000, 907) definition of urban planning as the "public production of space."

63. The framework of the relational production of space challenges politically disabling assumptions that space is an inert background or stage on which already constituted subjects and processes play out the dramas of collective life. It also contests the usual, unthinking association between large-scale processes and mental processes of abstraction, as well as their inverse—associating the concrete with small-scale processes (Angelo and Goh 2020). Small-scale activities can involve abstraction like social practices and spatial imaginaries, while large-scale activities can be decisively concrete.

64. D. Harvey 2009, cited in G. Hart 2016, 380.

65. These feminist perspectives emphasize social ontology (Ruddick et al. 2018), difference and the politics of subjectivity (Oswin 2018; Roy 2016), and Lefebvrian takes on everyday life (Buckley and Strauss 2016) to contest notions of a universal urban ontology or an epistemology of the urban without an outside found in the planetary urbanization school (Merrifield 2013; N. Brenner and Schmid 2015). Some see in the planetary urbanization school not just old tendencies to universalize the Euro-American urban experience but the hubris of totalization (Derickson 2018), while others argue that Lefebvre worked with dialectical social totalities, social wholes made of various interconnected parts that one always must analyze from a particular vantage point (Goonewardena 2018).

66. "The Rise and Fall of Londongrad," *The Economist*, March 5, 2022, 50, https://www.economist.com/britain/2022/03/05/the-rise-and-fall-of-londongrad.

67. A special issue of *Íconos: Revista de Ciencias Sociales*, titled "Economía popular: Entre la informalidad y la reproducción ampliada" (Gago, Cielo, and Gachet 2018), outlines many key dynamics (Tovar 2018; Cielo 2018; Álvarez 2018).

68. See Breman and van der Linden 2014. A broad literature describes these trends as economic restructuring, flexibilization, and austerity politics as generalized conditions of insecurity and precarity (Brenner and Theodore 2002; D. Harvey 2005; Neilson and Rossiter 2008; Sassen 1998; Storper 2000).

69. See Neilson and Rossiter 2008; Mosoetsa, Stillerman, and Tilly 2016. In the United States, New Deal labor protections explicitly excluded both domestic employees and agriculture workers, barring both groups from organizing. These exclusions were a "proxy to exclude most black employees" in the South as part of a compromise to appease racist southern legislators (Perea 2011, 100).

70. See Barrantes 1992. There is significant variation between domains of "informal work," which include unregistered petty commodity producers supplying cheap inputs into capitalist production processes and reducing costs for formal firms; own account operators, such as waste pickers and street vendors; and informal employees, such as day laborers or domestic workers. Pioneering researchers like Keith Hart (1973) considered informal economies as the survival-oriented labor of the poor. In the 1970s and 1980s scholars of development imagined a separate transitional informal sector, a so-called dual economy that, according to the stage theories of the time, signified underdevelopment and incomplete modernities (Lewis 1954; Rostow 1960). Neo-Marxists retorted that the informal economic sector was instead a structural, subordinated subsidization

of capitalist expansion (Moser 1978; Portes, Castells, and Benton 1989). Today, most researchers recognize extensive linkages between formal and informal economies. However, there persists a misperception that informal economies are outside of state control, a view promoted by free-market enthusiasts like Hernando de Soto (1989) and labor scholars (ILO 2002; Meagher 2013).

71. In its 2018 report, the International Labour Organization noted that Uruguay had the lowest rates of informal employment (24.5 percent) in South America, while Bolivia had the highest (83.1 percent) (ILO 2018, 93).

72. Moser 1978.

73. Li 2010; Sanyal 2013.

74. Rosaldo (2016) and Rosaldo, Tilly, and Evans (2012) analyze the power of organized informal workers, while Pithouse (2012) critiques orthodox Marxist assumptions about agency and the male industrial worker.

75. Millar 2018; Roig 2017.

76. O'Hare 2020; J. Ferguson 2015.

77. Chen et al. 2005.

78. Tucker and Anantharaman 2020.

79. Gago 2017; Sheppard, Sparks, and Leitner 2020.

80. Sarria Icaza and Tiribia 2004, 177.

81. Gidwani 2008.

82. Schuster 2015; Gago and Mezzadra 2017.

83. Personal communication, municipal official, March 8, 2015, Ciudad del Este.

84. A long lineage of critical, feminist, and postcolonial scholars emphasizes the relationship between power and knowledge (Foucault 1978, 1994; Haraway 1988; Stoler 2002). All forms of knowing have occlusions and blinds spots, for there is no detached, distant, Archimedean perspective from which to know the whole.

85. Collins 1986; Harding 1986; Stacey 1988; and D. Smith 1987.

86. Bush 2002.

87. Visweswaran 1994; Bell, Butlin, and Heffernan 1995; N. Smith and Godlewska 1994; Roy 2006; Cheah 2008.

88. Roy 2009.

89. The book is not the result of ethnographic immersion in subaltern worlds in order to excavate ontological difference, as in the classical anthropological model.

90. "Convocan otra marcha para exigir transparencia en comuna de CDE," *Vanguardia*, September 8, 2014, http://www.vanguardia.com.py/v1/index.php/component/k2/item/21464-convocan-otra-marcha-para-exigir-transparencia-en-comuna-de-cde.

CHAPTER 1. Notorious Markets

1. Personal communication, Sofía Espíndola, November 15, 2013.

2. Ciudad del Este is only mentioned one other time in the 475-page book (Lambert and Nickson 2013).

3. Webber is cited in Lambert and Nickson 2013, 374. See also Webber 2010.

4. Tom Slater (2015) and Loïc Wacquant, Tom Slater, and Virgílio Borges Pereira (2014) use the term *territorial stigmatization* to critique the policy-focused "neighbor-

hood effects" debates, which imagine that spaces of cultural dysfunction, like so-called ghettos, reproduce poverty.

5. The report used stock language to describe Ciudad del Este's "longstanding reputation as a hotbed of piracy and counterfeiting of all kinds of products" (USTR 2016).

6. USTR 2021.

7. Karaganis and Flynn 2011, 90.

8. In 2003 the CIA identified about fifty so-called lawless zones around the world (see Keefe 2013).

9. Jennifer Robinson 2006; Roy 2009; Watson 2009b.

10. Roy 2011a.

11. N. Smith 2010; Gilmore 2002; Sheppard 2012; Werner 2015.

12. Chang 2002.

13. Capitalist modernity is relationally produced through multilinear, co-constitutive trajectories across highly asymmetrical power relations and through the long histories of empire that make up what Gregory (2004) might call our "colonial present." The dominance of Euro-America was never preordained but forged through historically specific dynamics, imperial relations of conquest, colonization, and a fair dose of accident (Anievas and Nisancioglu 2013).

14. Capitalist cheerleaders like Walt Rostow (1960) and Niall Ferguson (2012) share with Marxist historians like Robert Brenner (1977) and Ellen Wood (1999) developmentalist perspectives on historical change that locate the origins of capitalism exclusively in western Europe. The stagist model of economic development has been roundly critiqued by many, including dependency theorists (Frank 1967; dos Santos 1970; Cardoso and Faletto 1979), economic geographers (D. Harvey 1982; Wright 2006; N. Brenner, Peck, and Theodore 2010), and economists (Alesina and Rodrik 1994; Stiglitz 2002; Piketty and Ganser 2014).

15. Blaut 1993.

16. Antunes de Oliveira 2019; Kay 2020; dos Santos 1970; Marini and Sader 1977; Bambirra 1999.

17. Raul Prebisch (1950) argues that the declining terms of trade lock in the underdevelopment of the Global South.

18. See also Emmanuel 1972.

19. See the estimate by economists Zak Cope and Timothy Kerswell, cited in Hickel 2017.

20. In their seminal texts, David Harvey (1982) and Neil Smith (2010) only cite Andre Gunder Frank and Samir Amin, a common reduction of the dependency school by English-language researchers that erases the *dependistas*. Frank simplified and dehistoricized the work of *dependistas*—especially in regard to their focus on national politics, alliances, and ideologies as structuring forces—yet Frank was often taken to represent the whole school (Cardoso 1977).

21. The move of manufacturing to peripheral regions within rich countries like northern England foreshadowed the outsourcing of production to the Global South (Massey 1995).

22. Dicken et al. 2001; Coe et al. 2004.

23. Capitalism requires this "hierarchical field of *possible* positions," as Marion Wer-

ner (2015, 11) says, for it is capital's restless movement among places that defends profits against their inevitable tendency to decline.

24. Werner 2015; Wright 2006.

25. Anthropologists and researchers from the region deconstruct how descriptors—informal, illegal, illicit, criminal—require and stabilize an imagined space of bounded legal economy (Manvoutouka 2013; Neffa 2009; Palacios 2011; Sequeda 2014; Waisgrais and Sarabia 2008; Kucera and Roncolato 2008). This imagined formal and legal economy then implies a noncompliant, problematic outside. Defining the outside in relation to the legal or formal economy then helps to epistemologically construct the spaces, practices, or people understood as requiring reform or expulsion. These descriptors also carry race-class connotations, with informality often implying the noncompliant economic practices of the poor. In contrast, corruption is used to describe the rule-breaking profiteering of the rich. Of course, everyday practice mixes activities that defy classification into binaries like illegal/legal and contraband/reexportation. The point is that the imagined hierarchies of valued, formal labor have material consequences.

26. Indeed, Harris (1993, 1714) describes whiteness as the "right to exclude" because the law worked through white supremacist logics to assess whose land claims were valid (white settlers') and whose would be excluded (Indigenous people's) and, further, what kinds of bodies were enslavable via exclusion from the very definition of personhood and therefore self-ownership (Black people's).

27. Racism produces the social categories of race, not the other way around (Fields and Fields 2014; Kendi 2016).

28. Demonstrating the extent of mass rape, a recent genetic study of Brazilians traced 70 percent of maternal lines back to Black and Indigenous women and 75 percent of paternal lines to European men (*Folha de S. Paulo* 2020).

29. E. Williams 1944; Rodney 1972; J. Moore 2018.

30. Telles and Paschel 2014.

31. Loveman 2014.

32. Quijano 2000.

33. De la Cadena 2001, 18.

34. See, for example, Fernando Ewerton, "Livre de Stroessner, Paraguai quer ser um paía sério," *Jornal do Brasil*, March 12, 1989, sec. Internacional, http://memoria.bn.br /DocReader/DocReader.aspx?bib=030015_10&Pesq=%22presidente%20stroessner %22&pagfis=185339; and Rosa Calmon Alves and Carols Max Torres, "Brasil garante ao Paraguai cooperação além de Itaipú," *Jornal do Brasil*, April 10, 1980, http:// memoria.bn.br/DocReader/docreader.aspx?bib=030015_10&pasta=ano%20198&pesq =porto%20stroessner&pagfis=4910.

35. The term *sacoleiro* derives from the Portuguese word *saco* (bag) and invokes the bags of merchandise these workers carted from Ciudad del Este to resell in street markets across Brazil, places associated with vibrant street vending, cheap prices, and counterfeit products.

36. This estimate is from a city transit official in 2013 and is higher than the U.S. Embassy estimate of fourteen hundred van and motorcycle drivers in 2006. Interview with transit official, June 13, 2013, Ciudad del Este; U.S. Embassy unclassified cable, March 13,

2006, Paraguay Political and Economic Update, March 4–10, 06ASUNCION270_a, accessed through Wikileaks. A leader of an association of taxi drivers estimated twenty-two hundred total drivers. Personal communication, taxi association president, March 12, 2015, Ciudad del Este.

37. See, for example, Coletto (2010, 10) or the video by AFP News Agency, "Ciudad del Este, South America's Tax-Free Free-for-All," YouTube, November 16, 2010, https://www.youtube.com/watch?v=UCtpcYLAfAI.

38. Gray is a potent metaphor. In his research on gray spaces, Oren Yiftachel (2009) emphasizes the power-laden processes that celebrate and protect spaces of privilege as they also condemn, criminalize, and expose spaces of poverty to violence and harm. I dislike black/white metaphors, as they invoke a racialized hierarchy of good and legal that is associated with whiteness while they associate deviance and illegality with blackness.

39. A 1999 *Vanguardia* article reported on undervaluation, while *Paraguay Vende* described it in a 2006 report. It remained active during my fieldwork through 2015. "Comisión de diputados investigará la mafia aduanera," *Vanguardia*, November 15, 1999.

40. Personal communication, June 10, 2013. Two factions of *contrabandistas*, each backed by different politicians, filed legal complaints against the other, bringing to light contraband logistics.

41. Personal communication, August 13, 2013, Ciudad del Este.

42. ISI policies relied on strategies proposed by Latin American dependency theorists and supported by the UN Economic Commission for Latin America and the Caribbean. By the 1980s ISI had fallen out of favor among development industry experts; however, ISI importantly enabled social and economic development in many Latin American countries (Baer and Birch 1984; Blouet and Blouet 2009).

43. Rabossi 2011a.

44. The history of this term lies in Adam Smith's triad: wages, profit, and rent. Rent results from payments flowing from land (or, later, resource) ownership.

45. *Lineamientos para el desarrollo de Ciudad del Este y su area metropolitana* (Secretaría Tecnica de Planificación, 1997).

46. Author's calculations with data from customs and the Treasury Department.

47. Ruiz Díaz 2012.

48. Penner 2006b, 8.

49. In 1971 Law 237/71 established the ten-hectare Zona Franca Internacional, and Law 523/95 established another duty-free zone, Zona Franca Global del Paraguay S.A. For a variety of reasons, most trade was not organized through these exceptional spaces.

50. Finance Ministry Resolution 210/85.

51. The 1972 provision set the overall tax burden between 27.75 and 39.25 percent. By 2010 the total tax rate was below 5 percent for items on the Tourism Regime lists. As taxes and tariffs on businesses dropped, sales tax increased (Ruiz Díaz 2011).

52. Ruiz Díaz 2011.

53. State Decree 26.730/72.

54. Observation, Nomei Haudenschild, September 11, 2013, Ciudad del Este.

55. Total tax rates, across five taxes and tariffs, were 4.1 percent on those goods in-

cluded in the amended Tourism Regime, like electronics. The Tourism Regime was amended in 2005 by Resolution 1021, followed by Law 1117/05 and the Secretariat of Taxation Resolutions 6406 and 6406 (Penner 2006b, 14).

56. O'Dougherty 2002, 24.

57. Pinheiro-Machado and Scalco 2020, 22.

58. Kregg Hetherington (2011) analyzed a related discursive closure that constructs *campesinos*—poor rural farmers—as unmodern and reads their habits as constitutively ill-suited for twenty-first-century democracy. Key to Paraguayan Cold War nationalism, land reform worked through an ideology of progress that constructed poor peasants— the majority of the population—as both the moral core of the Paraguayan nation and incompletely modern subjects. The spatiality of this imaginary is marked by Calle Ultima, or the Last Street, which correlates the edges of modern Paraguay with the spatial limits of the capital city and *campesinos* as democracy's other.

59. I thank Thainara Granero de Melo, PhD, for her research assistance building an archive of Brazilian spatial and racial imaginaries of Paraguay and Paraguayans.

60. C. Rodrigues (2015) analyzed Brazilian discourses about Paraguay in the media after the parliamentary coup ousting Fernando Lugo, as well as historical narratives of the War of the Triple Alliance.

61. A. Souza 1996.

62. This nationalist position is popular on the Paraguayan Right and Left, as both view the early dictatorial period as a noble anti-imperialist stance against the coercive extension of British trading relationships and capital markets.

63. Mauro Silveira 2007, 62.

64. Pires Junior 2015.

65. "Contamos mais una victoria," *Paraguay Ilustrado!* 6 (September 1865): 3.

66. "Anecdotas," *Paraguay Illustrado!* 4 (August 1865): 3.

67. Brandalise 2017, 8.

68. Brandalise 2017, 12.

69. Brandalise 2017, 1.

70. The free-trade position asserts that IPR violations cause "significant financial losses for U.S. right holders and legitimate businesses, [and] undermine critical U.S. comparative advantages in innovation and creativity to the detriment of American workers" (USTR 2019).

71. "Lei dos sacoleiros não emplaca e procura por importações é muito baixa," *Paraná TV*, Globo.com, accessed February 5, 2021, http://g1.globo.com/pr/parana/paranatv -2edicao/videos/t/edicoes/v/lei-dos-sacoleiros-nao-emplaca-e-procura-por -importacoes-e-muito-baixa/2036568/.

72. "Sacoleiro pagará 25% de imposto e poderá importar até R$ 110 mil por ano," *Globo*, September 10, 2009, http://g1.globo.com/Noticias/Economia_Negocios /0,,MUL1299479-9356,00-SACOLEIRO+PAGARA+DE+IMPOSTO+E+PODERA+IM PORTAR+ATE+R+MIL+POR+ANO.html.

73. Interview, Dionel Pérez, August 13, 2013, Ciudad del Este.

74. João Paulo, resident of Foz do Iguaçu, cited in Brandalise 2017, 9.

75. Interview, Dionel Pérez, August 13, 2013, Ciudad del Este.

76. Bantz Craddock, "Posture Statement of General Bantz Craddock, United States

Army Commander in Chief United States Southern Command before the 109th Congress Senate Armed Services Committee," presented at the House Armed Services Committee, Washington, D.C., March 16, 2006, p. 4, https://loveman.sdsu.edu/supplement/docs/GeneralCraddockMarch2006; "A Theater Strategy of Focused Cooperation and Mutual Security," United States Southern Command, 2005, p. 7, https://loveman.sdsu.edu/supplement/docs/SC_Theater_Strategy.pdf.

77. Giménez Béliveau 2011, 8.

78. Schemo 1998.

79. Coffin 2004, citing George W. Bush.

80. Interpol described illicit trade as the crime of the twenty-first century (Pinheiro-Machado 2018, 9), and similar language echoed across other development agencies (see also Aguiar 2010).

81. *Capitalismo Amarillo* 2008; Aguiar 2010; Jáuregui 2008.

82. Webber 2010.

83. Schemo 1998.

84. Jeffrey Robinson (2002), cited in Rabossi 2010, 24.

85. Rohter 2001; Goldberg 2002; Junger 2002.

86. Costa and Schulmeister 2007. In 2004 the 3 + 1 Group on Tri-Border Area Security (Paraguay, Brazil, and Argentina plus the United States) issued a communiqué stating that "no operational activities of terrorism have been detected at the tri-border area" (U.S. Department of State, "Communique of the 3 + 1 Group on Tri-Border Area Security," 2004, short releases, Bureau of Public Affairs, U.S. Department of State, https://2001-2009.state.gov/s/ct/rls/other/39706.htm).

87. During the Cold War, *Jane's Intelligence Review* was originally *Jane's Soviet Intelligence Review* and was later linked to the misinformation behind British prime minister Tony Blair's "Dodgy Dossier," used to justify the Iraq War.

88. Parks and Russo 2014.

89. Parks and Russo 2014, 26–27.

90. U.S. Embassy quotes are all from cables leaked between 2004 and 2010 through Wikileaks. See "hotbed of illicit activities" ("Interagency Cooperation on Tri-Border Area," August 20, 2007, 07ASUNCION688_a); "a haven for contraband, piracy, and other illegal activity" ("Paraguay: The Duarte Administration at Two Years," September 26, 2005, 05ASUNCION1218_a).

91. "Corruption in Paraguay's political and economic system undermines its efforts to modernize" (U.S. Embassy cable, "Scene-Setter for Codel Reid," November 20, 2007, 07ASUNCION970_a). The cable notes "protection not only for drug traffickers, but for terrorist fundraisers, IPR pirates and other organized crime kingpins" (U.S. Embassy cable, "Cabral Is Back," August 19, 2005, 05ASUNCION1045_a).

92. U.S. Embassy cable, "Paraguay Scenesetter for Southcom Commander," April 4, 2007, 07ASUNCION285_a. "Bloated but weak state institutions" is part of the stock language used by the embassy to describe Paraguay. I found similar language in fourteen other cables.

93. U.S. Embassy cable, "Maintaining MCC Momentum in Paraguay," December 10, 2007, 07ASUNCION1011_a.

94. Horacio Cartes was elected president of Paraguay in 2013 on the heels of the

speedy 2012 parliamentary coup of the country's only modern Left-leaning president, Fernando Lugo.

95. In 2019 Brazilian officials sought his arrest for money laundering in connection with the massive Car Wash corruption scandal. While on the lam, he hid out on the ranch of Fahd Jamil Georges, a notorious Brazilian drug trafficker.

96. For instance, U.S. Embassy cable, "ZA-09-0007 / YAZ1K Martinetti, Julio et al / Operation Heart of Stone Case Coordination Meeting," January 5, 2010, 10BUENOSAIRES5_a.

97. "Paraguay: South America's New Emerging Leader," *Forbes* (blog), February 28, 2018, https://www.forbes.com/custom/2018/03/01/paraguay/.

98. U.S. Embassy cable, "Managing Expectation for New SEPRELAD Director," August 27, 2007, 07ASUNCION714_a.

99. For instance, a U.S. Embassy cable describes a district judge as "on the take" ("Paraguay Political and Economic Update," August 14–20, 05ASUNCION1053, accessed through Wikileaks).

100. "Cartes piensa crear fuentes de trabajo, pero no dice cómo," *ABC Color*, March 7, 2012, http://www.abc.com.py/edicion-impresa/politica/cartes-piensa-crear-fuentes-de -trabajo-pero-no-dice-como-374467.html.

101. Akhil Gupta (2012) shows how the everyday practice of corruption brings into view an unbounded, fragmented state that manages poverty through the systemic production of arbitrariness, itself a source of structural violence toward the poor.

102. Other critical scholars of corruption use the term *corruption talk* (Kim 2020; Prouse 2021).

103. The liberal epistemology of corruption assumes rule following as the norm, or at least as an aspirational ideal, and then compares everyday dealmaking or schemes like *la tablita* to this norm, finding deviation and deviance. This perspective starts from the abstract presupposition that the law represents the common will of the people, accumulated over time to protect the safety and well-being of the populace. Individuals, the story goes, can expect to be treated equally before the law, and this equal treatment signifies modern democracies. The liberal epistemology of corruption holds even in the face of countervailing evidence demonstrating that the law upholds the interests of those with the power to write it and to selectively enforce it. Of course, in many places, social norms and customary practices hold sway over legal compliance. Obeying the law is one guide for action among many and often not the strongest. For both rich and poor, enforcement of the law is often negotiable.

104. This is the dominant definition of corruption (Harrison 2007). See "Anticorruption Fact Sheet," text/HTML, World Bank, February 19, 2020, https://www.worldbank .org/en/news/factsheet/2020/02/19/anticorruption-fact-sheet.

105. Wedel 2012.

106. Engelmann 2020.

107. E. Brown and Cloke 2004, 287. These views justified privatization and other structural adjustment policies. After the disasters and dislocations of Latin America's "lost decade," the World Bank revised its views, acknowledging the need for functioning institutions and good governance, yet the anticorruption industry retains its antistate bias.

108. Doshi and Ranganathan 2017.

109. J. Souza 2019.

110. Barkan thinks with Agamben to analyze contemporary corporate power. Agamben argues that sovereign power resides in the political reason of the state of exception, that is, in the power of the state to declare an emergency and suspend the law. Originating in archaic Roman law's logic of sovereign power, the state of exception today is brutally realized in Guantánamo via the U.S. juridical designation of enemy combatants as outside all legal protection.

111. Historically chartered grants—the forerunner to the corporate form we know today—formed a "sovereign gift" that offered "legally authorized suspensions" of the law on the grounds that these exceptions served the general interest (Barkan 2013, 8, 18). This history clarifies how both corporate and state power is ontologically rooted in the political reason of the exception.

112. Barkan 2013, 4.

113. Cartes's businesses inhabit both the light and the shadows. They include formal firms like juice companies and a soccer team and shadowy dealings with contraband cigarettes, fraud, and money laundering.

114. The popular vernacular of *blanqueamiento* stands in stark contrast to another use of the same term: the state project of whitening promoted by racist modernizers. This form of eugenicist *blanqueamiento* sought to lighten, contain, or eliminate Black and Indigenous bodies and cultures through European immigration, racial mixing, forced assimilation, and cultural genocide.

115. *Blanqueamiento* resonates with Oren Yiftachel's (2009) notions of gray space but with specific attention to the practices of the powerful and the racialized dynamics outside Israel's ethnocracy.

116. "Paraguay: South America's New Emerging Leader"; H.J. 2013.

117. Likewise, these performances are gendered. Cartes shares with Trump and Bolsonaro the patriarchal political style of the overly confident man who is callous to the suffering of others, unperturbed by facts, and uninterested in agonistic engagement with an adversary, promoting instead the annihilation of enemies. All use a posttruth style of speech that Will Davies (2016, 133) suggests is endemic to current neoliberal forms that abandon the pretense of credibly representing reality for "performative utterances which seek to preserve the status quo" and dominate discursive space.

118. Settler ownership is stabilized through the performance of Lockean improvements, or individualized projects of making what John Locke called "the wasteland" productive. This includes performing bureaucratic legibility through individual land titles (Whitehead 2010; Porter 2010). The project is one of elimination (Wolfe 2006). It all rests on the lies of terra nullius and the doctrine of discovery, the colonial reading of the "new world" as empty or only inhabited by nomads who are unwilling to make lands productive and therefore the idea that the land is open for the taking.

119. Lipsitz 2011, 3.

CHAPTER 2. Contraband Urbanism

1. Shopping Cristal, a lightning-rod business in the zone of the fourth stage, was standing through the end of August 2014. "Quedó por demoler solo el Shopping Cristal

en CDE," *ABC Color*, August 19, 2014, http://www.abc.com.py/edicion-impresa/interior /quedo-por-demoler-solo-el-shopping-cristal-en-cde-1277438.html.

2. "Comercio de CDE paralizado por protestas," *Ultima Hora*, August 12, 2014, https:// www.ultimahora.com/comercio-cde-paralizado-protestas-n820048.html.

3. Personal communication, local journalist, September 1, 2014, Ciudad del Este.

4. Personal communication, Kelembu, March 15, 2015, Ciudad del Este.

5. Various estimates of trade volume, all necessarily imprecise, are discussed in chapter 1.

6. As described in the introduction, theories of the social production of space refute dominant conceptualizations of space as an inert stage or empty container without force in the world. Modeled on how Marx demystified the commodity as a set of hidden labor relations and social processes, Lefebvre denaturalized space. Every society, each with its own set of social relationships of production and reproduction, produces its own sort of space. Doreen Massey (2005) offers a comprehensive critique of dominant, aspatial theories that propose time as the medium of change and locus of agency, both structuralist and poststructuralist, including Althusser, Bergson, Laclau, and Derrida.

7. Roy 2011b.

8. The hegemony of global urbanism is well documented by critical urban scholars (Jennifer Robinson 2006; Pieterse 2008; Bunnell and Maringanti 2010; McFarlane 2011; Sheppard, Leitner, and Maringanti 2013).

9. Logan and Molotch (2007) explore the politics of models imagining the city as a growth machine.

10. Lefebvre uses the term *the urban* rather than *the city* because the latter assumes a bounded, discrete, unproblematic unit of analysis, missing the historically produced, spatially expansive, interconnected processes of urbanization that are at once symbolic and structural. This same point is made by Brenner and Schmid (2015) in their thesis on planetary urbanization, although, as noted by others, they elevate epistemology over ontology and thereby miss the everyday as constitutive of social life and, crucially, as a site of resistance, rebellion, difference, and possibility (Ruddick et al. 2018).

11. Elden 2004, 177.

12. Kanai (2014) discusses Manaus, while Arboleda (2015) studies the mining boom in the Huasco Valley. Young and Keil (2010) look at Toronto.

13. "Informes ratifican impunidad en la franja de Itaipú durante era Cartes," *ABC Ultima Hora*, September 18, 2019, https://www.ultimahora.com/informes-ratifican -impunidad-la-franja-itaipu-era-cartes-n2844417.html.

14. These goods were imported into Paraguay either through Panama's free trade zone in Colón or through Paraguay's custom warehouse in the port of Paranaguá, Brazil.

15. These factories are under multiple investigations, including one stemming from a Brazilian lawsuit contending that they are the main source of counterfeit cigarettes flooding the regional market.

16. Guevara et al. 2009.

17. "Contrabando en la franja de Itaipú sigue pese a operativos realizados," *Ultima Hora*, August 20, 2019, https://www.ultimahora.com/contrabando-la-franja-itaipu-sigue -pese-operativos-realizados-n2839073.html; "Informes ratifican impunidad."

18. Slater 2015; Wacquant, Slater, and Pereira 2014.

19. "Investigación de los puertos ilegales de Ciudad del Este está paralizada," *ABC Color*, March 23, 2013, http://www.abc.com.py/edicion-impresa/economia/investigacion -de-los-puertos-ilegales-de-ciudad-del-este-esta-paralizada-552686.html.

20. USTR 2016, 18.

21. USTR 2015, 20; 2017, 32.

22. "Reclaman intervención en Ciudad del Este," *La Nación*, June 22, 2016, http:// www.lanacion.com.py/2016/06/09/210539/.

23. Drivers' associations cut deals with municipal officials to access street space by obtaining either a license or unofficial permission to sell without a license. A leader of an association of taxi drivers reported two umbrella unions with thirty-four associations organized by zone. He estimated twenty-two hundred total drivers. Personal communication, taxi association president, March 12, 2015, Ciudad del Este.

24. Observations, September 11, 2013, Ciudad del Este.

25. Haudenschild proposed more strategic use of three negotiated customs lists that reduced tax rates for 649 consumer goods, aiming to both support reexportation and protect national industry (often hurt by cheap imports).

26. Personal communication, municipal director, June 2013, Ciudad del Este.

27. Interview, Cinthia Ayala, May 19, 2013, Ciudad del Este.

28. Taniguchi worked with the famous architect Jamie Lerner in the 1970s on Curitiba's renowned master plan. (Lerner later became the city's mayor.)

29. Interview, architect, March 12, 2015, Ciudad del Este.

30. Personal communication, resident, May 29, 2013, Ciudad del Este.

31. Personal communication, traffic officer, May 17, 2013, Ciudad del Este.

32. Personal communication, transit official, June 13, 2013, Ciudad del Este.

33. What the officer called the "reduced fine" was 320,000 guaranies (about U.S.$74 in 2013).

34. Observation, Lucho Zacarías, September 11, 2013, Ciudad del Este.

35. Bhowmik 2005; Crossa 2009; Watson 2009a.

36. Devlin 2011; Holland 2015; Tucker 2017.

37. Cardenas 2007, 162–63.

38. Article 123 of Municipal Tax Law (Law 620) and Ordinance 027/98 of the City Council of Ciudad del Este.

39. Fernando Rabossi (2011b) argues that the precarious use tax constituted vendors as "legally precarious" because the law authorized the local state not only to extend permission to occupy public space but also to revoke that permission.

40. Personal communication, street vendor, October 14, 2013, Ciudad del Este.

41. Other vendors lost large brick-and-mortar stalls and opposed the plan on the grounds that it downsized their claims.

42. The municipality signed a deal, called a *convenio*, with the street vendors' association, the Federation.

43. Interview, municipal official, June 13, 2013, Ciudad del Este.

44. The Pilot Plan required vendors to apply to the city council for recognition of their claims. After approval, the municipality assigned the vendor to a spot in standard-

ized, state-owned stalls. The vendor paid a monthly fee, the "precarious use tax" (*canon del uso precario*), which had long been on the books but was unenforced. The tax applied to street vendors across the city, but the Pilot Plan accentuated its importance.

45. Personal communication, Raul Muñoz, August 15, 2021, Ciudad del Este.

46. "Ciudad del Este: Shopping Paris," SkyscraperCity, 2015, https://www.skyscrapercity.com/showthread.php?t=1850147.

47. The national newspaper *ABC Color* calls the Jebai Center "a time bomb" due to the precarious structure and deplorable electrical system. "Jebai Center, una bomba de tiempo en microcentro de Ciudad del Este," *ABC Color*, December 26, 2011, http://www.abc.com.py/edicion-impresa/interior/jebai-center-una-bomba-de-tiempo-en-microcentro-de-ciudad-del-este-349094.html.

48. Observation, taxi driver, May 14, 2013, Ciudad del Este; personal communication, street vendor, March 27, 2013, Ciudad del Este.

49. Taniguchi proposed a second bridge to ease congestion and facilitate trade, as well as improvements to road layouts, the building of pedestrian bridges over the street market, and the creation of a business district in place of Remansito, a poor, riverfront barrio.

50. Whitehead and More 2007; N. Smith 1996.

51. Royal Investments financed construction of Shopping del Este, a corporation led by Walid Amine Sweid, a Lebanese importer-exporter, and Juan Carlos Sosa Barreto, the son of the port town's first mayor, appointed by Stroessner. Both are likely connected to contraband.

52. Dávila 2016, 88.

CHAPTER 3. Schemes and State Power

1. Senate proceedings, May 24, 1990, "Diario de sesiones," 15–19. During the expropriation hearings, Senator Ovelar explained the terms of the social interest: to "relocate three thousand street vendors, fellow citizens who work in the street. This is the purpose [of expropriation], and also to bring some order to our streets and guarantee that this site does not just benefit a single individual."

2. "We see the extent of the greed of this former president, a dictator, who would not even pay 10,000 guaranies," Senator Ovelar said. Senate proceedings, May 24, 1990, "Diario de sesiones," 15–19.

3. Personal communication, Raul Muñoz, September 13, 2013, Ciudad del Este.

4. Personal communication, Cinthia Ayala, June 1, 2013, Ciudad del Este.

5. Kregg Hetherington (2011) describes a similar politics of paper in disputes over rural land claims and the contested process of interpreting piles of documents, from land titles to boundary measurements.

6. Kim 2020; Roy 2002; Weinstein 2008; Yiftachel 2009.

7. Alonso 1995; Ballvé 2012; Eilenberg 2012; Tsing 2005; Uribe 2017; M. Watts 1992.

8. Hansen and Stepputat 2006.

9. Dunbar-Ortiz and Gilio-Whitaker 2016.

10. Liberalism constructs and depends on its outsides, those considered not capable of citizenship's responsibilities, like the landless, the enslaved, and Indigenous people.

While those categorized as outside change, the project of securing these borders of exclusion requires violence (Losurdo 2011).

11. José Gaspar Rodríguez de Francia served as consul of the republic between 1813 and 1840, a period interrupted by the brief rule of Fulgencio Yegros. In 1814 Francia declared himself supreme dictator. Historian Milda Rivarola (2010, 5) described Francia's political project as "Jacobin egalitarianism." Both Eduardo Galeano (1975) and Augusto Roa Bastos (1987) argue that Francia's project of egalitarian nationalism was threatened by imperialist forces and justified his dictatorial tendencies.

12. Landlocked, Paraguay depended on river routes to ports controlled by Buenos Aires and Montevideo. In geopolitical conflicts, Argentina sometimes denied passage or charged exorbitant fees for Paraguayan cargo. Thus, nationalist self-sufficiency also responded to Argentine control of access to external markets.

13. Saeger 2007.

14. The numbers of Paraguayan deaths are controversial. Academic estimates range from a low of twenty-one thousand (Reber 1988) to 69 percent of the prewar population (Whigham and Potthast 1999). Regardless, the country had a small population before the war, a few hundred thousand, and after the war the skewed male-female ratio led some commentators to call Paraguay "a land of women" (Cannon 1946, 1).

15. Bethell 1996, 13.

16. Roa Bastos (1987, 217) described the War of the Triple Alliance in anti-imperialist terms: "The economic interests of the British Empire . . . could not allow the dangerous utopia of self-determination in this little landlocked country to continue to exist."

17. Indeed, the secret Treaty of the Triple Alliance between Brazil and Argentina, which predated the war, delineated which part of the Paraguayan territory each of the three countries would lay claim to after the war.

18. Paraguay first entered international credit markets, facilitated by London brokerages, through the Eight Per Cent Public Works Loan of 1871 (Schuster 2015).

19. Vázquez 2006, 23; Abente-Brun 1989.

20. Vázquez 2006, 24.

21. Barrett 1910, 37.

22. Data from the Dirección General de Estadísticas Encuestas y Censos. Ciudad del Este is in the department of Alto Paraná, which was formed in 1945. In the early 1900s, the settlement of Alto Paraná was limited to a few small pioneer communities, a few state-funded but unsuccessful Catholic missions, and a lone health outpost.

23. Instability marked the first half of the twentieth century as the people of Paraguay witnessed two civil wars and frequent factionalist coups. Between 1904 and 1939, twenty-two presidents served, nearly all from the Liberal Party. Stroessner rose in the military ranks through his loyalty to the Fascist, pro-Nazi president Higinio Morínigo (1940–48) and led military campaigns to quash worker rebellions in the 1947 Barefoot Revolution.

24. For a discussion of racial projects, see Omi and Winant (1986).

25. Maybury-Lewis and Howe 1980; Reed 1995. Beyond land theft, researchers accused the Stroessner regime of committing genocide against the Aché and other groups, seeking their land for agriculture and mining (Arens 1976; Miinzel 1976; R. Smith and Meliá 1978).

26. Kleinpenning 1987; Pastore 1979.

27. Land reform allotted 74 percent of total land to 2.5 percent of recipients, contributing to one of the most unequal distributions of land in the world ("La reforma" 2006, 15). More than 60 percent of recipients accessed land through fraudulent deals (Guereña 2016, 15; Fogel and Riquelme 2005). Land reform often fails to provide farmland to the poor (Borras and Franco 2010; Zoomers and Van der Haar 2000).

28. See note 58, chapter 1. Over the last three decades, the Colorado Party has largely abandoned *campesino* constituencies in its support of export-oriented industrial monocultures, especially soy, rather than state-subsidized smallholder farming. Today, the Colorado Party and national media outlets construe *campesino* organizing as a criminal invasion of private property (Nagel 1999).

29. Hetherington 2011.

30. Presidential Decree 24.634, January 28, 1957.

31. Parodi 2002; Silva 2007. Both countries claimed the massive Guaíra waterfalls, which led to a militarized territorial dispute that continued into the 1960s.

32. Fogel 2008, 279.

33. "Stronista" refers to the governing style of Alfredo Stroessner.

34. Presidential Decree 25.209, February 27, 1957.

35. Saba bought one hundred hectares of state land at fire-sale prices, 4 million guaranies, or about $5,300 in inflation-adjusted U.S. dollars, promising to draw up an urbanization plan and to fund the construction of roads and homes (Silva 2007, 345). His master plan proposed an urban zone radiating outward from the foot of the planned International Friendship Bridge, an industrial zone ringing the city center, and a rural-urban boundary beyond which land was zoned for farming.

36. Rivarola 2007; Morínigo 2008.

37. McSherry (2012) and Grandin (2007) detail the U.S. backing of authoritarian violence and its far-reaching, antidemocratic impacts.

38. Due to a labor shortage, an army regiment joined construction crews to build the airport, later excavating the Lake of the Republic, through donations collected by Ynsfrán from other municipalities.

39. Guernica (2003, 142) calls this a "vast patronage machinery." Rather than transactional trades, Mbembe's (2001, 45, emphasis in original) concept of the salary captures how "*the state created debts on society*" through patronage networks. As much as generating loyalty, the salary disciplines political imaginations, limiting the kinds of claims indebted state subjects make on the state.

40. Predicting a pattern of manufacturing-driven urban development, planners zoned an industrial district at the imagined urban edge, not far from the center city.

41. The state expropriated land from private companies, the yerba plantations of the Industria Paraguaya, and a few *latifundistas,* including Don Domingo Barthe. These lands remain contested by landless peasants (Fogel 2012).

42. Stroessner gifted one parcel to the Brazilian ex-president Kubitschek, gave another to his loyal personal secretary, Mario Abdo Benítez, and gave a third parcel to himself. Together, the seven hectares claimed by Stroessner and the two claimed by Abdo Benítez form the Nine Hectares.

43. Tully 1982.

44. P. Harvey 2014.

45. Interview, importer-exporter, September 11, 2013, Ciudad del Este.

46. Itaipú held the title of world's largest dam until, in 2010, the Three Gorges Dam went on line. While Three Gorges is physically bigger, Itaipú still produces more electricity.

47. Folch 2013, 45.

48. Holston 1989.

49. Holston 2008.

50. Interview, Carlos Barreto Sarubbi, September 19, 2013, Ciudad del Este.

51. Juan Manuel Salinas, "La muerte de Barreto Sarubbi y el ¿silencio cómplice?," *Epa!* (blog), February 22, 2018, http://www.epa.com.py/2018/02/22/la-muerte-de-barreto -sarubbi-y-el-silencio-complice/. Miranda (2000) and Aguirre (2008) also detail Barreto's links to contraband networks, which are also open secrets.

52. Historian Aníbal Miranda cited in Salinas, "La muerte."

53. Woods 1998, 101.

54. Centro de Documentación y Archivo para la Defensa de los Derechos Humanos (CDyA), box 61, folder 1151, Asunción.

55. A frontier politician illustrated this by quipping, "The Paraguayan state is a gang of friends [*una banda de amigos*]," while Kregg Hetherington (2011, 238) described the Colorado Party as a "self-serving private association."

56. Officially the Archives of Terror are called the Center for the Documentation and Archive for the Defense of Human Rights (Centro de Documentación y Archivo para la Defensa de los Derechos Humanos, Asunción), which I denote as CDyA. Contraband, in the Archives of Terror, invoked different registers of meaning, including an image problem to be managed by the regime and an anti-Stronista critique in the discourse of dissidents. Opposition to the Stroessner regime regularly critiqued "industrial contraband" or "contraband as philosophy" (CDyA, box 61, folder 1151), while the regime itself translated English-language news reports that, for instance, described how "70% of Paraguayan foreign trade is based in contraband" (CDyA, box 66, folder 2482).

57. CDyA, box 27, folder 1691.

58. CDyA, box 9, folder 1495.

59. CDyA, box 25, folder 1139.

60. In this document the authorizing letter was called a *nota de remisión*.

61. Interview, architect and member of Puerto Presidente Stroessner's administrative commission, October 5, 2013, Asunción.

62. CDyA, box 47, folder 127.

63. In an interview, an Administrative Commission appointee called these letters *cartas permisorias* (September 19, 2013, Ciudad del Este).

64. Silva 2007, 51, my translation, but quotation marks and capitalization are reproduced as they appear in the original.

65. Emancipation Paraguay, 1986, CDyA, box 27, folder 1691, my translation.

66. Comaroff and Comaroff 1999, 281, emphasis in original.

67. Historian Milda Rivarola called this consolidation of control by local alliances the "decentralization of corruption" (phone interview, September 17, 2013, Ciudad del Este).

68. Personal communication, street vendor block president, March 8, 2015, Ciudad del Este.

69. "Convocan otra marcha."

70. Personal communication, Emilio Sosa, March 11, 2015, Ciudad del Este.

71. The first free municipal elections were held in May 1991.

72. Heller 2001.

73. "Crean nueva coordinadora para buscar reactivación," *Vanguardia*, September 25, 2001.

74. "Hoy no habrá clases en colegios y universidades," *Vanguardia*, September 12, 2001.

75. "Hoy no habrá clases."

76. Puenteguýpe, *Vanguardia*, September 17, 2001.

77. "Quemaron muñeco alegórico al Presidente González Macchi," *Vanguardia*, September 12, 2001.

78. "Por temor, brasileños ayer no cruzaron el Puente," *Vanguardia*, September 14, 2001. The figure U.S.$23 million is an estimate adjusted for inflation.

79. The agreement also included a plan to give public jobs to residents of Alto Paraná and prohibited members of the national military from entering the "primary zone," the strip along the border that is subject to separate laws.

80. Aníbal Amado Nuñez, "Los siete puntos de la vergüenza," *Vanguardia*, September 15–16, 2001.

81. Law 12/90.

82. Political speech, Elias Fox, March 8, 2015.

83. Here I use Stuart Hall and Doreen Massey's (2010) interpretation of the Gramscian conjuncture as a temporarily settled social arrangement punctuated by crises that shape but never determine the resolution of the crisis.

84. Given the prominence of the Federation, it is not possible to anonymize the name of this group, as I have done for all other community organizations. All individuals associated with the Federation are anonymized.

85. This coalition argued that the land should, in its entirety, benefit street vendors through subsidized rents. The Federation, in contrast, argued that entrepreneurial vendors were capable of shouldering business risks. The coalition opposed the secretive contract negotiated between the municipality and the Federation.

86. While the Federation fought for expropriation, it ultimately abandoned its claims on the Nine Hectares. Critics suspect that the Federation cut deals with Javier Zacarías, selling out its constituency. Federation leadership, in contrast, argued that vendors lacked the power to contest the urban growth machine. They also argued that the streets of Ciudad del Este would never be clear of vendors, so relocation to the Nine Hectares would only expose their members to more competition from new arrivals.

87. Article 3 of Law 533/95 states that "the purpose of the expropriation is the relocation of vendors from the public thoroughfare and occupants of green spaces in the municipal public domain of Ciudad del Este, to the effect that the same establish their businesses in the expropriated properties, the totality of which will be used for this purpose."

88. Supreme Court Decision 415/95, "Acción de inconstitucionalidad: Contra la ley 533/95," December 20, 1995, Supreme Court judges Oscar Paciello Candia, Raul Sapena Brugada, and Luis Lezcano Claude.

89. Senate proceedings, May 24, 1990, "Diario de sesiones," 15–19.

90. In the Paraguayan Constitution, private property is inviolable, with expropriation limited to exceptional cases of the social interest. Expropriation required compensating landholders, even in cases of *tierra malhabida*.

91. S. Moore 1978.

92. Sometime around 2011, officials from Itaipú—which funded construction of vending infrastructure upgrades for some vendors—requested the census of regularized street vendors so they could be charged for electricity. Invoking the autonomy of local governments under decentralization, municipal officials refused to provide the census (interview, municipal director of urban affairs, September 24, 2013, Ciudad del Este).

93. Interview, street vendor association president, August 28, 2013, Ciudad del Este.

94. A lawyer explained how the Tribunal de Cuentas became a parallel institution displacing the National Comptroller: "The Comptroller does not enter to audit the municipal administration. And the judge, obedient to the political will, against the Constitution, which establishes the Comptroller's Office as the only oversight body and against all the regulations, against the constitutional order, the judge grants a protection order to the municipality, prohibiting the Comptroller's Office to exercise its constitutional role. It is incredible. And so this administration was not audited, their accounting was not reviewed or supervised from that time to today. It is an administration that functions as a private administration" (interview, March 19, 2015, Ciudad del Este).

95. Observation, municipality lobby, October 8, 2015, Ciudad del Este.

96. Personal communication, journalist, February 11, 2019.

CHAPTER 4. Urban Livelihood Rights

1. Observation, Emilio Sosa, March 11, 2015, Ciudad del Este.

2. Laclau (2005) argues this friend/enemy binary is key to populism.

3. Sosa observation.

4. Early associations unsuccessfully sought to limit the number of allowable vendors to the original 108 vendors affiliated with the United Association of Sunglasses Sellers (Asociación de Lenteros Unidos) and the Association of Vendors of Artisanal Goods (Asociación de Vendedores de Artículos Típicos).

5. Eizenberg 2012.

6. Rosaldo 2022.

7. Scholars in the postdevelopment school, like Arturo Escobar (2011), elide the extent to which the desires of oppressed people are shaped by capitalism, racism, patriarchy, and other structures of oppression. These approaches seek to chart a path beyond capitalism by excavating subaltern knowledges and centering their political ontologies. Asher and Wainwright (2019) critique the postdevelopment school for romanticizing the local and essentializing subaltern politics as resistance to development. The result is a politically disabling politics of cultural difference that is insufficiently attentive to the historical and geographic dynamics of capitalism, as well as to the ways that hegemonic forces shape culture and desire.

8. Street vending is a common and *placed* urban-economic practice. Its ends vary widely, with many vending as a survival strategy and earning little, while a much smaller

number earn a decent living as small-scale capitalists (Bromley 2000). Both groups provide cheap goods and services as an important part of the urban fabric (Bhowmik 2005). Extensive scholarship on the importance of street vendors has not stopped a recent worldwide wave of evictions (Skinner and Balbuena 2019).

9. Street vendors are managed through uncertainty (Tucker and Devlin 2019), electorally useful forbearance (Holland 2015), and the privatization of public space (Crossa 2009).

10. Indeed, as state action shapes landscapes of wealth and poverty through selective investment and disinvestment, the state produces informality. More than the official power to draw and redraw the line between legal and illegal (Portes, Castells, and Benton 1989), state practice itself works through "unceasing negotiability" (Roy 2002, 18), power-laden processes (Yiftachel 2009; Varley 2013), and dealmaking (Pieterse 2013).

11. Ethnographers also demonstrate that arbitrariness (Gupta 2012) and illegibility (Das and Poole 2004) condition the slow violence of state poverty management projects.

12. Spivak 1988.

13. Miraftab 2009, 33.

14. Use value refers to the qualities of a commodity or space that serve a useful purpose by meeting a human want or need, while exchange value is determined by the market.

15. Affect is alternately theorized as felt experience, lived intensity (Massumi 2002), "unstructured potential" (Shouse 2005), or Spinozan bodily capacity underwriting action (Bennett 2009). Scholars concerned with the ontological grounds of the political, in particular, consider affect to be noncognitive, interpersonal, nonrepresentational, even "irreducibly bodily and automatic" (Massumi 2002, 28). However, this sharp delineation between affect and cognition is contested for neglecting feminist scholarship on the body (Hemmings 2005), resting on a binary between biology and culture or rationality and emotion (Leys 2011), and eliding the necessary project of giving reasons for promoting select affective states over others (Barnett 2008, 187). I use *affect* to connote the emotional realm of lived experience ambiguously related to cognitive processing and do not claim to be able to sharply differentiate between emotion and affect.

16. Ahmed 2013; Berlant 2011; Hemmings 2005.

17. Foucault 1978, vol. 1.

18. Spivak 1988.

19. Cockayne 2016.

20. E. James 2010.

21. Adams 2012, 211.

22. Berlant, Vishmidt, and Helms 2010, 3; see also Anderson 2014.

23. Observations, June 11, 2013, Ciudad del Este.

24. Observation, municipal official, June 2013, Ciudad del Este.

25. Paraphrase of multiple conversations, Ña Gabriela, June 14 and 16, 2013, Ciudad del Este.

26. Personal communication, street vendor, October 14, 2013, Ciudad del Este.

27. Personal communication, street vendor, June 11, 2013, Ciudad del Este.

28. Personal communication, Ña Gabriela, June 14, 2013, Ciudad del Este.

29. Observations, June 13, 2013, Ciudad del Este.

30. Personal communication, Ña Isabel, August 20, 2013, Ciudad del Este.

31. Interview, Ña Lucia, October 25, 2013, Ciudad del Este.

32. I thank Mariela Cuevas for this translation.

33. The base verb of the construction *ne'ẽveima*, "to speak or create" (*ne'ẽ*), attributes the force of conjuring *¡chake!* to "they," the municipal officials. Ña Lucia curtailed that force, declaring it over through conjugating *ne'ẽ* in the negative and past tense, the equivalent of adding "not anymore" (*veima*) alongside the root verb.

34. Interview, Obdulio, October 29, 2013, Ciudad del Este.

35. These practices do not amount to an abstract sovereign capacity to activate a state of exception, which assumes a stable legal order that can be suspended (Agamben 2005). Nor are they the practices of calculation, measurement, and mapping often described as enabling state power through particular modes of seeing, of rendering space and subjects knowable through measurement (Mitchell 1999; James Scott 1998).

36. Interview, Santiago Torres, June 27, 2013, Ciudad del Este.

37. I argue that the political emotion of uncertainty is simultaneously a collective experience, an embodied affect, and an emotive field through which municipal officials govern. This reading follows Ben Anderson (2014, 17), who differentiates between structures of feeling, a Spinozan bodily capacity, and a Foucauldian object-target, that is, a population-level phenomenon through which state actors attempt to govern. With structures of feeling, Raymond Williams (1978) connects individual felt experience with collective, historical processes. "Practical consciousness" or "meanings and values as they are actively lived and felt" articulate social forms at other scales: institutions, ideologies, and the like (R. Williams 1978, 132). Structures of feeling can be progressive or regressive, fueling xenophobic movements or freedom struggles. For Anderson, affect becomes an object-target when state projects target, channel, and measure it. For instance, consumer confidence is both an enabling affective condition of economic growth and an object of calculation and intervention.

38. Observation, June 2013, Ciudad del Este. *Ambulantes* are hawkers with no fixed claims to space, while *casilleros* command established vending stalls with on-site storage. Obduilo is a *mesitero*, a street vendor with a table, a more secure status than a hawker but controlling less space than a *casillero*.

39. Personal communication, Ña Lucia, October 25, 2013, Ciudad del Este.

40. Thompson 1993.

41. Personal communication, Hugo Domínguez, June 2013, Ciudad del Este.

42. Ghertner 2015; Watson 2009a.

43. Interview, Ña Lucia, October 25, 2013, Ciudad del Este.

44. Lefebvre 2003, 18–21.

45. Personal communication, Magdalena, August 8, 2013, Ciudad del Este.

46. Observation, June 27, 2013, Ciudad del Este.

47. Observation, June 6, 2013, Ciudad del Este.

48. Observation, street vendor, June 6, 2013, Ciudad del Este.

49. Observation, June 6, 2013, Ciudad del Este.

50. Personal communication, Celia, June 28, 2013, Ciudad del Este.

51. As Saba Mahmood (2011, 14) insists, "The meaning and sense of agency cannot be fixed in advance." Instead of focusing on (authentic or deluded) expressions of individual

will and desire, this feminist approach starts from embodied action to ask what kinds of subjects those actions produce and how intersubjective relations perform, reiterate, and contest relations of rule.

52. Fraser and Gordon 1994.

CHAPTER 5. Enclosure Devices

1. Observations, July 12, 2013, Ciudad del Este.
2. Personal communication, journalist, July 12, 2013, Ciudad del Este.
3. Observations, July 12, 2013, Ciudad del Este.
4. Recorded in field notes, August 15, 2015.
5. Álvarez 2018; Cielo 2018; Gago 2018, 34; Gago, Cielo, and Gachet 2018; Tovar 2018.
6. See note 70 of the introduction.
7. Fraser 2014.
8. Bear et al. 2015.
9. Gago 2017; Sheppard, Sparks, and Leitner 2020.
10. Bromley 2000; Dias 2016; Duneier, Hasan, and Carter 2000.
11. Marx (1894, 874–75) writes that primitive accumulation "can be nothing other than the process which divorces the worker from the ownership of the conditions of his own labour."
12. Geographers and anthropologists, in particular, have outlined how dispossession today casts millions into the worlds of wagelessness (Denning 2010; Li 2010; M. Watts 2011; Perreault 2013; Sanyal 2013; Soederberg 2012; Sassen 2014).
13. Gidwani and Maringanti 2016; Inverardi-Ferri 2018; Samson 2015.
14. A. Davis 1983; De Angelis 2004.
15. While Gibson-Graham perhaps overestimate the power of discursive structures and economic imaginaries in shaping material social relations, their work has neverthe-less been crucial to directing our attention to these important social fields of power.
16. See the introduction for further discussion.
17. Even further, in many places working for a wage remains a condition for effective citizenship. Barchiesi (2011, 10) calls this the "work-citizenship nexus," while Nancy Fra-ser and Linda Gordon (1994) trace the gendered genealogy that codes the male bread-winner who earns a family wage as independent, obscures the various dependencies in-herent in the labor relation, and pathologizes other relationships like so-called welfare dependency.
18. Katz 2001.
19. The tenacity of the deficit definition echoes dynamics that render invisible value-producing domains, like women's unpaid household labor and social reproduction more broadly (Katz 2001), as well as the essential inputs of nature.
20. For the neoliberal view, see Maloney (2004).
21. Formalization encompasses different policies, including decriminalizing infor-mal work; licensing businesses; enforcing tax, labor, and environmental regulations; and aligning activities with zoning and use-of-space codes. As Manisha Anantharaman and I (2020, 292) note, legalistic projects value rule following for its own sake, center Eurocen-tric urban knowledge, and "fail to understand the diverse realities of most cities."
22. Procacci 1991; A. Goldstein 2012.

23. Poynter (1969) analyzes the English poor laws, while Jankiewicz (2012) describes street traders as a particularly troublesome class problem for bourgeois society.

24. Personal communication, Lina, March 22, 2013, Ciudad del Este.

25. Hsing 2010; Kuruvilla, Lee, and Gallagher 2011; Lin, Cai, and Li 2003.

26. "Intendente de Foz insiste en suspender fiscalización," *Vanguardia*, September 20, 2001.

27. "Gobierno y coordinadora ceden y se flexibizarán los controles," *Vanguardia*, September 27, 2001. More than a decade later, one former CPCA organizer emphasized that their efforts eventually resulted in more sales jobs for Paraguayans (interview, CPCA leader, March 25, 2015, Ciudad del Este). Another community leader complained about the ten thousand Brazilians earning a salary in Ciudad del Este but spending it across the bridge, uninvested in local development. "We never see the hand of the state in the issue of inspections," he commented (interview, street vendors' association president, April 3, 2013, Ciudad del Este).

28. Personal communication, Lina, July 8, 2013, Ciudad del Este.

29. Interview, Lina, July 15, 2011, Ciudad del Este.

30. A *sacoleiro* named Sandra interviewed by Eric Cardin (2014, 108) also described her work as more autonomous and better paid than waged jobs: "First, it's an easier job: you don't need to wake early, there isn't a required schedule, nor a boss you have to deal with every day. And you earn more than minimum wage. Here in Foz, if you work all month, obeying orders, you earn a salary of four or five hundred reais. But if you work in Paraguay, maybe twice, you would earn this. So people around here ask themselves, Why work a full month, eight hours a day, if by traveling the highway two nights, I earn the same amount that I would earn working a full month in a regular job? . . . [W]e are doing this to survive, there is little work, and I am not going to steal."

31. Personal communication, taxi driver, September 23, 2013, Ciudad del Este. The minimum salary for elementary schoolteachers in 2020 was 2,502,847 guaranies per month, or about 15,600 guaranies per hour (about U.S.$2.26).

32. ILO 2002.

33. Personal communication, resident, May 19, 2013, Ciudad del Este.

34. The Threshold Project—investing in developing what it called "state capacity"— funded Paraguay Vende's research into formalizing the electronics trade. For seven years (2003–10), USAID funded Paraguay Vende (Paraguay Vende 2008), which published several reports on formalization and reexportation (Penner 2006a, 2006b), while Penner (1988) published an earlier report with the central bank.

35. Based on the neoliberal philosophy that increasing exports reduces poverty, U.S. development policy promoted industrializing the frontier region, hoping for jobs in the export-oriented private sector. A chart in Paraguay Vende's glossy annual report tracked the rise of exports with slight declines in poverty rates, suggesting a causal relationship. The group's strategic focus was the countryside, where its programs trained "peasants and producers to start acting like minibusinessmen" (recorded in fieldnotes, April 15, 2013). USAID also sought to reduce competition for transnational corporations taking a hit from booming markets for pirated goods.

36. Interview, Adrien Ojeda, Finance Ministry employee, September 12, 2013, Asunción.

37. Penner 2006b, 4.

38. Interview, Reinaldo Penner, April 15, 2013, Asunción.

39. Ojeda interview.

40. Penner 2006b, 29–30. Undervaluation, described in chapter 1, involves customs officials clearing entire containers of high-value electronics by weight and underreporting the value of merchandise in order to slash tax bills.

41. Penner 2006b, 29–30, quotation marks in original.

42. Penner 2006a, 19.

43. Penner 2006a, 14.

44. Ojeda interview; phone interview, Milda Rivarola, September 17, 2013, Ciudad del Este.

45. Observation, importer-exporter, September 11, 2013, Ciudad del Este.

46. U.S. Embassy quotes are all from the following leaked cables: "potentially explosive social reaction" ("GSP/IPR: Brazil's Emerging Initiatives," December 3, 2004, 04BRASILIA2253_a); Fernando Lugo's "economic justice" platform ("Paraguayan Priest Lugo's Conversion to Politics a Work in Progress," March 29, 2007, 07ASUNCION256_a).

47. Ojeda interview.

48. Penner interview.

49. Pinheiro-Machado 2017, 81.

50. Pinheiro-Machado 2017, 3.

51. Pinheiro-Machado 2017, 56.

52. Pinheiro-Machado 2017, 59.

53. Pinheiro-Machado 2017, 55, 74.

54. Rabossi 2018, 270.

55. Pinheiro-Machado (2017, 83) cites border officials in Foz do Iguaçu who estimated the number of bridge crossers at twenty thousand to forty thousand each day in 2002, although this is much higher than U.S. Embassy estimates of six thousand people crossing each day in 2005 ("CODEL Dodd Meets with President Kirchner," January 20, 2005, 05BUENOSAIRES138_a). Numbers have since dropped drastically. See "Portal brasileño destaca la drástica reducción de sacoleiros en Foz," *Ultima Hora*, October 3, 2016, https://www.ultimahora.com/portal-brasileno-destaca-la-drastica-reduccion-sacoleiros-foz-n1028649.html.

56. Rosana Pinheiro-Machado compared the fate of merchants from Taiwan and mainland China (2017, 100). Chinese merchants from Taiwan, benefiting from Paraguay's preferential migration policies, successfully mobilized connections and accumulated capital to set up formalized businesses in new cities after they left Ciudad del Este. Mainland Chinese shopkeepers were more precariously situated in border trade. With fewer connections and capital and without legal status as Paraguayan residents, some ended up as vendors, selling trinkets like sunglasses associated with Paraguay vendors, thereby signaling their descent down the economic hierarchy.

57. Pinheiro-Machado 2017, 156.

58. Pinheiro-Machado 2017, 143–45.

59. The meaning of *muamba* is also contested. Brazilians conceptualized piracy, in different moments, as a national embarrassment or a challenge to a system that protected corporate profits at the expense of ordinary people (Dent 2012, 44).

60. Trade agreements require ratification by each country. In Brazil, Law RTU

11.898/2009 was later modified by Instrução Normativa da Secretaria da Receita Federal do Brasil as Law 1.098/2010. In Paraguay, the plan was called the RFC (Regimen Fronterizo de Comercialización, or Regime of Frontier Commerce).

61. Brazil passed enabling legislation in 2012 with Law 12.723/2012 de Lojas Franca.

62. Interview, journalist, August 13, 2013, Ciudad del Este; interview, Secretariat of Taxation employee, October 26, 2013, Asunción.

63. Tariffs vary based on product, origin, and other factors. In 2013 Brazil's maximum bound tariff rate for industrial products was 35 percent. Local and state taxes can double costs. See USTR 2013.

64. Interview, secretary of taxation official, October 31, 2013, Asunción.

65. In 2013 the fixed cost for a registered taxi to cross the International Friendship Bridge was 400 reais. Interview, secretary of taxation official, October 31, 2013, Asunción.

66. "Calling All Smugglers—Brazilian 'Sacoleiro' Bill," May 20, 2008, 08b708_a.

67. During two rounds of trade negotiations (2006–7) Brazil pushed for a flat 42 percent tax rate, while Paraguayan negotiators pressed for 18 percent based on Paraguayan studies suggesting that anything higher than 22 percent would be economically unfeasible for *sacoleiros*. The two countries settled on 25 percent.

68. "Fábrica de frazada concreta la primera exportación al Brasil," *Ultima Hora*, February 25, 2009, https://www.ultimahora.com/fabrica-frazada-concreta-la-primera -exportacion-al-brasil-n207073.html.

69. U.S. Embassy, "Paraguay's Threshold Program Working to Formalize Ciudad del Este," December 19, 2001, 08ASUNCION847.

70. Personal communication, street vendor, July 13, 2013, Ciudad del Este.

71. Observation, May 10, 2013, Ciudad del Este.

72. Observation, regional official with the Ministry of Industry and Commerce, May 27, 2013, Ciudad del Este.

73. Recorded in fieldnotes, May 21, 2013.

74. Personal communication, street vendor, May 7, 2013, Ciudad del Este.

75. This transformation paralleled another moment in which importer-exporters sought monopolies. A few Paraguayans kept a foothold in the small-scale import-export business, but competition tightened, and bigger importer-exporters successfully sought to drive out competition. For instance, before she switched to selling blankets, Lina herself traveled to Iquique, Chile, to buy fans and shoes from East Asian SEZs from her contacts in the free-trade zone. But it seemed to be getting harder for vendors to self-provision.

CONCLUSION

1. Prieto formed his own party, Movimiento Conciencia Democrática del Este (CDE), after the Colorado Party refused to allow him to register and run as a Colorado.

2. Opposition parties also won in Presidente Franco, Minga Guazú, and Hernanderias. The lead-up to Prieto's election was dramatic. After years of anticorruption protests, in 2018 national auditors opened an investigation into the leadership of Mayor Sandra McLeod de Zacarías. Auditors found dozens of irregularities and tens of millions of U.S. dollars in missing funds. As McLeod faced removal, her allies strategized to avoid elections for her replacement, timing her resignation to avoid elections and cutting a deal to

hand power to their archrival turned ally, Kelembu, the ostensible anticorruption activist we met in chapter 2. When that power grab was thwarted by the city council, voters elected Prieto to fill out the remainder of McLeod's term.

3. In 2021 Prieto won again, winning with 81,186 votes, more than twice as many votes as Sandra McLeod de Zacarías in 2015 (40,371 votes), the candidate with the next highest vote count. "Electores del Este dejaron claro mensaje a partidos tradicionales," *Ultima Hora*, October 21, 2021, https://www.ultimahora.com/electores-del-este-dejaron-claro -mensaje-partidos-tradicionales-n2966038.html.

4. "Ejecutan operativo de despeje en mercado de CDE—ABC en el Este—ABC Color," *ABC Color*, January 10, 2022, https://www.abc.com.py/este/2022/01/10/ejecutan -operativo-de-despeje-en-mercado-de-cde/.

5. "Suspenden a funcionario tras incidente violento con Kelembu," *Ultima Hora*, January 16, 2020, https://www.ultimahora.com/suspenden-funcionario-incidente-violento -kelembu-n2865152.html, emphasis added. A scuffle between Kelembu and Prieto's new transportation police came to blows when officers refused to allow Kelembu to remove the impounded motorcycle of a driver unofficially authorized by a politician, possibly Kelembu himself, rather than through the official authorization process.

6. The municipality's own census uncovered layered and contradictory claims to city space, further complicating proposals that law will solve the dilemmas of urban occupancy.

7. As of 2022, the accusations include illicit enrichment, overinvoicing, and breach of trust, many of the same charges leveled against Javier Zacarías and Sandra McLeod.

8. Jennifer Robinson 2011.

9. I developed many of the ideas in this section with my collaborator, Thainara Granero de Melo, PhD.

10. Foucault 1995, 272; see also Thompson 1993. Here, economy can be understood as both the wealth unleashed by illegalities and the careful management of those illegalities.

11. During the early modern ancien régime in France, both the rich and poor enjoyed widespread forbearance due to the sovereign's inability to effectively enforce the law. Yet in the vast social transformations accompanying the emerging capitalist social order, the bourgeoisie sought to limit and punish customary uses on the lands they claimed by criminalizing foraging, grazing, hunting, and wood gathering, both enforcing old laws and generating new ones. Peasants rebelled against these assaults on their lives, livelihoods, and culture, contesting the transformation of their illegalities of rights into illegalities of property.

12. Foucault 1995, 87.

13. As Marx (1894) details in his analysis of primitive accumulation, the struggle to create the waged worker by enclosing the common lands and thereby dispossessing the peasantry of their lifeways took centuries, from the late 1500s through the mid-1800s. The landed gentry first transgressed law in their efforts toward enclosure and only later developed the "bloody legislation," as Marx famously called it, justifying dispossession and criminalizing vagabondage. Likewise, settlers first stole Indigenous land, and only afterward did the apparatus of law generate the justifications for the theft. These historical transgressions form capitalism's conditions of possibility.

14. These anxieties go back not only to colonial administrators' need for entrepôt cit-

ies to circulate stolen bounty and the fruits of slavery from the metropole to the center but also to their nervousness about how workers and Black people used these hubs to circulate news of rebellion and develop dangerous notions of freedom (Julius Scott 2018).

15. Writing about the birth of the prison in Europe, Foucault (1995) did not consider the geographic management of illegalities. His concern was how this differential administration was effected in industrializing Europe through a juridical-epistemological ensemble of the police, the prison, and delinquency. Policing was concentrated in working-class areas, defusing crimes away from political and collective forms into depoliticized forms. Policing also predictably funneled "criminals" into spatially enclosed prisons, places that highlight the illegalities of property by the poor even as they actually produce delinquency by creating a class of stigmatized and unemployable people disconnected from community and channeled into lives of criminality for survival. These people, constructed as delinquents, then shore up the myth of an underclass that is criminal in nature. Around the police-prison-delinquency ensemble arose a whole field of knowledge-based practitioners—lawmakers, philanthropists, and, later, researchers and social workers—aiming to reform a delinquency that came to stand in for all criminality.

16. Hudson and Fitzgibbon 2021.

17. Taddonio 2021.

18. In 2009 the pink tide included Frenández de Kirchner (Argentina), Morales (Bolivia), Da Silva (Brazil), Bachelet (Chile), Correa (Ecuador), Funes (El Salvador), Colom (Guatemala), Zelaya (Honduras), Ortega (Nicaragua), Lugo (Paraguay), Vásquez (Uruguay), and Chávez (Venezuela). In 2019 it included Morales (Bolivia), Cerén (El Salvador), López Obrador (Mexico), Ortega (Nicaragua), Vásquez (Uruguay), and Madura (Venezuela).

19. Miller and Uriegas 2019.

20. J. Watts 2017.

21. Nolen 2019.

22. The Brazilian media portrayed Judge Moro and the Lava Jato prosecutors as the "nation's heroes" on a noble crusade against evil, while a Brazilian action-drama series produced by Netflix, *O mecanismo* (The mechanism), depicted a neutral legal team fearlessly confronting a corrupt political underworld. "O Brasil tem um novo herói: Um juiz anticorrupção," *Público*, October 26, 2015, https://tinyurl.com/eypymwws.

23. Jinkings, Doria, and Cleto 2016; Allan et al. 2018; Valim 2018.

24. Andrew Fishman, Leandro Demori, Amanda Audi, and Rafael Moro Martins, "'The Risk Is Well Paid Lol,'" *The Intercept* (blog), July 26, 2019, https://theintercept.com /2019/07/26/brazil-car-wash-deltan-dallagnol-paid-speaking/; Andrew Fishman, Rafael Moro Martins, Leandro Demori, Alexandre de Santi, and Glenn Greenwald, "Breach of Ethics," *The Intercept* (blog), June 9, 2019, https://theintercept.com/2019/06/09/brazil -lula-operation-car-wash-sergio-moro/.

25. F. Rodrigues 2019.

26. Glenn Greenwald, "In Brazil, Major New Corruption Scandals Engulf the Faction That Impeached Dilma," *The Intercept* (blog), November 25, 2016, https://theintercept .com/2016/11/25/in-brazil-major-new-corruption-scandals-engulf-the-faction-that -impeached-dilma/.

27. "Brazil's Bolsonaro Says He Ended 'Car Wash' Corruption Probe," *AlJazeera*, Octo-

ber 8, 2020, https://www.aljazeera.com/news/2020/10/8/operation-car-wash-bolsonaro-says-he-ended-graft-probe.

28. Gallego 2019; Merlin 2019.

29. In sequence, these are Zezé Perrella, Waldemir Moka, and Magno Malta. *Senado Federal*, August 25, 2016, https://tinyurl.com/4hpfpbac.

30. Five conservative conglomerates control an estimated 50 percent of the most consumed media. The largest conglomerates—the groups Globo, Folha, Estadão, Abril, Record, and Bandeirantes—own eleven television networks, twelve radio stations, seventeen print media, and ten online media vehicles. *Media Ownership Monitor*, https://brazil.mom-rsf.org.

31. Populist politics are ideologically heterogeneous and variable over space and time, with both left-wing and right-wing expressions.

32. This contrasts with Left populism, which condemns elite collaboration with imperial and global capitalist interests.

33. For example, Carlos Menem in Argentina, Fernando Collor de Mello in Brazil, and Alberto Fujimori in Peru.

34. Maria C. Trevisan, "Where Was the Afro-Brazilian Community at the Protests against Dilma Rousseff?," *Jornalistas Livres* (blog), March 28, 2016, https://medium.com/jornalistas-livres/where-was-the-afro-brazilian-community-at-the-protests-against-dilma-rousseff-35395123e82f.

35. Donna Goldstein and Drybread 2018, 307.

36. Drybread 2018, 347.

37. Costa Vargas 2004.

38. Alves 2014; Penglase 2014.

39. The police killed 6,416 people, 79 percent of whom were young men of color. *Anuário brasileiro de segurança pública 2021* (São Paulo: Forum Brasileiro de Segurança Pública, 2021), 15:14, https://dossies.agenciapatriciagalvao.org.br/dados-e-fontes/pesquisa/anuario-brasileiro-de-seguranca-publica-fbsp-2021/.

40. In the wake of Rousseff's ouster, Franco (2018, 138) wrote of the generalized distrust of the political class by *favela* residents, exacerbated "as the dominant classes succeed in spreading the idea that the most serious problem facing Brazil is not inequality, but corruption."

41. Loureiro 2020.

42. Franco 2016, cited in Loureiro 2020, 54.

43. Brazil is an ex-slaveholder society with entrenched racial hierarchies and the largest Black population outside of Nigeria. The country's colonial history of *mestizaje* (race mixing) feeds a "myth of racial democracy" where race is supposedly less salient than in old apartheid race regimes like the United States and South Africa (Munanga 2010, 169).

44. Cited in Berth 2016.

45. During a debate, Djamila Ribeiro questioned Moro's defense of the law in the context of mass incarceration and state violence, one of the few times Judge Moro was publicly challenged. *Brazil Forum UK 2017*, https://youtu.be/LOdwq1rHoho.

46. Berth 2016.

47. Franco 2014, 123.

48. Mariana Silveira 2020, 226; Pereira and Silva 2021.

49. As unemployment rose to new highs and underpaid frontline workers faced exposure to the deadly virus, professionals turned their homes into workplaces and unhooked from the urban grid as remote work enabled unprecedented mobility.

50. Many Languages One Voice, LA Street Vendor Campaign, Street Vendor Project, and Street Vendors Association of Chicago, "National Agenda for Street Vendor Justice," *Medium* (blog), May 13, 2020, https://medium.com/@carinamariakg/national-agenda -for-street-vendor-justice-ba55e2d2e51d; "8M 2021—Pliego de demandas del paro internacional feminista," *LatFem* (blog), March 8, 2021, https://latfem.org/8m-2021-pliego -de-demandas-del-paro-internacional-feminista/.

51. Marchiori and Assis 2021.

52. Marchiori and Assis 2021, 15.

53. Marchiori and Assis 2021, 22.

54. In one poor barrio, Bañado Sur, a community soup kitchen fed three thousand people in 2020 and almost two thousand people in 2021. Personal communication, member of the Coordinator of Bañado Sur, May 25, 2022.

55. Law 6603 allocated nearly U.S.$2.2 million to community soup kitchens (Law 6603: Of Support and Assistance for Popular Kitchens Organized throughout Paraguayan Territory during the Pandemic Declared to Be the Cause of COVID-19 by the World Health Organization).

56. Gilmore 2007, 178.

57. Tucker and Anantharaman 2020.

58. West 2019.

APPENDIX

1. Interview, Secretariat of Taxation official, October 31, 2013, Asunción.

WORKS CITED

Abente-Brun, Diego. 1989. "Foreign Capital, Economic Elites and the State in Paraguay during the Liberal Republic (1870–1936)." *Journal of Latin American Studies* 21 (1): 61–88.

Abínzano, Roberto Carlos. 2005. "El contrabando no es delito para quienes viven en la frontera." *El Territorio*, December 4, sec. Foja Cero. http://www.aporrea.org/tecno /n58772.html.

Abrams, Philip. 1988. "Notes on the Difficulty of Studying the State (1977)." *Journal of Historical Sociology* 1 (1): 58–89.

Abu-Lughod, Janet L. 2000. *New York, Chicago, Los Angeles: America's Global Cities.* Minneapolis: University of Minnesota Press.

Adams, Vincanne. 2012. "The Other Road to Serfdom: Recovery by the Market and the Affect Economy in New Orleans." *Public Culture* 24 (1 [66]): 185–216.

Agamben, Giorgio. 2005. *State of Exception.* Translated by Kevin Attell. Chicago: University of Chicago Press.

Agbiboa, Daniel E. 2016. "'No Condition Is Permanent': Informal Transport Workers and Labour Precarity in Africa's Largest City." *International Journal of Urban and Regional Research* 40 (5): 936–57.

Aguiar, José Carlos G. 2010. "La piratería como conflicto: Discursos sobre la propiedad intelectual en México." *FLACSO sede Ecuador* 38 (September): 143–56. http:// repositorio.flacsoandes.edu.ec/handle/10469/2584.

Aguirre, Osvaldo. 2008. *La conexión latina: De la mafia corsa a la ruta Argentina de la heroína.* Barcelona: Tusquets.

Ahmed, Sara. 2013. *The Cultural Politics of Emotion.* New York: Routledge.

Alesina, Alberto, and Dani Rodrik. 1994. "Distributive Politics and Economic Growth." *Quarterly Journal of Economics* 109 (2): 465–90.

Allan, Nasser Ahmad, Gabriela Shizue Soares de Araujo, Marcelo Labanca Corrêa de Araújo, Paula Saleh Arbs, Charlotth Back, Tiago Resende Botelho, Cristiane Brandão, Weida Zancaner Brunini, Flavio Crocce Caetano, and Roberto de Figueiredo Caldas. 2018. *Comments on a Notorious Verdict: The Trial of Lula.* Buenos Aires: CLACSO.

Alonso, Ana María. 1995. *Thread of Blood: Colonialism, Revolution, and Gender on Mexico's Northern Frontier.* Tucson: University of Arizona Press.

Álvarez, María Inés Fernández. 2018. "Más allá de la precariedad: Prácticas colectivas y subjetividades políticas desde la economía popular argentina." *Íconos: Revista de Ciencias Sociales* 62 (August): 21–38.

Alvino da Silva, Micael. 2018. "The Triple Frontier Again: The Terrorism Nexus and What Has Changed in the Argentina, Brazil, and Paraguay Borderland Since 2001." *Mural Internacional* 9 (2): 175–81.

Alves, Jaime Amparo. 2014. "From Necropolis to Blackpolis: Necropolitical Governance and Black Spatial Praxis in São Paulo, Brazil." *Antipode* 46 (2): 323–39.

Amin, Samir. 1976. *Unequal Development: An Essay on the Social Formations of Peripheral Capitalism*. Translated by Brian Pierce. New York: Monthly Review Press.

Anderson, Ben. 2014. *Encountering Affect: Capacities, Apparatuses, Conditions*. Farnham, U.K.: Ashgate Publishing.

Andreas, Peter. 2013. *Smuggler Nation: How Illicit Trade Made America*. Oxford: Oxford University Press.

Angelo, Hillary, and Kian Goh. 2020. "Out in Space: Difference and Abstraction in Planetary Urbanization." *International Journal of Urban and Regional Research* 45 (4): 732–44.

Anievas, Alexander, and Kerem Nisancioglu. 2013. "What's at Stake in the Transition Debate? Rethinking the Origins of Capitalism and the 'Rise of the West.'" *Millennium* 42 (1): 78–102.

Antunes de Oliveira, Felipe. 2019. "The Rise of the Latin American Far-Right Explained: Dependency Theory Meets Uneven and Combined Development." *Globalizations* 16 (7): 1145–64.

Arboleda, Martín. 2015. "Financialization, Totality and Planetary Urbanization in the Chilean Andes." *Geoforum* 67 (December): 4–13.

Arens, Richard. 1976. *Genocide in Paraguay*. Philadelphia, Pa.: Temple University Press.

Aretxaga, Begoña. 2003. "Maddening States." *Annual Review of Anthropology* 32 (1): 393–410.

Asher, Kiran, and Joel Wainwright. 2019. "After Post-development: On Capitalism, Difference, and Representation." *Antipode* 51 (1): 25–44.

Baer, Werner, and Melissa H. Birch. 1984. "Expansion of the Economic Frontier: Paraguayan Growth in the 1970s." *World Development* 12 (8): 783–98.

Ballvé, Teo. 2012. "Everyday State Formation: Territory, Decentralization, and the Narco Landgrab in Colombia." *Environment and Planning D: Society and Space* 30 (4): 603–22.

———. 2019. "Narco-Frontiers: A Spatial Framework for Drug-Fuelled Accumulation." *Journal of Agrarian Change* 19 (2): 211–24.

———. 2020. *The Frontier Effect: State Formation and Violence in Colombia*. Ithaca, N.Y.: Cornell University Press.

Bambirra, Vania. 1999. *El capitalismo dependiente latinoamericano*. Mexico City: Siglo XXI.

Barchiesi, Franco. 2011. *Precarious Liberation: Workers, the State, and Contested Social Citizenship in Postapartheid South Africa*. Albany: SUNY Press.

Barkan, Joshua. 2013. *Corporate Sovereignty: Law and Government under Capitalism*. Minneapolis: University of Minnesota Press.

Barnett, Clive. 2008. "Political Affects in Public Space: Normative Blind-Spots in Non-representational Ontologies." *Transactions of the Institute of British Geographers* 33 (2): 186–200.

Barrantes, César A. 1992. "Del sector informal urbano a la economía popular." *Ciencias Sociales* 57:97–108.

Barrett, Rafael. 1910. *Lo que son los yerbales*. Montevideo: OM Bertani.

Bear, Laura, Karen Ho, Anna Tsing, and Sylvia Yanagisako. 2015. "Gens: A Feminist Manifesto for the Study of Capitalism—Cultural Anthropology." *Fieldsights*, March. https://culanth.org/fieldsights/gens-a-feminist-manifesto-for-the-study-of-capitalism.

Bell, Morag, Robin Alan Butlin, and Michael J. Heffernan. 1995. *Geography and Imperialism, 1820–1940*. Manchester: Manchester University Press.

Bennett, Jane. 2009. *Vibrant Matter: A Political Ecology of Things*. Durham, N.C.: Duke University Press.

Berlant, Lauren. 2011. *Cruel Optimism*. Durham, N.C.: Duke University Press.

Berlant, Lauren, Marina Vishmidt, and Gesa Helms. 2010. "Affect and the Politics of Austerity: An Interview with Lauren Berlant." *Variant* 39 (1): 3–6.

Berth, Joice. 2016. "Como é proposta no Brasil, pauta contra a corrupção é racista." *Justificando* (blog). May 18. https://portal-justificando.jusbrasil.com.br/noticias/339124541/como-e-proposta-no-brasil-pauta-contra-a-corrupcao-e-racista?ref=amp.

Bethell, Leslie. 1996. *The Paraguayan War: History and Historiography*. London: University of London, Institute of Latin American Studies.

Bhattacharyya, Gargi. 2005. *Traffick: The Illicit Movement of People and Things*. 1st ed. Ann Arbor, Mich.: Pluto Press.

Bhowmik, Sharit K. 2005. "Street Vendors in Asia: A Review." *Economic and Political Weekly*, May 28–June 4, 2256–64.

Blaut, James M. 1993. *The Colonizer's Model of the World: Geographical Diffusionism and Eurocentric History*. New York: Guilford Press.

Blouet, Brian W., and Olwyn M. Blouet. 2009. *Latin America and the Caribbean: A Systematic and Regional Survey*. Hoboken, N.J.: John Wiley & Sons.

Bondi, Liz. 2005. "Making Connections and Thinking through Emotions: Between Geography and Psychotherapy." *Transactions of the Institute of British Geographers* 30 (4): 433–48.

Borras, Saturnino M., and Jennifer C. Franco. 2010. "Towards a Broader View of the Politics of Global Land Grab : Rethinking Land Issues, Reframing Resistance." *Journal of Agrarian Change* 10 (1): 1–32.

Brandalise, Roberta. 2017. "O estigma da falsificação ou da pirataria, a circulação dos sentidos propostos pela televisão brasileira e a resistência na fronteira Paraguai-Brasil." Paper presented at the 40th Congresso Brasileiro de Ciências da Comunicação, Curitiba, Brazil, September 9.

Braudel, Fernand. 1992. *The Perspective of the World*. Vol. 3 of *Civilization and Capitalism, 15th–18th Century*. Berkeley: University of California Press.

Breman, Jan, and Marcel van der Linden. 2014. "Informalizing the Economy: The Return of the Social Question at a Global Level." *Development and Change* 45 (5): 920–40.

Brenner, Neil. 1998. "Global Cities, Glocal States: Global City Formation and State Territorial Restructuring in Contemporary Europe." *Review of International Political Economy* 5 (1): 1–37.

Brenner, Neil, Jamie Peck, and Nik Theodore. 2010. "Variegated Neoliberalization: Geographies, Modalities, Pathways." *Global Networks* 10 (2): 182–222.

Brenner, Neil, and Christian Schmid. 2015. "Towards a New Epistemology of the Urban?" *City* 19 (2–3): 151–82.

Brenner, Neil, and Nik Theodore. 2002. "Cities and the Geographies of 'Actually Existing Neoliberalism.'" *Antipode* 34 (3): 349–79.

Brenner, Robert. 1977. "The Origins of Capitalist Development: A Critique of Neo-Smithian Marxism." *New Left Review* 104 (1): 25–92.

———. 2003. *Merchants and Revolution: Commercial Change, Political Conflict, and London's Overseas Traders, 1550–1653.* London: Verso.

Bromley, Ray. 2000. "Street Vending and Public Policy: A Global Review." *International Journal of Sociology and Social Policy* 20 (1/2): 1–28.

Brown, Ed, and Jonathan Cloke. 2004. "Neoliberal Reform, Governance and Corruption in the South: Assessing the International Anti-corruption Crusade." *Antipode* 2: 272–94.

Brown, Rachel. 2009. "The Tri-Border Area: A Profile of the Largest Illicit Economy in the Western Hemisphere." Financial Transparency Coalition. https://financial transparency.org/the-tri-border-area-a-profile-of-the-largest-illicit-economy-in-the -western-hemisphere/.

Brown, Wendy. 2015. *Undoing the Demos: Neoliberalism's Stealth Revolution.* New York: Zone Books.

Buckley, Michelle, and Kendra Strauss. 2016. "With, against and beyond Lefebvre: Planetary Urbanization and Epistemic Plurality." *Environment and Planning D: Society and Space* 34 (4): 617–36.

Bunnell, Tim, and Anant Maringanti. 2010. "Practising Urban and Regional Research beyond Metrocentricity." *International Journal of Urban and Regional Research* 34 (2): 415–20.

Bush, George W. 2002. "The President's State of the Union Address." Washington, D.C., January 29. https://georgewbush-whitehouse.archives.gov/news/releases/2002/01 /20020129-11.html.

Byrd, Jodi A., Alyosha Goldstein, Jodi Melamed, and Chandan Reddy. 2018. "Predatory Value: Economies of Dispossession and Disturbed Relationalities." *Social Text* 36 (2 [135]): 1–18.

Caldeira, Teresa. 2001. *City of Walls: Crime, Segregation, and Citizenship in São Paulo.* Berkeley: University of California Press.

———. 2016. "Peripheral Urbanization: Autoconstruction, Transversal Logics, and Politics in Cities of the Global South." *Environment and Planning D: Society and Space* 35 (1): 3–20.

Callejas, John Sebastián Zapata. 2014. "La teoría del estado fallido: Entre aproximaciones y disensos." *Revista de Relaciones Internacionales, Estrategia y Seguridad* 9 (1): 87–110.

Cannon, Mary M. 1946. "Women Workers in Paraguay." Washington, D.C.: U.S. Department of Labor Women's Bureau.

Capitalismo Amarillo. 2008. "Culturas de la modernidad pirateada." https://capitalismo amarillo.net/acerca-de/.

Cárdenas, Hugo Martínez. 2007. *Mil días de historia: Ciudad Presidente Stroessner.* Ciudad del Este, Paraguay: self-published.

Cardin, Eric Gustavo. 2006. "Sacoleiros e laranjas na tríplice fronteira: Uma análise da precarização do trabalho no capitalismo contemporâneo." Master's thesis, Universidade Estadual Paulista (UNESP).

———. 2012. "Trabalho e práticas de contrabando na fronteira do Brasil com o Paraguai." *Revista Geopolíticas* 3 (2): 207–34.

———. 2014. "La historia de una vida en situación de frontera: Migración, superación y trabajo en el 'circuito sacoleiro.'" *Revista de Estudios Sociales* 48 (January): 100–109.

———. 2015. *A expansão do capital e as dinâmicas das fronteiras.* Jundiaí, Brazil: Paco Editorial.

Cardoso, Fernando Henrique. 1977. "The Consumption of Dependency Theory in the United States." *Latin American Research Review* 12 (3): 7–24.

Cardoso, Fernando Henrique, and Enzo Faletto. 1979. *Dependency and Development in Latin America.* Berkeley: University of California Press.

Castells, Manuel. 2010. *The Information Age: Economy, Society, and Culture.* Vol. 3 of *End of Millennium.* New York: John Wiley & Sons.

Césaire, Aimé. 1950. *Discourse on Colonialism.* New York: NYU Press.

Chabal, Patrick, and Jean-Pascal Daloz. 1999. *Africa Works: Disorder as Political Instrument.* Bloomington, IN: International African Institute.

Chang, Ha-Joon. 2002. *Kicking Away the Ladder: Development Strategy in Historical Perspective.* London: Anthem Press.

Chari, Sharad, and Vinay Gidwani. 2005. "Introduction: Grounds for a Spatial Ethnography of Labor." *Ethnography* 6 (3): 267–81.

Cheah, Pheng. 2008. "Universal Areas: Asian Studies in a World in Motion." In *The Postcolonial and the Global,* edited by Revathi Krishnaswamy and John Charles Hawley, 54–68. Minneapolis: University of Minnesota Press.

Chen, Martha, Joann Vanek, Francie Lund, James Heintz, Renata Jhabvala, and Christine Bonner. 2005. *Women, Work & Poverty.* New York: UNIFEM.

Chiodelli, Francesco, Tim Hall, and Ray Hudson, eds. 2017. *The Illicit and Illegal in Regional and Urban Governance and Development: Corrupt Places.* New York: Routledge.

Cielo, Cristina. 2018. "La productividad de la contingencia en economías populares del sur global: Diálogo con AbdouMaliq Simone." *Íconos: Revista de Ciencias Sociales* 62 (August): 153–64.

Cockayne, Daniel G. 2016. "Entrepreneurial Affect: Attachment to Work Practice in San Francisco's Digital Media Sector." *Environment and Planning D: Society and Space* 34 (3): 456–73.

Coe, Neil M., Martin Hess, Henry Wai-chung Yeung, Peter Dicken, and Jeffrey Henderson. 2004. "'Globalizing' Regional Development: A Global Production Networks Perspective." *Transactions of the Institute of British Geographers* 29 (4): 468–84.

Coffin, Bill. 2004. "Global Perspectives: Fighting the Global Scourge of IP Theft." *Risk Management.* https://go.gale.com/ps/i.do?id=GALE%7CA119615275&sid

=googleScholar&v=2.1&it=r&linkaccess=abs&issn=00355593&p=AONE&sw =w&userGroupName=nm_p_oweb&isGeoAuthType=true.

Colectivo Situaciones, ed. 2009. *Conversaciones en el impasse: Dilemas políticas del presente*. Colección de mano en mano. Buenos Aires: Tinta Limón.

Coletto, D. 2010. *The Informal Economy and Employment in Brazil: Latin America, Modernization, and Social Changes*. New York: Springer.

Collins, Patricia Hill. 1986. "Learning from the Outsider Within: The Sociological Significance of Black Feminist Thought." *Social Problems* 33 (6): S14–32.

Colmán Gutiérrez, Andrés. 2007. *El último vuelo del pájaro campana*. Asunción, Paraguay: Servilibro.

Comaroff, Jean, and John L. Comaroff. 1999. "Occult Economies and the Violence of Abstraction: Notes from the South African Postcolony." *American Ethnologist* 26 (2): 279–303.

Corning, Owens. 2017. "Companies That Likely Hold Profits in Tax Havens." Institute on Taxation and Economic Policy. https://itep.org/fortune-500-companies-hold-a -record-26-trillion-offshore/.

Coronil, Fernando. 1996. "Beyond Occidentalism: Toward Nonimperial Geohistorical Categories." *Cultural Anthropology* 11 (1): 51–87.

———. 2011. "The Future in Question: History and Utopia in Latin America." In *Business as Usual: The Roots of the Global Financial Meltdown*, edited by Craig Calhoun and Georgi Derluguian, 231–64. New York: New York University Press.

Costa, Thomaz G., and Gastón H. Schulmeister. 2007. "The Puzzle of the Iguazu Tri-Border Area: Many Questions and Few Answers Regarding Organised Crime and Terrorism Links." *Global Crime* 8 (1): 26–39.

Costa Vargas, João H. 2004. "Hyperconsciousness of Race and Its Negation: The Dialectic of White Supremacy in Brazil." *Identities* 11 (4): 443–70.

Cowen, Deborah. 2010. "A Geography of Logistics: Market Authority and the Security of Supply Chains." *Annals of the Association of American Geographers* 100 (3): 600–620.

———. 2014. *The Deadly Life of Logistics: Mapping Violence in Global Trade*. Minneapolis: University of Minnesota Press.

Crossa, Veronica. 2009. "Resisting the Entrepreneurial City: Street Vendors' Struggle in Mexico City's Historic Center." *International Journal of Urban and Regional Research* 33 (1): 43–63.

Das, Veena, and Deborah Poole. 2004. *Anthropology in the Margins of the State*. Santa Fe, N.M.: SAR Press.

Davies, William. 2016. "The New Neoliberalism." *New Left Review* 101: 121–34.

Dávila, Arlene. 2016. *El Mall: The Spatial and Class Politics of Shopping Malls in Latin America*. Berkeley: University of California Press.

Davis, Angela Y. 1983. *Women, Race, & Class*. New York: Vintage.

Davis, Mike. 2006. *Planet of Slums*. New York: Verso.

De Angelis, Massimo. 2004. "Separating the Doing and the Deed: Capital and the Continuous Character of Enclosures." *Historical Materialism* 12 (2): 57–87.

de la Cadena, Marisol. 2001. "Reconstructing Race: Racism, Culture and Mestizaje in Latin America." *NACLA* 34 (6): 16–23.

Denning, Michael. 2010. "Wageless Life." *New Left Review* 66 (November/December): 79–97.

Dent, Alexander. 2012. "Piracy, Circulatory Legitimacy, and Neoliberal Subjectivity in Brazil." *Cultural Anthropology* 27 (1): 28–49.

Derickson, Kate. 2018. "Masters of the Universe." *Environment and Planning D: Society and Space* 36 (3): 556–62.

de Soto, Hernando. 1989. *The Other Path: The Invisible Revolution in the Third World.* New York: Harper Collins.

Devlin, Ryan Thomas. 2011. "'An Area That Governs Itself': Informality, Uncertainty and the Management of Street Vending in New York City." *Planning Theory* 10 (1): 53–65.

Dias, Sonia Maria. 2016. "Waste Pickers and Cities." *Environment and Urbanization* 28 (2): 375–90.

Dicken, Peter, Philip F. Kelly, Kris Olds, and Henry Wai-Chung Yeung. 2001. "Chains and Networks, Territories and Scales: Towards a Relational Framework for Analysing the Global Economy." *Global Networks* 1 (2): 89–112.

Doshi, Sapana, and Malini Ranganathan. 2017. "Contesting the Unethical City: Land Dispossession and Corruption Narratives in Urban India." *Annals of the American Association of Geographers* 107 (1): 183–99.

———. 2018. "Towards a Critical Geography of Corruption and Power in Late Capitalism." *Progress in Human Geography* 43 (3): 436–57.

dos Santos, Theotônio. 1970. "The Structure of Dependence." *American Economic Review* 60 (2): 231–36.

Drybread, K. 2018. "When Corruption Is Not a Crime: 'Innocent' White Politicians and the Racialisation of Criminality in Brazil." *Culture, Theory and Critique* 59 (4): 332–53.

Du Bois, William Edward Burghardt. 1935. *Black Reconstruction in America: An Essay toward a History of the Part Which Black Folk Played in the Attempt to Reconstruct Democracy in America, 1860–1880.* Oxford: Oxford University Press.

Dunbar-Ortiz, Roxanne, and Dina Gilio-Whitaker. 2016. *"All the Real Indians Died Off": And 20 Other Myths about Native Americans.* Boston: Beacon Press.

Duneier, Mitchell, Hakim Hasan, and Ovie Carter. 2000. *Sidewalk.* 1st ed. New York: Farrar, Straus and Giroux.

Easterling, Keller. 2014. *Extrastatecraft: The Power of Infrastructure Space.* London: Verso.

Eilenberg, Michael. 2012. *At the Edges of States: Dynamics of State Formation in the Indonesian Borderlands.* Leiden: KITLV Press.

Eizenberg, Efrat. 2012. "Actually Existing Commons: Three Moments of Space of Community Gardens in New York City." *Antipode* 44 (3): 764–82.

Elden, Stuart. 2004. *Understanding Henri Lefebvre.* London: Continuum International Publishing Group.

Emmanuel, Arghiri. 1972. *Unequal Exchange: A Study of the Imperialism of Trade.* New York: Monthly Review Press.

Engelmann, Fabiano. 2020. "The 'Fight against Corruption' in Brazil from the 2000s: A Political Crusade through Judicial Activism." *Journal of Law and Society* 47:S74–89.

Escobar, Arturo. 2011. *Encountering Development: The Making and Unmaking of the Third World.* Princeton, N.J.: Princeton University Press.

Fanon, Frantz. 1963. *The Wretched of the Earth.* New York: Grove Atlantic.

Federici, Silvia. 2004. *Caliban and the Witch.* Brooklyn, N.Y.: Autonomedia.

Ferguson, James. 1994. *The Anti-politics Machine: "Development," Depoliticization, and Bureaucratic Power in Lesotho*. Minneapolis: University of Minnesota Press.

———. 2013. "Declarations of Dependence: Labour, Personhood, and Welfare in Southern Africa." *Journal of the Royal Anthropological Institute* 19 (2): 223–42.

———. 2015. *Give a Man a Fish: Reflections on the New Politics of Distribution*. Durham, N.C.: Duke University Press.

Ferguson, Niall. 2012. *Empire: How Britain Made the Modern World*. London: Penguin UK.

Fields, Karen E., and Barbara Jeanne Fields. 2014. *Racecraft: The Soul of Inequality in American Life*. London: Verso.

Fogel, Ramón. 2008. "La región de la Triple Frontera: Territorios de integración y desintegración." *Sociologias* 20:270–90.

———. 2012. "El movimiento de los carperos." *Novapolis* 5 (October): 11–30.

Fogel, Ramón, and Marcial Antonio Riquelme. 2005. *Enclave sojero: Merma de soberanía y pobreza*. Asunción, Paraguay: Centro de Estudios Rurales Interdisciplinarios.

Folch, Christine. 2013. "Surveillance and State Violence in Stroessner's Paraguay: Itaipú Hydroelectric Dam, Archive of Terror." *American Anthropologist* 115 (1): 44–57.

Folha de S. Paulo. 2020. "Estudo com 1.200 genomas mapeia diversidade da população brasileira." September 23. https://www1.folha.uol.com.br/ciencia/2020/09/estudo-com-1200-genomas-mapeia-diversidade-da-populacao-brasileira.shtml.

Foucault, Michel. 1978. *The History of Sexuality*. 4 vols. Translated by Robert Hurley. London: Penguin Books.

———. 1994. *The Order of Things: An Archaeology of the Human Sciences*. Reissue ed. New York: Vintage.

———. 1995. *Discipline & Punish: The Birth of the Prison*. Translated by Alan Sheridan. New York: Vintage Books.

Franco, Marielle. 2014. "UPP–A redução da favela a três letras: Uma análise da política de segurança pública do estado do Rio de Janeiro." PhD dissertation, Universidade Federal Fluminense, Niteroi, Brazil.

———. 2018. "After the Take-Over: Mobilizing the Political Creativity of Brazil's Favelas." *New Left Review* 110 (March/April): 135–40.

Frank, Andre Gunder. 1967. *Capitalism and Underdevelopment in Latin America: Historical Studies of Chile and Brazil*. Revised and enlarged ed. New York: Monthly Review Press.

Fraser, Nancy. 2014. "Behind Marx's Hidden Abode for an Expanded Conception of Capitalism." *New Left Review* 86: 55–72.

Fraser, Nancy, and Linda Gordon. 1994. "A Genealogy of Dependency: Tracing a Keyword of the U.S. Welfare State." *Signs* 19 (2): 309–36.

Gago, Verónica. 2014. *La razón neoliberal: Economías barrocas y pragmática popular*. Buenos Aires: Tinta Limón.

———. 2017. *Neoliberalism from Below: Popular Pragmatics and Baroque Economies*. Durham, N.C.: Duke University Press.

———. 2018. "What Are Popular Economies? Some Reflections from Argentina." *Radical Philosophy* 202: 31–38.

Gago, Verónica, Cristina Cielo, and Francisco Gachet. 2018. "Presentación del dossier."

Economía popular: Entre la informalidad y la reproducción ampliada." *Íconos: Revista de Ciencias Sociales* 62: 11–20.

Gago, Verónica, and Sandro Mezzadra. 2017. "A Critique of the Extractive Operations of Capital: Toward an Expanded Concept of Extractivism." *Rethinking Marxism* 29 (4): 574–91.

Galeano, Eduardo. 1975. *Open Veins of Latin America: Five Centuries of the Pillage of a Continent.* New York: NYU Press.

Galemba, Rebecca Berke. 2017. *Contraband Corridor: Making a Living at the Mexico-Guatemala Border.* Stanford, Calif.: Stanford University Press.

Gallego, Esther Solano. 2019. "Quem é o inimigo? Retóricas de inimizade nas redes sociais no período de 2014–2017." In *Brasil em transe: Bolsonarismo, nova direita e desdemocratização,* edited by Rosana Pinheiro-Machado and Adriano Freixo, 83–98. Rio de Janeiro: Oficina.

Ghertner, D. Asher. 2015. *Rule by Aesthetics: World-Class City Making in Delhi.* New York: Oxford University Press.

Gibler, John. 2010. "Outsourcing the Blood: Letter from the Drug War in Mexico." *Left Turn: Notes from the Global Intifada* (blog). December 1. https://www.leftturn.org /Outsourcing-the-blood.

Gibson-Graham, J. K. 2006. *The End of Capitalism (as We Knew It): A Feminist Critique of Political Economy.* Minneapolis: University of Minnesota Press.

Gidwani, Vinay. 2008. *Capital, Interrupted: Agrarian Development and the Politics of Work in India.* Minneapolis: University of Minnesota Press.

Gidwani, Vinay, and Anant Maringanti. 2016. "The Waste-Value Dialectic: Lumpen Urbanization in Contemporary India." *Comparative Studies of South Asia, Africa and the Middle East* 36 (1): 112–33.

Gillespie, Tom. 2016. "Accumulation by Urban Dispossession: Struggles over Urban Space in Accra, Ghana." *Transactions of the Institute of British Geographers* 41 (1): 66–77.

Gilmore, Ruth Wilson. 2002. "Fatal Couplings of Power and Difference: Notes on Racism and Geography." *Professional Geographer* 54 (1): 15–24.

———. 2007. *Golden Gulag: Prisons, Surplus, Crisis, and Opposition in Globalizing California.* Berkeley: University of California Press.

Gilroy, Paul. 1993. *The Black Atlantic: Modernity and Double Consciousness.* Cambridge, Mass.: Harvard University Press.

Giménez Béliveau, Verónica. 2011. "La 'Triple Frontera' y sus representaciones: Políticos y funcionarios piensan la frontera." *Frontera Norte* 23 (46): 7–34.

Glassman, Jim. 2006. "Primitive Accumulation, Accumulation by Dispossession, Accumulation by 'Extra-Economic' Means." *Progress in Human Geography* 30 (5): 608–25.

Goldberg, Jeffrey. 2002. "In the Party of God." *New Yorker,* October 7. https://www .newyorker.com/magazine/2002/10/14/in-the-party-of-god.

Goldstein, Alyosha. 2012. *Poverty in Common: The Politics of Community Action during the American Century.* Durham, N.C.: Duke University Press.

Goldstein, Daniel M. 2016. *Owners of the Sidewalk: Security and Survival in the Informal City.* Durham, N.C.: Duke University Press.

Goldstein, Donna M., and K. Drybread. 2018. "The Social Life of Corruption in Latin America." *Culture, Theory and Critique* 59 (4): 299–311.

Gonzáles Solís, José Luis. 2013. "Neoliberalismo y crimen organizado en México: El surgimiento del estado narco." *Frontera Norte* 25 (50): 7–34.

Goonewardena, Kanishka. 2018. "Planetary Urbanization and Totality." *Environment & Planning D: Society & Space* 36 (3): 456–73.

Grandin, Greg. 2007. *Empire's Workshop: Latin America, the United States, and the Rise of the New Imperialism*. New York: Macmillan.

Gregory, Derek. 2004. *The Colonial Present: Afghanistan, Palestine, Iraq*. Malden, Mass.: Wiley-Blackwell.

Gregson, Nicky, and Mike Crang. 2017. "Illicit Economies: Customary Illegality, Moral Economies and Circulation." *Transactions of the Institute of British Geographers* 42 (2): 206–19.

Gudynas, Eduardo. 2009. "Diez tesis urgentes sobre el nuevo extractivismo." In *Extractivismo, política y sociedad*, edited by Jürgen Schuldt, Alberto Acosta, Alberto Barandiarán, Anthony Beggington, and Mauricio Folchi, 187–225. Quito: Centro Andino de Acción Popular and Centro Latinoamericano de Ecología Social.

Guereña, Arantxa. 2016. "Unearthed: Land, Power and Inequality in Latin America." *Oxfam*, November. https://oi-files-d8-prod.s3.eu-west-2.amazonaws.com/s3fs-public /file_attachments/bp-land-power-inequality-latin-america-301116-en.pdf.

Guernica, Edward. 2003. "The Legal Coup: Impeachment Politics in Paraguay." PhD dissertation, Tulane University.

Guevara, Marina Walker, Mabel Rehnfeldt, Marcelo Soares, and Daniel Santor. 2009. "El gran 'duty free': Paraguay es uno de los mayores productores mundiales de cigarrillos de contrabando." International Consortium of Investigative Journalists, June 29. https://www.icij.org/investigations/tobacco-underground/el-gran-duty -free/.

Gupta, Akhil. 2012. *Red Tape: Bureaucracy, Structural Violence, and Poverty in India*. Durham, N.C.: Duke University Press.

Haberly, Daniel, and Dariusz Wójcik. 2015. "Tax Havens and the Production of Offshore FDI: An Empirical Analysis." *Journal of Economic Geography* 15 (1): 75–101.

Hall, Stuart. 1986. "Gramsci's Relevance for the Study of Race and Ethnicity." *Journal of Communication Inquiry* 10 (2): 5–27.

Hall, Stuart, and Doreen Massey. 2010. "Interpreting the Crisis." *Soundings* 44 (44): 57–71.

Hansen, Thomas Blom, and Finn Stepputat. 2001. *States of Imagination: Ethnographic Explorations of the Postcolonial State*. Durham, N.C.: Duke University Press.

———. 2006. "Sovereignty Revisited." *Annual Review of Anthropology* 35:295–315.

Haraway, Donna J. 1988. "Situated Knowledges: The Science Question in Feminism and the Privilege of Partial Perspective." *Feminist Studies* 14 (3): 575–99.

Harding, Sandra G. 1986. *The Science Question in Feminism*. Ithaca, N.Y.: Cornell University Press.

Harris, Cheryl I. 1993. "Whiteness as Property." *Harvard Law Review* 106 (8): 1707–91.

Harrison, Elizabeth. 2007. "Corruption." *Development in Practice* 17 (4–5): 672–78.

Hart, Gillian. 2006. "Denaturalizing Dispossession: Critical Ethnography in the Age of Resurgent Imperialism." *Antipode* 38 (5): 977–1004.

———. 2016. "Relational Comparison Revisited: Marxist Postcolonial Geographies in Practice." *Progress in Human Geography* 42 (3): 371–94.

Hart, Keith. 1973. "Informal Income Opportunities and Urban Employment in Ghana." *Journal of Modern African Studies* 11 (1): 61–89.

Harvey, David. 1982. *The Limits to Capital*. Oxford: Blackwell.

———. 2001. "Globalization and the 'Spatial Fix.'" *Geographische Revue* 2:23–30.

———. 2003. *The New Imperialism*. New York: Oxford University Press.

———. 2005. *A Brief History of Neoliberalism*. 1st ed. New York: Oxford University Press.

———. 2009. *Social Justice and the City*. Athens: University of Georgia Press.

———. 2017. *Marx, Capital, and the Madness of Economic Reason*. New York: Oxford University Press.

Harvey, Penelope. 2014. "Infrastructures of the Frontier in Latin America." *Journal of Latin American and Caribbean Anthropology* 19 (2): 280–83.

Heller, Patrick. 2001. "Moving the State: The Politics of Democratic Decentralization in Kerala, South Africa, and Porto Alegre." *Politics and Society* 29 (1): 131–63.

Hemmings, Clare. 2005. "Invoking Affect." *Cultural Studies* 19 (5): 548–67.

Hetherington, Kregg. 2011. *Guerrilla Auditors: The Politics of Transparency in Neoliberal Paraguay*. Durham, N.C.: Duke University Press.

Heyman, Josiah McConnell. 1999. *States and Illegal Practices*. Oxford: Berg.

Hickel, Jason. 2017. "How to Stop the Global Inequality Machine." *The Guardian*, May 18, sec. Global Development Professionals Network. https://www.theguardian.com /global-development-professionals-network/2017/may/18/how-to-stop-the-global -inequality-machine.

H.J. 2013. "The New Face of the Colorados." *The Economist*, December 20. https://www .economist.com/americas-view/2013/12/20/the-new-face-of-the-colorados.

Holland, Alisha C. 2015. "The Distributive Politics of Enforcement." *American Journal of Political Science* 59 (2): 357–71.

Holston, James. 1989. *The Modernist City: An Anthropological Critique of Brasilia*. Chicago: University of Chicago Press.

———. 2008. *Insurgent Citizenship: Disjunctions of Democracy and Modernity in Brazil*. Princeton, N.J.: Princeton University Press.

———. 2009. "Dangerous Spaces of Citizenship: Gang Talk, Rights Talk and Rule of Law in Brazil." *Planning Theory* 8 (1): 12–31.

Hsing, You-tien. 2010. *The Great Urban Transformation: Politics of Land and Property in China*. New York: Oxford University Press.

Hudson, Michael, and Will Fitzgibbon. 2021. "Pandora Papers Caps Off 2021 with Consequences Felt around the Globe." International Consortium of Investigative Journalists. https://www.icij.org/investigations/pandora-papers/pandora-papers-caps-off -2021-with-consequences-felt-around-the-globe/.

Hudson, Rex. 2003. "Terrorist and Organized Crime Groups in the Tri-Border Area (TBA) of South America." Federal Research Division, Library of Congress. https:// www.ojp.gov/ncjrs/virtual-library/abstracts/terrorist-and-organized-crime-groups -tri-border-area-tba-south.

Ignatiev, Noel. 2008. *How the Irish Became White*. New York: Routledge.

ILO (International Labour Organization). 2002. "Decent Work and the Informal Economy." https://www.ilo.org/public/english/standards/relm/ilc/ilc90/pdf/rep-vi.pdf.

———. 2018. "Women and Men in the Informal Economy: A Statistical Picture. Third

Edition." http://www.ilo.org/global/publications/books/WCMS_626831/lang--en/index.htm.

Inverardi-Ferri, Carlo. 2018. "The Enclosure of 'Waste Land': Rethinking Informality and Dispossession." *Transactions of the Institute of British Geographers* 43 (2): 230–44.

Jaffe, Rivke. 2013. "The Hybrid State: Crime and Citizenship in Urban Jamaica." *American Ethnologist* 40 (4): 734–48.

James, Cyril Lionel Robert. 2001. *The Black Jacobins: Toussaint L'Ouverture and the San Domingo Revolution*. London: Penguin.

James, Erica Caple. 2010. "Ruptures, Rights, and Repair: The Political Economy of Trauma in Haiti." *Social Science & Medicine* 70 (1): 106–13.

Jankiewicz, Stephen. 2012. "A Dangerous Class: The Street Sellers of Nineteenth-Century London." *Journal of Social History* 46 (2): 391–415.

Jáuregui, Jorge Mario. 2008. *La ciudad en devenir: Economías informales / espacios efímeros*. Catálogo Post-It City. Ciudades Ocasionales. Barcelona: CCCB, SEACEX, Turner.

Jinkings, Ivana, Kim Doria, and Murito Cleto. 2016. *Por que gritamos golpe? Para entender o impeachment e a crise política no Brasil*. São Paulo: Boitempo.

Joseph, Gilbert, and David Nugent. 1994. *Everyday Forms of State Formation: Revolution and the Negotiation of Rule in Modern Mexico*. Durham, N.C.: Duke University Press.

Junger, Sebastian. 2002. "Terrorism's New Geography." *Vanity Fair*, December. https://archive.vanityfair.com/article/2002/12/terrorisms-new-geography.

Kanai, Juan Miguel. 2014. "On the Peripheries of Planetary Urbanization: Globalizing Manaus and Its Expanding Impact." *Environment and Planning D: Society and Space* 32 (6): 1071–87.

Kanai, Juan Miguel, and Rafael da Silva Oliveira. 2014. "Paving (through) Amazonia: Neoliberal Urbanism and the Reperipheralization of Roraima." *Environment and Planning A: Economy and Space* 46 (1): 62–77.

Karaganis, Joe, and Sean Flynn. 2011. "Networked Governance and the USTR." In *Media Piracy in Emerging Economies*, edited by Joe Karaganis. New York: Social Science Research Council.

Karras, Alan L. 2010. *Smuggling: Contraband and Corruption in World History*. Lanham, Md.: Rowman & Littlefield.

Katz, Cindi. 2001. "Vagabond Capitalism and the Necessity of Social Reproduction." *Antipode* 33 (4): 709–28.

Kay, Cristóbal. 2020. "Theotonio Dos Santos (1936–2018): The Revolutionary Intellectual Who Pioneered Dependency Theory." *Development and Change* 51 (2): 599–630.

Keefe, Patrick Radden. 2013. "The Geography of Badness: Mapping the Hubs of the Illicit Global Economy." In *Convergence: Illicit Networks and National Security in the Age of Globalization*, edited by Michael Miklaucic and Jacqueline Brewer, 97–110. Washington, D.C.: National Defense University Press.

Kelley, Robin D. G. 2003. *Freedom Dreams: The Black Radical Imagination*. Boston: Beacon Press.

Kendi, Ibram X. 2016. *Stamped from the Beginning: The Definitive History of Racist Ideas in America*. London: Hachette UK.

Kim, Hun. 2020. "Corruption as Infrastructure: Rendering the New Saigon Global." *International Journal of Urban and Regional Research* 44 (6): 1057–71.

Kleinpenning, Jan M. G. 1987. *Man and Land in Paraguay.* West Lafayette, Ind.: Purdue University Press.

Krupa, Christopher, and David Nugent. 2015. *State Theory and Andean Politics: New Approaches to the Study of Rule.* Philadelphia: University of Pennsylvania Press.

Kucera, David, and Leanne Roncolato. 2008. "El trabajo informal: Dos asuntos clave para los programas políticos." *Revista Internacional del Trabajo* 127 (4): 357–87.

Kuruvilla, Sarosh, Ching Kwan Lee, and Mary E. Gallagher. 2011. *From Iron Rice Bowl to Informalization: Markets, Workers, and the State in a Changing China.* Ithaca, N.Y.: Cornell University Press.

Laclau, Ernesto. 2005. *On Populist Reason.* London: Verso.

Laclau, Ernesto, and Chantal Mouffe. 1985. *Hegemony and Socialist Strategy: Towards a Radical Democratic Politics.* London: Verso.

Lambert, Peter, and Andrew Nickson, eds. 2013. *The Paraguay Reader: History, Culture, Politics.* Durham, N.C.: Duke University Press.

"La reforma agraria en Paraguay: Informe de la misión investigadora sobre el estado de la realización de la reforma agraria en tanto obligación de derechos humanos." 2006. FIAN Informe R8. FIAN and La Vía Campesina. https://www2.ohchr.org/english/bodies/cescr/docs/info-ngos/fianparaguay.pdf.

Lefebvre, Henri. 1991. *The Production of Space.* Malden, Mass.: Wiley-Blackwell.

———. 1996. "The Right to the City." In *Writings on Cities,* translated and edited by Eleonore Kofman and Elizabeth Lebas, 63–181. Malden, Mass.: Wiley-Blackwell.

———. 2002. *Critique of Everyday Life.* Vol. 2. London: Verso.

———. 2003. *The Urban Revolution.* Minneapolis: University of Minnesota Press.

———. 2017. *Key Writings.* London: Bloomsbury Publishing.

Lewis, W. Arthur. 1954. "Economic Development with Unlimited Supplies of Labour." *Manchester School* 22 (2): 139–91.

Leys, Ruth. 2011. "The Turn to Affect: A Critique." *Critical Inquiry* 37 (3): 434–72.

Li, Tania Murray. 2010. "To Make Live or Let Die? Rural Dispossession and the Protection of Surplus Populations." *Antipode* 41 (s1): 66–93.

Lin, Justin Yifu, Fang Cai, and Zhou Li. 2003. *The China Miracle: Development Strategy and Economic Reform.* Hong Kong: Chinese University Press.

Lipsitz, George. 2011. *How Racism Takes Place.* Philadelphia: Temple University Press.

Logan, John R., and Harvey L. Molotch. 2007. "The City as Growth Machine." In *Urban Fortunes: The Political Economy of Place.* Berkeley: University of California Press.

Losurdo, D. 2011. *Liberalism: A Counter-History.* London: Verso.

Loureiro, Gabriela Silva. 2020. "To Be Black, Queer and Radical: Centring the Epistemology of Marielle Franco." *Open Cultural Studies* 4 (1): 50–58.

Loveman, Mara. 2014. *National Colors: Racial Classification and the State in Latin America.* Oxford: Oxford University Press.

Luke, Timothy W., and Gerard Toal. 1998. "The Fraying Modern Map: Failed States and Contraband Capitalism." *Geopolitics* 3 (3): 14–33.

Luxemburg, Rosa. 1921. *The Accumulation of Capital.* London: Routledge.

Mahmood, Saba. 2011. *Politics of Piety: The Islamic Revival and the Feminist Subject.* Princeton, N.J.: Princeton University Press.

Maloney, William F. 2004. "Informality Revisited." *World Development* 32 (7): 1159–78.

Manvoutouka, Tine. 2013. "¿Hasta qué punto y cómo puede conceptualizarse el trabajo informal?" *Laboreal* 9 (2). https://journals.openedition.org/laboreal/5674?lang=en.

Marchiori, Teresa, and Mariana Prandini Assis. 2021. "The Impact of COVID-19 Laws on Street Vendors and Market Traders: Trends and Insights from Latin America." Women in Informal Employment: Globalizing and Organizing. https://www.wiego .org/publications/impact-covid-19-laws-street-vendors-and-market-traders-trends -and-insights-latin.

Marez, Curtis. 2004. *Drug Wars: The Political Economy of Narcotics*. Minneapolis: University of Minnesota Press.

Mariátegui, José Carlos. 1970. *Peruanicemos al Perú*. Lima: Amauta.

Merrifield, Andy. 2013. *The Politics of the Encounter: Urban Theory and Protest under Planetary Urbanization*. Geographies of Justice and Social Transformation 19. Athens: University of Georgia Press.

Marini, Ruy Mauro, and Emir Sader. 1977. *Dialéctica de la dependencia*. Mexico City: Ediciones Era México.

Marx, Karl. 1894. *Capital*. Vol. 1. London: Penguin Classics.

Massey, Doreen. 1995. *Spatial Divisions of Labor: Social Structures and the Geography of Production*. London: Psychology Press.

———. 2004. "Geographies of Responsibility." *Geografiska Annaler: Series B, Human Geography* 86 (1): 5–18.

———. 2005. *For Space*. London: Sage.

Massumi, Brian. 2002. *Parables for the Virtual: Movement, Affect, Sensation*. Durham, N.C.: Duke University Press.

Mathews, Gordon, Gustavo Lins Ribeiro, and Carlos Alba Vega, eds. 2012. *Globalization from Below: The World's Other Economy*. London: Routledge.

Maybury-Lewis, David, and James Howe. 1980. *The Indian Peoples of Paraguay: Their Plight and Their Prospects*. Cambridge, Mass.: Cultural Survival.

Mbembe, Achille. 2001. *On the Postcolony*. Berkeley: University of California Press.

McClintock, Anne. 1995. *Imperial Leather: Race, Gender, and Sexuality in the Colonial Contest*. New York: Routledge.

McFarlane, Colin. 2011. *Learning the City: Knowledge and Translocal Assemblage*. RGS-IBG Book Series 56. Malden, Mass.: Wiley-Blackwell.

McKittrick, Katherine. 2006. *Demonic Grounds: Black Women and the Cartographies of Struggle*. Minneapolis: University of Minnesota Press.

McSherry, J. Patrice. 2012. *Predatory States: Operation Condor and Covert War in Latin America*. Lanham, Md.: Rowman & Littlefield.

Meagher, Kate. 2013. "Unlocking the Informal Economy: A Literature Review on Linkages between Formal and Informal Economies in Development Countries." Women in Informal Employment: Globalizing and Organizing. https://www.wiego.org/sites /default/files/migrated/publications/files/Meagher-Informal-Economy-Lit-Review -WIEGO-WP27.pdf.

Melamed, Jodi. 2015. "Racial Capitalism." *Critical Ethnic Studies* 1 (1): 76–85.

Melamed, Jodi, and Chandan Reddy. 2019. "Using Liberal Rights to Enforce Racial Capitalism." *Items: Insights from the Social Sciences* (blog). July 30. https://items.ssrc.org /race-capitalism/using-liberal-rights-to-enforce-racial-capitalism/.

Merlin, Nora. 2019. "Colonização da subjetividade e neoliberalismo." *Revista GEARTE* 6 (2). https://seer.ufrgs.br/gearte/article/view/92906.

Mezzadra, Sandro, and Brett Neilson. 2013. "Extraction, Logistics, Finance." *Radical Philosophy* 178:8–18.

Midnight Notes Collective. 1990. "The New Enclosures." *Midnight Notes* 10:1–9. https://www.e-flux.com/legacy/2013/05/1.-Midnight-Notes-The-New-Enclosures.pdf?b8c429.

Miinzel, Mark. 1976. *The Aché: Genocide Continues in Paraguay.* Copenhagen: IWGIA Documents.

Millar, Kathleen M. 2018. *Reclaiming the Discarded: Life and Labor on Rio's Garbage Dump.* Durham, N.C.: Duke University Press.

Miller, Ben, and Fernanda Uriegas. 2019. "Latin America's Biggest Corruption Cases: A Retrospective." *Americas Quarterly*, July 11. https://americasquarterly.org/article/latin-americas-biggest-corruption-cases-a-retrospective/.

Miraftab, Faranak. 2009. "Insurgent Planning: Situating Radical Planning in the Global South." *Planning Theory* 8 (1): 32–50.

———. 2016. "Insurgency, Planning and the Prospect of a Humane Urbanism." Keynote presented at the World Congress of Planning Schools, Rio de Janeiro, Brazil, July 3. https://pdfs.semanticscholar.org/68b8/3103db898622430c93ebeff8637ad07ad412.pdf.

Miraftab, Faranak, Ken Salo, Efadul Huq, Atyeh Ashtari, and David Aristizabal Urrea. 2019. *Constructing Solidarities for a Humane Urbanism.* Publishing Without Walls.

Miranda, Anibal. 2000. *Dossier Paraguay: Los dueños de grandes fortunas.* Asunción, Paraguay: Miranda & Asociados.

Mitchell, Timothy. 1999. "Society, Economy, and the State Effect." In *State/Culture: State-Formation after the Cultural Turn*, edited by George Steinmetz, 76–97. Ithaca, N.Y.: Cornell University Press.

Moore, Donald. 2005. *Suffering for Territory: Race, Place, and Power in Zimbabwe.* Cambridge: Cambridge University Press.

Moore, Jason W. 2018. "The Capitalocene Part II: Accumulation by Appropriation and the Centrality of Unpaid Work/Energy." *Journal of Peasant Studies* 45 (2): 237–79.

Moore, Sally Falk. 1978. *Law as Process: An Anthropological Approach.* Oxford: Oxford University Press.

Moreton-Robinson, Aileen. 2015. *The White Possessive: Property, Power, and Indigenous Sovereignty.* Minneapolis: University of Minnesota Press.

Morínigo, José Nicolás. 2008. "Clientelismo y padrinazgo en la práctica patrimonialista del gobierno en el Paraguay." *Novapolis* 3:7–29.

Moser, Caroline. 1978. "Informal Sector or Petty Commodity Production: Dualism or Dependence in Urban Development?" *World Development* 6 (9–10): 1041–64.

Mosoetsa, Sarah, Joel Stillerman, and Chris Tilly. 2016. "Precarious Labor, South and North: An Introduction." *International Labor and Working-Class History* 89:5–19.

Muehlmann, Shaylih. 2013. *When I Wear My Alligator Boots: Narco-Culture in the U.S. Mexico Borderlands.* Berkeley: University of California Press.

Munanga, Kabengele. 2010. "Teoria social e relações raciais no Brasil contemporâneo." *Cadernos PENESB* 12:169–203.

Murilo de Carvalho, José. 1998. *Pontos e bordados: Escritos de história e política*. 3rd ed. Belo Horizonte, Brazil: Editora UFMG.

Nagel, Beverly Y. 1999. "'Unleashing the Fury': The Cultural Discourse of Rural Violence and Land Rights in Paraguay." *Comparative Studies in Society and History* 41 (1): 148–81.

Neffa, Julio César. 2009. "Sector informal, precariedad, trabajo no registrado." In *Noveno Congreso Nacional de Estudios del Trabajo, Buenos Aires*. https://aset.org.ar /congresos-anteriores/9/ponencias/p8_Neffa.pdf.

Negrey, Cynthia, Jeffery L. Osgood, and Frank Goetzke. 2011. "One Package at a Time: The Distributive World City." *International Journal of Urban and Regional Research* 35 (4): 812–31.

Neilson, Brett, and Ned Rossiter. 2008. "Precarity as a Political Concept, or, Fordism as Exception." *Theory, Culture & Society* 25 (7–8): 51–72.

Nickson, Andrew. 1981. "Brazilian Colonization of the Eastern Border Region of Paraguay." *Journal of Latin American Studies* 13 (1): 111–31.

———. 2005. "Colonización brasilera en la región oriental del Paraguay." In *Enclave sojero: Merma de soberanía y pobreza*, edited by Fogel Ramón and Marcial Antonio Riquelme, 219–46. Asunción, Paraguay: Centro de Estudios Rurales Interdisciplinarios.

Nickson, Andrew, and Peter Lambert. 2002. "State Reform and the 'Privatized State' in Paraguay." *Public Administration and Development* 22 (2): 163–74.

Nolen, Stephanie. 2019. "The Corruption Scandal That Shook Latin America." *The Walrus*, September 4. https://thewalrus.ca/corruption-the-corruption-scandal-that -shook-latin-america/.

Nordstrom, Carolyn. 2007. *Global Outlaws: Crime, Money, and Power in the Contemporary World*. Berkeley: University of California Press.

Nugent, David. 2009. "Building the State, Making the Nation: The Bases and Limits of State Centralization in 'Modern' Peru." *American Anthropologist* 96 (2): 333–69.

Observatoria de Economía Internacional. 2014. "Informe especial de comercio exterior 2014." http://www.cadep.org.py/uploads/2014/12/Informe-Especial-de-Comercio -Exterior-2014-full-color.pdf.

O'Dougherty, Maureen. 2002. *Consumption Intensified: The Politics of Middle-Class Daily Life in Brazil*. Durham, N.C.: Duke University Press.

O'Hare, Patrick. 2020. "'We Looked After People Better When We Were Informal': The 'Quasi-Formalisation' of Montevideo's Waste-Pickers." *Bulletin of Latin American Research* 39 (1): 53–68.

Omi, Michael, and Howard Winant. 1986. *Racial Formation in the United States*. 3rd ed. New York: Routledge.

Ong, Aihwa. 2006. *Neoliberalism as Exception: Mutations in Citizenship and Sovereignty*. Durham, N.C.: Duke University Press.

Oswin, Natalie. 2018. "Planetary Urbanization: A View from Outside." *Environment and Planning D: Society and Space* 36 (3): 540–46.

Palacios, Rosario. 2011. "¿Qué significa 'trabajador informal'? Revisiones desde una investigación etnográfica." *Revista Mexicana de Sociología* 73 (4): 591–616.

Paley, Dawn. 2014. *Drug War Capitalism*. Oakland, Calif.: AK Press.

Paraguay Vende. 2008. "Paraguay Poverty Reduction Program Work Plan." Chemonics. https://pdf.usaid.gov/pdf_docs/Pdacr590.pdf.

Parks, Ande, and Anthony Russo. 2014. *Ciudad*. Portland, Ore.: Oni Press.

Parodi, Carlos A. 2002. *The Politics of South American Boundaries*. Westport, Conn.: Greenwood Publishing Group.

Pastore, Carlos. 1979. *La lucha por la tierra en el Paraguay*. Montevideo, Uruguay: Editorial Antequera.

Penglase, R. Ben. 2014. *Living with Insecurity in a Brazilian Favela: Urban Violence and Daily Life*. New Brunswick, N.J.: Rutgers University Press.

Penner, Reinaldo. 1998. "Movimiento comercial y financiero de Ciudad del Este y sus perspectivas dentro del proceso de integración." Banco Central del Paraguay. https://repositorio.bcp.gov.py/handle/123456789/144?show=full.

———. 2006a. "Formalización de empresas de Ciudad del Este." Informe final del Centro de Facilitación de Comercio (CFC) de Paraguay Vende. Asunción, Paraguay: Paraguay Vende & USAID.

———. 2006b. *Segundo informe sobre el comercio de productos informáticos en Ciudad del Este*. Asunción, Paraguay: Paraguay Vende & USAID.

Perea, Juan F. 2011. "The Echoes of Slavery: Recognizing the Racist Origins of the Agricultural and Domestic Worker Exclusion from the National Labor Relations Act." *Loyola University Chicago* 72 (1): 95–138.

Pereira, Mateus Henrique de Faria, and Daniel Pinha Silva. 2021. "Is Sérgio Moro a Negationist? Operation 'Lava Jato,' Updatism Transparency and Negation of Politics." *Revista Brasileira de História* 41 (July): 135–59.

Perelman, Michael. 2000. *The Invention of Capitalism: Classical Political Economy and the Secret History of Primitive Accumulation*. Durham, N.C.: Duke University Press.

Perreault, Tom. 2013. "Dispossession by Accumulation? Mining, Water and the Nature of Enclosure on the Bolivian Altiplano." *Antipode* 45 (5): 1050–69.

Pieterse, Edgar. 2008. *City Futures: Confronting the Crisis of Urban Development*. London: Zed Books.

———. 2013. "Grasping the Unknowable: Coming to Grips with African Urbanisms." In *Rogue Urbanism: Emergent African Cities*, edited by AbdouMaliq Simone and Edgar Pieterse, 19–35. Cape Town, South Africa: University of Cape Town.

Piketty, Thomas, and L. J. Ganser. 2014. *Capital in the Twenty-First Century*. Cambridge, Mass.: Harvard University Press.

Pinheiro-Machado, Rosana. 2008. "China–Paraguai–Brasil: Uma rota para pensar a economia informal." *Revista Brasileira de Ciências Sociais* 23 (67): 117–92.

———. 2010. "Caminos del contrabando: La fiscalización en el puente de la amistad y sus efectos en la cotideanidad de la Triple Frontera." In *La Triple Frontera: Dinámicas culturales y procesos transnacionales*, edited by Verónica Giménez Béliveau and Silvia Montenegro, 89–109. Buenos Aires: Espacio Editorial.

———. 2017. *Counterfeit Itineraries in the Global South: The Human Consequences of Piracy in China and Brazil*. New York: Routledge.

Pinheiro-Machado, Rosana, and Lucia Mury Scalco. 2020. "From Hope to Hate: The Rise of Conservative Subjectivity in Brazil." *HAU: Journal of Ethnographic Theory*.

Pires Junior, Arnaldo Lucas. 2015. "Imagens em guerra: Imprensa, nacionalismo e formação do estado brasileiro na guerra do Paraguai." PhD dissertation, Universidade Federal do Rio de Janeiro.

Pithouse, Richard. 2012. "Thought amidst Waste." *Journal of Asian and African Studies* 47 (5): 482–97.

Porter, Libby. 2010. *Unlearning the Colonial Cultures of Planning.* Farnham, U.K.: Ashgate Publishing.

Portes, Alejandro, Manuel Castells, and Lauren A. Benton. 1989. *The Informal Economy: Studies in Advanced and Less Developed Countries.* Baltimore, Md.: Johns Hopkins University Press.

Poynter, John Riddoch. 1969. *Society and Pauperism: English Ideas on Poor Relief, 1795–1834.* London: Routledge & Kegan Paul.

Prebisch, Raul. 1950. "The Economic Development of Latin America and Its Principal Problems." *Economic Bulletin for Latin America 1962* 7. https://archivo.cepal.org /pdfs/cdPrebisch/002.pdf.

Procacci, Giovanna. 1991. "Social Economy and the Government of Poverty." In *The Foucault Effect: Studies in Governmentality,* edited by Graham Burchell, Colin Gordon, and Peter Miller, 151–68. Chicago: University of Chicago Press.

Prouse, Carolyn. 2021. "Articulating Corruption of Infrastructural Upgrading Projects in Rio de Janeiro." *Political Geography* 84 (January): 102305.

Pulido, Laura. 2017. "Geographies of Race and Ethnicity II: Environmental Racism, Racial Capitalism and State-Sanctioned Violence." *Progress in Human Geography* 41 (4): 524–33.

Quijano, Aníbal. 2000. "Colonialidad del poder, Eurocentrismo y América Latina." In *La colonialidad del saber: Eurocentrismo y ciencias sociales. Perspectivas latinoamericanas,* edited by Edgardo Lander, 201–46. Buenos Aires: CLASCO.

Rabossi, Fernando. 2008. *En las calles de Ciudad del Este: Una etnografía del comercio de frontera.* Asunción, Paraguay: Centro de Estudios Antropológicos de la Universidad Católica.

———. 2010. "Negocios en el límite: El comercio de frontera desde las calles de Ciudad Del Este." PhD dissertation, Universidade Federal do Río de Janeiro.

———. 2011a. "Economías ilegales en la Triple Frontera Paraguay, Argentina y Brasil." http://www.slideshare.net/gatoramiro/economas-ilegales-en-la-triple-frontera -paraguay-argentina-y-brasil-fernando-rabossi.

———. 2011b. "Negociações, associações e monopólios: A política da rua em Ciudad del Este (Paraguai)." *Etnográfica* 15 (1): 83–107.

———. 2012. "Ciudad del Este and Brazilian Circuits of Commercial Distribution." In *Globalization from Below: The World's Other Economy,* edited by Gordon Mathews, Gustavo Lins Ribeiro, and Carlos Alba Vega, 54–68. New York: Routledge.

———. 2018. "Smuggling Realities: On Numbers, Borders, and Performances." *HAU: Journal of Ethnographic Theory* 8 (1–2): 265–81.

Ranganathan, Malini, David L. Pike, and Sapana Doshi. 2023. *Corruption Plots: Stories, Ethics, and Publics of the Late Capitalist City.* Ithaca, N.Y.: Cornell University Press.

Reber, Vera Blinn. 1988. "The Demographics of Paraguay: A Reinterpretation of the Great War, 1864–70." *Hispanic American Historical Review* 68 (2): 289–319.

Reed, Richard K. 1995. *Prophets of Agroforestry: Guarani Communities and Commercial Gathering.* Austin: University of Texas Press.

Rivarola, Milda. 2007. "El clientelismo: Motor del estado paraguayo." Decidamos. http://www.portalguarani.com/1686_milda_rivarola_espinoza/15367_el_clientelismo_motor_del_estado_paraguayo_milda_rivarola_.html.

———. 2010. *Vagos, pobres & soldados: La domesticación estatal del trabajo en el Paraguay del siglo XIX*. 2nd ed. Asunción, Paraguay: Editorial ServiLibro.

Roa Bastos, Augusto Antonio. 1987. "Fragments from a Paraguayan Autobiography." *Third World Quarterly* 9 (1): 212–28.

Robinson, Cedric J. 1983. *Black Marxism: The Making of the Black Radical Tradition*. Chapel Hill: University of North Carolina Press.

Robinson, Jeffrey. 2002. *The Merger: The International Conglomerate of Organized Crime*. 1st ed. Overlook TP.

Robinson, Jennifer. 2002. "Global and World Cities: A View from off the Map." *International Journal of Urban and Regional Research* 26 (3): 531–54.

———. 2006. *Ordinary Cities: Between Modernity and Development*. London: Routledge.

———. 2011. "Cities in a World of Cities: The Comparative Gesture." *International Journal of Urban and Regional Research* 35 (1): 1–23.

Rodney, Walter. 1972. *How Europe Underdeveloped Africa*. London: Bogle-L'Ouverture Publications.

Rodrigues, Carolina Samara. 2015. "Construções discursivas sobre o Paraguai: O impeachment de Fernando Lugo." PhD dissertation, Universidade Federal da Grande Dourados. http://repositorio.ufgd.edu.br/jspui/handle/prefix/1542.

Rodrigues, Fabiana Alves. 2019. "Operação Lava Jato: Aprendizado institucional e ação estratégica na justiça criminal." PhD dissertation, Universidade de São Paulo.

Roediger, David. 2017. *Class, Race, and Marxism*. London: Verso.

Rohter, Larry. 2001. "Terrorists Are Sought in Latin Smugglers' Haven." *New York Times*, September 27, sec. World. http://www.nytimes.com/2001/09/27/world/terrorists-are-sought-in-latin-smugglers-haven.html.

Roig, Alexandre. 2017. "Financiarización y derechos de los trabajadores de la economía popular." In *Economía popular: Los desafíos del trabajo sin patrón*, edited by Emilio Pérsico, 87–102. Buenos Aires: Colihue.

Rosaldo, Manuel. 2016. "Revolution in the Garbage Dump: The Political and Economic Foundations of the Colombian Recycler Movement, 1986–2011." *Social Problems* 63 (3): 351–72.

———. 2022. "The Antinomies of Successful Mobilization: Colombian Recyclers Manoeuvre between Dispossession and Exploitation." *Development and Change* 53 (2): 251–78.

Rosaldo, Manuel, Chris Tilly, and Peter Evans. 2012. "A Conceptual Framework on Informal Work and Informal Worker Organizing." UCLA Institute for Research on Labor and Employment. https://irle.ucla.edu/wp-content/uploads/2017/05/EOIWConceptualFramework-Rosaldo-Evans-Tilly-03.12.pdf.

Rostow, Walt W. 1960. *The Stages of Economic Growth: A Non-Communist Manifesto*. Cambridge: Cambridge University Press.

Roy, Ananya. 2002. *City Requiem, Calcutta: Gender and the Politics of Poverty*. Minneapolis: University of Minnesota Press.

———. 2006. "Praxis in the Time of Empire." *Planning Theory* 5 (1): 7–29.

———. 2009. "The 21st-Century Metropolis: New Geographies of Theory." *Regional Studies* 43 (6): 819–30.

———. 2011a. "Slumdog Cities: Rethinking Subaltern Urbanism." *International Journal of Urban and Regional Research* 35 (2): 223–38.

———. 2011b. "Urbanisms, Worlding Practices and the Theory of Planning." *Planning Theory* 10 (1): 6–15.

———. 2016. "Who's Afraid of Postcolonial Theory?" *International Journal of Urban and Regional Research* 40 (1): 200–209.

Roy, Ananya, and Aihwa Ong, eds. 2012. *Worlding Cities: Asian Experiments and the Art of Being Global.* Malden, Mass.: Wiley-Blackwell.

Ruddick, Sue, Linda Peake, Gökbörü S. Tanyildiz, and Darren Patrick. 2018. "Planetary Urbanization: An Urban Theory for Our Time?" *Environment and Planning D: Society and Space* 36 (3): 387–404.

Ruiz Díaz, Francisco. 2011. "La política comercial del Paraguay en el proceso de integración en el Mercosur: Desvíos del AEC y costos de la protección." Asunción, Paraguay: Centro de Análisis y Difusion de la Economía Paraguaya.

———. 2012. "Mythbuster: Explorando el comercio exterior paraguayo." Centro de Análisis y Difusión de la Economía Paraguaya. http://www.cadep.org.py/2015/10/mythbusters-explorando-el-comercio-exterior-paraguayo-2/.

Saeger, James Schofield. 2007. *Francisco Solano López and the Ruination of Paraguay: Honor and Egocentrism.* Lanham, Md.: Rowman & Littlefield.

Samson, Melanie. 2015. "Accumulation by Dispossession and the Informal Economy: Struggles over Knowledge, Being and Waste at a Soweto Garbage Dump." *Environment and Planning D: Society and Space* 33 (5): 813–30.

Santos, Boaventura de Sousa. 2018. *The End of the Cognitive Empire: The Coming of Age of Epistemologies of the South.* Durham, N.C.: Duke University Press.

Sanyal, Kalyan. 2013. *Rethinking Capitalist Development: Primitive Accumulation, Governmentality and Post-colonial Capitalism.* London: Routledge.

Sarria Icaza, Ana Mercedes, and Lia Tiribia. 2004. "Economía popular." In *La otra economía,* edited by Antonio David Cattani, 173–86. Buenos Aires: Editorial Altamira.

Sassen, Saskia. 1998. *Globalization and Its Discontents: Essays on the New Mobility of People and Money.* New York: New Press.

———. 2001. *The Global City: New York, London, Tokyo.* Princeton, N.J.: Princeton University Press.

———. 2014. *Expulsions.* Cambridge, Mass.: Harvard University Press.

Schemo, Diana Jean. 1998. "In Paraguay Border Town, Almost Anything Goes." *New York Times,* March 15, sec. World. https://www.nytimes.com/1998/03/15/world/in-paraguay-border-town-almost-anything-goes.html.

Schneider, Friedrich, and Dominik Enste. 2000. "Shadow Economies around the World: Size, Causes, and Consequences." *Journal of Economic Literature* 38:77–144.

———. 2013. *The Shadow Economy: An International Survey.* Cambridge: Cambridge University Press.

Schuster, Caroline E. 2015. *Social Collateral: Women and Microfinance in Paraguay's Smuggling Economy.* Oakland: University of California Press.

Scott, James C. 1998. *Seeing Like a State: How Certain Schemes to Improve the Human Condition Have Failed.* New Haven, Conn.: Yale University Press.

Scott, Julius. 2018. "Common Wind: Afro-American Organization in the Revolution against Slavery." London: Verso.

Sequeda, María Teresa Ferreira. 2014. "Las nociones de trabajo informal y trabajo precario en el análisis de la calidad del empleo en Colombia." *Revista Lebret* 6:29–58.

Setrini, Gustavo. 2010. "Twenty Years of Paraguayan Electoral Democracy: From Monopolistic to Pluralistic Clientelism." Asunción, Paraguay: Centro de Análisis y Difusión de la Economía Paraguaya. http://www.cadep.org.py/2010/09/proyecto-bicentenario-el-clientelismo-en-los-anos-de-democracia/.

Sheppard, Eric. 2012. "Trade, Globalization and Uneven Development Entanglements of Geographical Political Economy." *Progress in Human Geography* 36 (1): 44–71.

Sheppard, Eric, Helga Leitner, and Anant Maringanti. 2013. "Provincializing Global Urbanism: A Manifesto." *Urban Geography* 34 (7): 893–900.

Sheppard, Eric, Tony Sparks, and Helga Leitner. 2020. "World Class Aspirations, Urban Informality, and Poverty Politics: A North-South Comparison." *Antipode* 52 (2): 393–407.

Shouse, Eric. 2005. "Feeling, Emotion, Affect." *M/C Journal* 8 (6): 26.

Silva, Fidel Miranda. 2007. *Historia de Alto Paraná: Formaciones de los pueblos del Paraná.* Ciudad del Este, Paraguay: Sanchos Libros.

Silveira, Mariana de Moraes. 2020. "Juristas e vida pública no Brasil: Trajetórias no tempo." In *Do fake ao fato: Des(actualizado) Bolsonaro*, edited by Bruna Stutz Klem, Mateus Henrique de Faria Pereira, and Valdei Lopes de Araujo, 225–38. Vitória, Brazil: MilFontes.

Silveira, Mauro César. 2007. "As marcas do preconceito no jornalismo brasileiro e a história do Paraguay illustrado." *Intercom: Revista Brasileira de Ciências da Comunicação* 30 (2): 41–66.

Skinner, Caroline, and Pilar Balbuena. 2019. "Where Are the Inclusive Cities? Street Vendors Globally Face Increasing Hostility." Women in Informal Employment: Globalizing and Organizing. http://www.wiego.org/blog/where-are-inclusive-cities-street-vendors-globally-face-increasing-hostility.

Slater, Tom. 2015. "Territorial Stigmatization: Symbolic Defamation and the Contemporary Metropolis." In *The Handbook of New Urban Studies*, edited by J. Hannigan and G. Richards, 111–25. London: Sage.

Smith, Dorothy. 1987. *The Everyday World as Problematic: A Feminist Sociology.* Toronto: University of Toronto Press.

Smith, Neil. 1986. *Uneven Development: Nature, Capital and the Production of Space.* Oxford: Blackwell.

———. 1996. *The New Urban Frontier: Gentrification and the Revanchist City.* Brighton, U.K.: Psychology Press.

———. 2010. *Uneven Development: Nature, Capital, and the Production of Space.* Athens: University of Georgia Press.

Smith, Neil, and Anne Godlewska. 1994. *Geography and Empire.* Oxford: Blackwell.

Smith, Robert J., and Bartomeu Meliá. 1978. "Genocide of Ache-Guayaki?" *Survival International Supplement* 3 (1): 8–13.

Soederberg, Susanne. 2012. "The Mexican Debtfare State: Dispossession, Micro-lending, and the Surplus Population." *Globalizations* 9 (4): 561–75.

Souza, Ana Claudia. 1996. "TV Gente." *Jornal do Brasil*, February 17.

Souza, Jessé. 2019. *A elite do atraso: Da escravidão à Lava-Jato.* Rio de Janeiro: Leya.

———. 2021. *Como o racismo criou o Brasil*. Rio de Janeiro: Editora Sextante.

Spivak, Gayatri Chakravorty. 1988. *A Critique of Postcolonial Reason: Toward a History of the Vanishing Present*. Cambridge, Mass.: Harvard University Press.

———. 2007. "Thinking about the Humanities: A Talk." Lecture, Columbia University, March 21.

———. 2013. *The Spivak Reader: Selected Works of Gayati Chakravorty Spivak*. London: Routledge.

Stacey, Judith. 1988. "Can There Be a Feminist Ethnography?" *Women's Studies International Forum* 11:21–27.

Stiglitz, Joseph E. 2002. *Globalization and Its Discontents*. New York: W. W. Norton & Company.

Stoler, Ann. 2002. *Carnal Knowledge and Imperial Power: Race and the Intimate in Colonial Rule*. Berkeley: University of California Press.

Storper, Michael. 2000. "Lived Effects of the Contemporary Economy: Globalization, Inequality, and Consumer Society." *Public Culture* 12 (2): 375–409.

Syal, Rajeev. 2009. "Drug Money Saved Banks in Global Crisis, Claims UN Advisor." *The Guardian*, December 13. http://www.theguardian.com/global/2009/dec/13/drug -money-banks-saved-un-cfief-claims.

Taddonio, Patrice. 2021. "Who's Using South Dakota as a Tax Haven for Foreign Wealth?" *Frontline*, November 9. https://www.pbs.org/wgbh/frontline/article /pandora-papers-tax-havens-south-dakota/.

Taibbi, Matt. 2012. "Outrageous HSBC Settlement Proves the Drug War Is a Joke." *Rolling Stone*, December 13, 2012. https://www.rollingstone.com/politics/politics-news /outrageous-hsbc-settlement-proves-the-drug-war-is-a-joke-230696/.

Telles, Edward. 2014. *Pigmentocracies: Ethnicity, Race, and Color in Latin America*. Chapel Hill: University of North Carolina Press.

Telles, Edward, and Tianna Paschel. 2014. "Who Is Black, White, or Mixed Race? How Skin Color, Status, and Nation Shape Racial Classification in Latin America." *American Journal of Sociology* 120 (3): 864–907.

Thompson, Edward Palmer. 1975. *Whigs and Hunters: The Origin of the Black Act*. New York: Pantheon Books.

———. 1993. *Customs in Common: Studies in Traditional Popular Culture*. New York: New Press.

Tilly, Charles. 1985. "War Making and State Making as Organized Crime." In *Bringing the State Back In*, edited by Peter B. Evans, Dietrich Rueschemeyer, and Theda Skocpol, 169–87. Cambridge: Cambridge University Press.

Tovar, Luisa Fernanda. 2018. "Formalización de las organizaciones de recicladores de oficio en Bogotá: Reflexiones desde la economía popular." *Íconos: Revista de Ciencias Sociales* 62: 39–63.

Trouillot, Michel-Rolph, Chris Hann, and Lszl Krti. 2001. "The Anthropology of the State in the Age of Globalization: Close Encounters of the Deceptive Kind." *Current Anthropology* 42 (1): 125–38.

Tsing, Anna Lowenhaupt. 2005. *Friction: An Ethnography of Global Connection*. Princeton, N.J.: Princeton University Press.

Tucker, Jennifer. 2017. "City-Stories: Narrative as Diagnostic and Strategic Resource in Ciudad del Este, Paraguay." *Planning Theory* 16 (1): 74–98.

Tucker, Jennifer, and Manisha Anantharaman. 2020. "Informal Work and Sustainable Cities: From Formalization to Reparation." *One Earth* 3 (3): 290–99.

Tucker, Jennifer, and Ryan Thomas Devlin. 2019. "Uncertainty and the Governance of Street Vending: A Critical Comparison across the North/South Divide." *International Journal of Urban and Regional Research* 43 (3): 460–75.

Tully, James. 1982. *A Discourse on Property: John Locke and His Adversaries.* Cambridge: Cambridge University Press.

Turner, Frederick Jackson. 1893. *The Frontier in American History.* New York: Henry Holt and Company.

Uribe, Simón. 2017. *Frontier Road: Power, History, and the Everyday State in the Colombian Amazon.* Hoboken, N.J.: John Wiley & Sons.

USTR. 2013. "National Trade Estimate Report on Foreign Trade Barriers Brazil." Office of the United States Trade Representative, Washington, D.C. https://ustr.gov/about-us /policy-offices/press-office/reports-and-publications/2013/NTE-FTB.

———. 2015. "Out of Cycle Review of Notorious Markets." Office of the United States Trade Representative, Washington, D.C. https://ustr.gov/sites/default/files/USTR -2015-Out-of-Cycle-Review-Notorious-Markets-Final.pdf.

———. 2016. "Out of Cycle Review of Notorious Markets." Office of the United States Trade Representative, Washington, D.C. https://ustr.gov/node/5520.

———. 2017. "Out of Cycle Review of Notorious Markets." Office of the United States Trade Representative, Washington, D.C. https://ustr.gov/sites/default/files/files /Press/Reports/2017%20Notorious%20Markets%20List%201.11.18.pdf.

———. 2019. "Out of Cycle Review of Notorious Markets." Office of the United States Trade Representative, Washington, D.C. https://ustr.gov/sites/default/files/2019 _Review_of_Notorious_Markets_for_Counterfeiting_and_Piracy.pdf.

———. 2021. "USTR Releases 2020: Review of Notorious Markets for Counterfeiting and Piracy, United States Trade Representative." January 14. United States Trade Representative, Washington, D.C. https://ustr.gov/about-us/policy-offices/press-office /press-releases/2021/january/ustr-releases-2020-review-notorious-markets -counterfeiting-and-piracy.

Valim, Rafael. 2018. "State of Exception: The Legal Form of Neoliberalism." *Zeitschrift für Politikwissenschaft* 28 (4): 409–21.

Van Schendel, Willem, and Itty Abraham. 2005. *Illicit Flows and Criminal Things: States, Borders, and the Other Side of Globalization.* Bloomington: Indiana University Press.

Varley, Ann. 2013. "Postcolonialising Informality?" *Environment and Planning D: Society and Space* 31 (1): 4–22.

Vasconcelos, José. (1925) 1997. *The Cosmic Race.* Baltimore, Md.: Johns Hopkins University Press.

Vázquez, Fabricio. 2006. "Territorio y población: Nuevas dinámicas regionales en el Paraguay." Población y Desarrollo. Asunción, Paraguay: United Nations Population Fund.

Visweswaran, Kamala. 1994. *Fictions of Feminist Ethnography.* Minneapolis: University of Minnesota Press.

Wacquant, Loïc, Tom Slater, and Virgílio Borges Pereira. 2014. "Territorial Stigmatization in Action." *Environment and Planning A: Economy and Space* 46 (6): 1270–80.

Waisgrais, Sebastián, and Marianela Sarabia. 2008. "Heterogeneidad social y productiva: Caracterización del trabajo informal en el gran Buenos Aires." In *Aportes a una nueva visión de la informalidad laboral en la Argentina*, edited by Ignacio Apella, 179–230. Buenos Aires: Banco Mundial, Ministerio de Trabajo, Empleo y Seguridad Social.

Watson, Vanessa. 2009a. "'The Planned City Sweeps the Poor Away . . .': Urban Planning and 21st Century Urbanisation." *Progress in Planning* 72 (3): 151–93.

———. 2009b. "Seeing from the South: Refocusing Urban Planning on the Globe's Central Urban Issues." *Urban Studies* 46 (11): 2259–75.

Watts, Jonathan. 2017. "Operation Car Wash: Is This the Biggest Corruption Scandal in History?" *The Guardian*, June 1. https://www.theguardian.com/world/2017/jun/01/brazil-operation-car-wash-is-this-the-biggest-corruption-scandal-in-history.

Watts, Michael J. 1992. "Space for Everything (a Commentary)." *Cultural Anthropology* 7 (1): 115–29.

———. 2011. "Planet of the Wageless." *Identities* 18 (1): 69–80.

Webber, Jude. 2010. "Ciudad del Este's Deadly Trade Route." *Financial Times*, March 13. https://www.ft.com/content/dd80bec8-2be5-11df-8033-00144feabdc0.

Wedel, Janine R. 2012. "Rethinking Corruption in an Age of Ambiguity." *Annual Review of Law and Social Science* 8 (1): 453–98.

Weeks, Kathi. 2011. *The Problem with Work: Feminism, Marxism, Antiwork Politics, and Postwork Imaginaries.* Durham, N.C.: Duke University Press.

Weinstein, Liza. 2008. "Mumbai's Development Mafias: Globalization, Organized Crime and Land Development." *International Journal of Urban and Regional Research* 32 (1): 22–39.

Werner, Marion. 2015. *Global Displacements: The Making of Uneven Development in the Caribbean.* Hoboken, N.J.: John Wiley & Sons.

West, Cornell. 2019. "2019 MLK Keynote Address." Presented at the Martin Luther King Jr. Series, Center for Social Equity & Inclusion, January 23. https://digitalcommons.risd.edu/studentaffairs_MLK/Keynotes/Presentations/13.

Whigham, Thomas L., and Barbara Potthast. 1999. "The Paraguayan Rosetta Stone: New Insights into the Demographics of the Paraguayan War, 1864–1870." *Latin American Research Review* 34 (1): 174–86.

Whitehead, Judy, and Nitin More. 2007. "Revanchism in Mumbai? Political Economy of Rent Gaps and Urban Restructuring in a Global City." *Economic and Political Weekly* 42 (25): 2428–34.

Williams, Eric. 1944. *Capitalism and Slavery.* Chapel Hill: University of North Carolina Press.

Williams, Raymond. 1978. *Marxism and Literature.* New York: Oxford University Press.

Wilson, Eric. 2009. *Government of the Shadows: Parapolitics and Criminal Sovereignty.* Ann Arbor, Mich.: Pluto Press.

Wolfe, Patrick. 2006. "Settler Colonialism and the Elimination of the Native." *Journal of Genocide Research* 8 (4): 387–409.

Wolford, Wendy. 2004. "This Land Is Ours Now: Spatial Imaginaries and the Struggle for Land in Brazil." *Annals of the Association of American Geographers* 94 (2): 409–24.

Wolpe, Harold. 1972. "Capitalism and Cheap Labour-Power in South Africa: From Segregation to Apartheid." *Economy and Society* 1 (4): 425–56.

Wood, Ellen Meiksins. 1999. *The Origin of Capitalism.* New York: Monthly Review Press.

Woods, Clyde. 1998. *Development Arrested: The Blues and Plantation Power in the Mississippi Delta*. London: Verso.

Wright, Melissa W. 2006. *Disposable Women and Other Myths of Global Capitalism*. New York: Routledge.

Yiftachel, Oren. 2009. "Theoretical Notes on 'Gray Cities': The Coming of Urban Apartheid?" *Planning Theory* 8 (1): 88–100.

Yiftachel, Oren, and Margo Huxley. 2000. "Debating Dominance and Relevance: Notes on the 'Communicative Turn' in Planning Theory." *International Journal of Urban and Regional Research* 24 (4): 907–13.

Ynsfrán, Edgar L. 1990. *Un giro geopolítico: El milagro de una ciudad*. Asunción, Paraguay: Editora Litocolor.

Young, Douglas, and Roger Keil. 2010. "Reconnecting the Disconnected: The Politics of Infrastructure in the In-Between City." In "The Suburban Question," edited by Andrew Kirby and Ali Modarres, special issue, *Cities* 27 (2): 87–95.

Zapatista Comité Clandestino Revolucionario Indígena—Comandancia General del Ejército Zapatista de Liberación Nacional. 1996. "Cuarta declaración de la Selva Lacandona," January 10. https://es.wikisource.org/wiki/EZLN:_Cuarta_Declaraci%C3%B3n_de_la_Selva_Lacandona.

Zoomers, Annelies, and Gemma van der Haar. 2000. *Current Land Policy in Latin America: Regulating Land Tenure under Neo-liberalism*. Amsterdam: KIT Publishers.

INDEX

GEOGRAPHIES OF JUSTICE AND SOCIAL TRANSFORMATION

Printed in the USA
CPSIA information can be obtained
at www.ICGtesting.com
LVHW041744160923
758411LV00001B/63